MERCURY RISING
MERCURY RISING
MERCURY RISING
MERCURY RISING
MERCURY RISING

MERCURY RISING

WOMEN, EVIL, AND THE TRICKSTER GODS

Deldon Anne McNeely

Spring Publications, Inc.
Woodstock, Connecticut

Published in 1996 by Spring Publications, Inc.
299 East Quassett Road, Woodstock, CT 06281
tel (860)974-3428

© 1996 by Spring Publications, Inc. All rights reserved

Distributed in the United States by Continuum Publishing Group; in Canada by McClelland and Stewart; in the United Kingdom, Eire, and Europe by Airlift Book Co.; in Europe by Daimon Verlag; and in Australia by Astam Books Pty Ltd.

Cover designed by Julia Hillman. Interior designed by Brian O'Kelley.

Library of Congress Cataloging-in-Publication Data

McNeely, Deldon Anne
Mercury Rising : women, evil, and the trickster gods / Deldon Anne McNeely.
 p. cm.
 Includes bibliographical references (p.198-208)
 ISBN 0-88214-366-2 (alk. paper)
 1. Archetype (psychology) 2. Trickster. 3. Women—Psychology.
BF175.5.A72M37 1996
155.2'64—dc21
 96-50485
 CIP

Printed in Canada

CONTENTS

INTRODUCTION   7
   Invocation

1. SUPERMAN IN HELL   13
   PART I: HEROES, CYNICS, CELEBRITIES, AND TRICKSTERS
      Defining the Realms of Heroes and Tricksters
   PART II: WANTED: ETHICS, DEAD OR ALIVE
      Divine Research on Greed - Progress's Shadow - Theoretical Ethics - Individuation and Integrity - Clowning Around in the Shadow - Shadow's Guide - Order's Shadow
   PART III: SOCIOPATHY, STAMINA, AND HOPE
      Sociability's Shadow - Heroes, Hermes, and Hubris - A Developmental View of Disorder - The Stamina to Hope
   CONCLUSION

2. THROUGH LENS AND LOOKING GLASS   58
   Reflection and Survival - Mirrors, Dreams, and Truth - Whoever Knows God Has an Effect on Him - Trickster as a Messenger of God's Plan - The Seen, the Unseen, and the Camera - Reflections on Reflection - The Matter of Narcissism - Trickster, Narcissism, and the Search for Soul - Longing for Center

3. SCRUPLES AND SOUL DOCTORS   87
   The Search for Meaning in Suffering - Trickster, Shaman, Healer - Freeing the Double-Bind - Doctors of Darkness - The Imaginal Trickster - Trickster and the Borderline - The Therapeutic Trickster - Trickster as Mediator - The Reverent Boundary

4. TRICKSTER WOMAN   109
   Woman-Threat - Trickster-Threat - Trickster and the Feeling Function - Woman and the Trickster Animus - Melusina, Soul of Mercurius - Sophia, Soul of Yahweh - Lilith, Soul of Satan - Binah, Soul of Chokmah - Goddesses of Transformation - Creative Crone Hecate - Sacred Eroticism - Women of Spiritual Power - Vivienne, Soul of Merlin - Earth Woman, Soul of Coyote

5. ETUDES IN PARANOIA   151
   Lies - Evil - Violence - Sex - Innocence

6. THE ANIMATED TRICKSTER   185
   The Dark Trickster and Anima - Parenting the Divine Child - Inclusiveness and Compassion - Devouring Giants: Exploitative Greed - Parenting Nature

ENDNOTES   199

ACKNOWLEDGMENTS

Deepest thanks to Jan Bauer, William Doty, and Anna Margaret Martin for generously reading and thoughtfully responding to the manuscript, as well as to Yseult Tyler, my daughter, for her fine editing of some parts. To the friends and patients whose contributions to this book came in gifts of trust, dialogue, and mutual interest in psyche, I am most grateful. May you always find a warm hearth and a star.

In addition, the author and publisher wish to thank those who have kindly given permission to excerpt from copyrighted materials.

INTRODUCTION

So much of importance has been written about the Trickster Archetype in its various representations by psychologists, anthropologists, and mythologists. Why put forth another book on this subject? I have three objectives: One is to expound the survival value of recognizing the Trickster Archetype in our individual and collective psyches; another is to raise the possibility of developing a more enlightened approach to ethics by our species, by attending to the Trickster as an agent in the differentiation of evil; a third is to explore the feminine side of an androgynous archetype which is portrayed universally as masculine.

My primary motivation for this work springs from a personal need to continually deepen my understanding of an archetype which has shaped my life. It was when first reading Karl Kerényi's *Hermes: Guide of Souls,* that I became enlightened in my attitude toward certain dark aspects of my life which had made dull sense to me at the time, but which, with Kerényi's inspiration, were imbued with meaning and motion. Mercurius had entered consciousness. Now I often recognize that potential for enlightenment in others as Mercurius enters through a dream or moment of inspiration. Usually such awareness must be quickly grasped, or it will as fleetingly disappear.

To those who may feel closed to admit that such a silly or chaotic figure as a trickster could offer anything of substance to an individual or developing society, I invite you to look more deeply into this subject. You may be surprised at the levels of perception which this door opens. New perceptions allow re-balancing of energies in the psyche, and lead to new solutions to problems.

To attempt to catch hold of an archetypal moment or pattern and verbalize the experience is the chore of clinicians particularly. I must apologize to those scholars whose task it is to cleanly articulate and place in context something as nebulous as the Trickster in its many manifestations and meanings. I am essentially doing the opposite here, as I blithely stir together gods, goddesses, folk-heroes, fools, magicians, and other creatures, real and imaginary, into some great archetypal stew.

I justify this in order to share an appreciation for the value of the Trickster Archetype as an amplifier and healer of splits in the individual and collective psyches. The healing quality makes Trickster an extremely relevant—perhaps the most relevant—archetype for our time of fragmented societies and personalities. The Coyote figure of Native American culture does not literally translate into African Legba, or alchemical Mercurius, but all carry a similar spirit, and their stories evoke the same profound truths, truths which I shall argue here are cogent and valuable for the questions which face us presently as a human race.

I must also ask my readers' forgiveness for leaping between examples of happenings in the collective psyche and individual psyches. I respond to the phenomena which I, as an archetypal psychologist, believe to be happening on both levels; while I am more qualified to describe individual experience, I cannot resist making comparisons between what I experience everyday in my clinical work with what I intuit from wider social interactions. One can relate to the collective experience as one would the images of one's own archetypal dream; this brings the large picture into personally meaningful focus. In any case, I hope that the combinations of personal examples, intuitions, and generalizations may be stimulating, if unscientific, as I look less for data than for awareness.

My second objective is to offer the hypothesis that our contemporary worldwide problems may be not just warnings of an immanent apocalypse, but an invitation to differentiate our comprehension of evil. I suggest that if we were to separate out certain truths that Trickster brings, from our very diffuse sense of good/evil, we could leap ahead to new ground in our ethical development. Trickster gods and goddesses, by their very nature, force us to question our premises regarding order and morality. Mercurial and paradoxical, tricksters always open us to something new, to something larger than our current state of awareness. The Trickster Archetype, old as mythology, has been held as an essential aspect of the divine by most cultures. But in the Judeo-Christian and Islamic theologies, whose approaches to morality dualistically polarize Good versus Evil, Trickster has no apparent place. In societies influenced by these contemporary theologies, Trickster's qualities are more often subsumed by the Devil, the principle of evil. Trickster's characteristics are also projected onto women as negative qualities, while not acknowledged as Trickster's. This pattern of suppression of the Trickster Archetype and then projection onto Satan and woman, will have unfortunate consequences for our civilization until we further differentiate our concept of evil.

The third objective for writing is to pose a question: Why are trickster figures usually portrayed as masculine? I propose we circumambulate this question without having to adopt one answer. I suspect that the inclusion of the feminine in our conceptualization of the Divine Trickster would considerably enhance the development of a wiser ethical vantage point. You will notice that I often refer to the Trickster as "it," and sometimes as "he" or "she." Regrettably, "it" connotes asexuality, while I would prefer a pronoun that connoted androgyny. The absence of such a word in the English language may be related to a culture-wide imbalance that renders the Trickster, an androgynous archetype, to be thought of as masculine.

On the subject of pronouns, I deliberately use the personal "we" in examples of particular personality types or traits. I do so to emphasize a strong belief: that understanding each other demands examining ourselves. Seeing in ourselves every possible component of human nature enhances communication and facilitates connection.

Jungian psychotherapists consider the Trickster Archetype to be the guide of the journey of individuation and of psychotherapy, much as alchemists saw Mercurius as the guide of the opus, and the Greeks saw Hermes as the guide of souls. We are influenced by Jung's treatment of Mercurius as mediator between the conscious world and the unconscious world which is unseen, has never been seen, or has been seen and banished from awareness as too frightening, too unworthy, too challenging, or too confusing.

An individual psyche requires a mediating or integrative function to tolerate the pushes and pulls of conflicting energies. Whether experienced as within the psyche, or projected outward onto a deity or ideal, the mediating experience establishes integrity; its absence results in disturbing feelings, such as emptiness and self-contempt, and then in protective devices against such unpleasant feelings. Examples of such devices which protect the personality from feelings of unabated inner-division include excessive narcissism, extreme arrogance, attempts at over-control of one's environment, and rationalizations of contradictions in behavior or beliefs, all among the traits included in the syndromes identified clinically as Personality Disorders. The Trickster Archetype is essentially related to these dynamics, dynamics which are abundantly evident in contemporary society.

In the collective psyche as well, the splits and shards of modern life invite a mediating principle. In the absence of such, societies will continue to be torn apart by chaotic governments, civil wars, moral anarchy, and the decline of culture. The Trickster Archetype provides this function when channeled constructively by a society, and given its due along with other archetypes.

I conceptualize our present archetypal situation as one in which the patriarchal Masculine Archetype is diminishing in prominence, and with him the Patriarchal Hero; the Feminine Archetype rises in importance, as does the archetype of transition, the Trickster. Because of the absence of images in our current day culture to house these archetypes, I borrow from other cultures to illustrate these relationships: for example, Tricksters like Coyote, Legba, Hermes; Patriarchal Heroes such as Apollo, Herakles, and Superman; the Feminine Centering Principle, such as Hestia, Mawu, Isis. These archetypes influence our behavior unconsciously until we find a way to bring them into awareness.

In the hermetic spirit of questioning and opening, this series of essays, each of which can be read independently of the others, examines the relationship of the Trickster Archetype to the problem of fragmentation in our individual and collective psyches. Chapter I, "Superman in Hell," explores the present trend of disdain for heroes and superior beings, for fixed criteria, and for universal ethical standards, as ordering or centering principles. In the absence of such principles the psyche exists in disharmony, vulnerable to sociopathic influences. This chapter considers the value of the Trickster in mediating the tendencies toward fragmentation, arrogance, disorder, and sociopathy of humankind in transition. The essay consists of three parts: Part One examines qualities of the Hero and Trickster Archetypes and their influences in the psyche; Part Two focuses on ethical issues; and Part Three explores the place of sociopathy in the individual psyche and its relationship to the Trickster Archetype.

Chapter II, "Through Lens and Looking Glass," focuses on the relationship of the Trickster to the need to be mirrored, and to seek in being seen a sense of meaning and of future—immortality at best—as a source of hope for something beyond the mundane pieces of our finite lives. Here the argument is raised that the narcissistic character of today's lifestyles is a manifestation of a desperate need for hope, a symptom of the missing integrative function.

In Chapter III, "Scruples and Soul Doctors," the attention is on the Trickster Archetype in the practice of psychotherapy, the need for centering of the personality in some experience of truth and reliability, and the dis-ordering of personality which occurs in the absence of such grounding, as seen, for example, in the Borderline personality dynamics.

Chapter IV, "Trickster-Woman," looks at the relationship of the Trickster Archetype to the feminine as described in myth and story. The intention of this essay is to recognize the juxtaposition of a current concentration of trickster aspects in our society and the arousal of feminine values and feminine voices of wisdom.

One way that feminine voices are being heard is through feminine influences in the philosophy of ethics. Chapter V, "Etudes in Paranoia," aims to articulate some attitudes toward evil, lying, violence, and sex in the hope of promoting dialogue and differentiation of these typically over-generalized and sentimentalized subjects. Chapter VI, "The Animated Trickster," explores one feminine ethicist's influence and proposes to separate more consciously the experience of the Trickster Archetype and of the Feminine Principle from the experience of evil in the individual and collective psyche.

I would like to believe that there are some ideas here for the adults among us to chew on, but I must admit that the greater impetus for writing comes from the child in me who loves Trickster and sees her as a rescuer of the young; a child who acknowledges death, but says, "Not yet," and wants to hope. The child's hope is that the Anima-ted, life-affirming Trickster will flourish and prevail over the death-dealing excesses that threaten to annihilate many species, including our own. This book is an effort toward that hope.

INVOCATION

You of many names…Trickster, Hermes, Mercurius, Melusina, Baubo, Thoth, Loki, Coyote, Eshu…I will call "Holy." For in the great mystery that we humans know only through a dim and short-spectrumed vision, You are a bright facet of the divine. You manifest, by hook or by crook, in each of us. If by hook, You catch hold of us and twist us about like little pawns until we find it difficult to walk a straight line. If by crook, Your impact is felt through projection; that is, You act through another to treat us to a glimpse of life's crookedness and unpredictability. You put your spin on us and our perspective changes, the straight and narrow is less discernible, boundaries which we count on to keep us safe and sure about our place in the cosmos become confused. Help us to keep a lively spirit at such times! In other days when our vision was less clouded we spoke of You in stories carefully preserved and told only in sacred spaces at auspicious times. The stories were more than entertainment; they invited the people to reflect on their perspectives, their values. Here's a prayer: hear us and enlighten us as we seek the essence of our humanity.

Chapter I

Superman in Hell

Superman is dead. The comic-book merchants of the early 1990s announced that they had him rubbed out, shameless about their motivation, to make even more money on his resurrection someday. This bit of pop-trivia strikes me as a fertile metaphor for our present time. We might say that every super-hero and super-heroine is imperiled today while the Joker has the upper hand. Of course, the high and mighty have always been an endangered species, threatened as they are from above by pigeon droppings, space debris, and lightning, and from below by envious rivals who aim to topple them or fawners underfoot who cause them to trip, as well as by the sheer weightiness of their crowns and egos. But something extraordinary seems to be at large today, working against idealization and undermining the established order. The Trickster Archetype, that representative of inverted values, paradox, and sacred foolishness, dominates our collective value system. A study of mythologies suggests that this is the case in times of transition, whenever the established principle, or high god, is able to be outwitted. What does this mythologizing mean for our modern condition?

We moderns are relatively unconscious of our mythological patterns. Typically we don't look for archetypal patterns, nor recognize that a Trickster Archetype exists and colors our values. Yet *awareness* of an archetype who holds dominion over boundaries and who guides us through ambiguity is crucial to our survival. Why crucial? Because acted-out unreflectively, the Trickster is unpredictable and possibly destructive, even sociopathic. Under its influence we can destroy other species and self-destruct as a species. On the other hand, an individual or society which can consciously and deliberately invoke and integrate the Trickster into its psyche will experience a creative and transforming archetype. We cannot afford to ignore the wisdom of the Trickster, though our culture does not have a name for this wisdom. This book does not make claims to wisdom or to be an answer to society's ills, nor is it a how-to book about handling tricksters. It is an invitation to contemplate and respect one of the oldest and most powerful archetypes within the collective psyche.

PART I: HEROES, CYNICS, CELEBRITIES, AND TRICKSTERS

> So-called facts are fraud
> They want us to allege and pledge and bow down to their God.
> We need a movement with quickness…
> You are the witness…
> To change and to counteract
> We have to take the power back.
>
> *Rage Against the Machine* (alternative rock band)

Lyrics of popular music such as these attest to the fact that cynicism, once a flag of the underground or counterculture, is now culture-wide. To know Trickster, we must consider the meaning of idealism and cynicism, of heroes and anti-heroes, of order and anarchy. Perhaps in our world society we have become too cynical to take anyone seriously as a superior hero. No sooner is a hero born than she or he is taken down by the anti-structural gravity of our current culture. In every profession the mighty have fallen; respected business leaders, statespeople, sports pros, men and women of the cloth, the military—found guilty. The word "patriarchy" inspires images of senility. Even the old patriarchal planet, Jupiter, has been bombarded by pesky comets recently.

Cynicism, which archetypal psychologist James Hillman has defined as "that sneer at our star," makes many of us too wary to want to empower any leader for very long. A public official appointed to investigate allegations of conflict of interest in the highest level of U.S. government described the situation as "cannibalism loose on the land." Comedians joked about "the failed presidency" even before the inauguration. And the bones of those giants of psychology, Freud and Jung, are being cleaned by their own followers as every rumor of character flaw is amplified. Many believers who had looked to the clergy as spiritual heroes, or to political leaders as men of integrity, feel betrayed when the intimate details of human frailty are exposed in the media.

So whom does society hold in highest esteem? Not clergy, educators, humanitarians, philosophers, artists, poets, dancers, creative scientists; they have little status, at least in America. Those unsung heroes, teachers, our cherished resource, are short-changed and often treated with disrespect or contempt. Judging by monetary rewards, comics, television hosts, and professional gossips are our valued sages and mentors; our heroes and heroines are sports figures, movie/T.V./pop-music celebrities, and business tycoons. And yet the rewards of honor are brief, envy and contempt are strong, and being in the public eye with all the media attention that ensues is an invitation to hubris—hubris that is tenuous because it is so hard to keep the media's attention. Bad sportsmanship can find applause, but it is not only sports celebrities who regard themselves as above the law, even to the extent of feeling entitled to harm their rivals. Tonya Harding, the figure skater whose boyfriend whacked the knee of her rival, made news, but she was not the first, nor will she be the last, to use foul play to get ahead.

Deliberately harming or undermining a competitor is something to which no traditionally honorable hero would stoop. In traditional folklore the wisdom-hero is never shifty, but is firmly planted in an ideal that demands honor above material advantage, even above death. But today we walk on the shifting sands of consumerism, where venality, and seldom an eternal value, dominates our tastes. Today "value" more often means money than merit. Once we spoke of the "seedy" elements of society, but now who can define "seedy?" What does it mean that we, the public, can't hear enough about the shabbiest aspects of the lives of other ordinary citizens, stars, and public servants? Many young people consider ours a society of liars and cheaters, where no values are sacred enough to escape ridicule, and anyone can be bought. If we as a society are becoming more "seedy," we need to ask what is being seeded.

DEFINING THE REALMS OF HEROES AND TRICKSTERS

In a speech to the Radio and Television Correspondents' Association, humorist Garrison Keillor urged journalists to hold to a standard of truth. He said, "When you slip into the field of fiction and entertainment, then you will be expected to be fascinating. This is going to shorten your careers." His distinction between the fields of entertainment and serious journalism is cogent, differentiating two different archetypal worlds, represented by such images as the gods Hermes and Apollo. This differentiation of the aegis of Hermes-Trickster, and the aegis of Apollo-solar hero of civilized life, is one we will continue to explore here.

For example, a lack of this differentiation is seen in the blurring of lines between serious art, simple amusements, entertainment, truth, and fiction, creating some artistic and literary nightmares. It is worth pondering why we make celebrities of our criminals and reward them for writing best-selling autobiographies. Or why we have pictures of serial-killers on record jackets and calendars ("Killer of the Month"). Or why opportunistic writers command attention and riches, not by any artistic talent of their own, but by writing sordid fictional biographies of living celebrities. Is the current state of the arts in danger of becoming a wasteland, as T. S. Eliot predicted, watered down to the point of absurdity? Woody Allen's futuristic movie *Sleeper* suggests so; its leading lady represents a vapid victim of cultural emptiness, reciting shallow verbiage which she passes off as poetry. She illustrates what happens when poorly educated consumers become the arbiters of taste. Of what value the classics when one can study wine-tasting and surfing for college credits? On the other hand, the classics and fine arts are accessible to, and possibly more appreciated by more people than ever before. Who can decide the standards for culture? Who is wise enough? Who is arrogant enough?[1] Woody Allen and Garrison Keillor are suggesting that we distinguish between serious art (or journalism, government, etc.) and light entertainment. Maybe it is a measure of our cultural flattening that this needs to be said. According to gossip columnist Liz Smith, "No one ever went broke underestimating the taste of the American public."[2]

In honoring heroic Apollo and Athena, the Greeks delineated divine realms of civilized forms and reason, such as government, medicine, military, and science; there, taking oneself and one's occupation seriously is expected because life/death repercussions are involved. In such professions, according to the ancients, Hermes plays a significant role as mediator and communicator, but does not usually usurp the responsibilities of these solar deities.[3] While tricksters of mythology often prod and poke at their more serious fellow-deities, they cannot destroy each other's power. Because in the modern world we lack awareness of these archetypal powers, we do not differentiate their realms, much less respect them. The comedy of Keillor and Allen fosters such awareness, and opens a space in the psyche for exploring: What matters? What is worth fighting for? Where has the passion gone? When do we play?

In the realm of serious professions where the responsibility for human lives is in the hands of a few, a fine line between dedication and arrogance can be discerned. For instance, the Iran-Contra affair divided the U.S. populace into those who saw the plan as a clever and justifiable trick of patriotic dedication and those who saw it as an arrogant betrayal of power. Such divisive judgments can be expected in a democracy, or in any situation where responsibility is given over cautiously, and supposedly respectfully, to those who represent our interests. Our representatives are easily able to rationalize exploiting us "for our own good," and we may have trouble recognizing when we have been used. A therapist may use his power to violate a boundary and seduce his patient in the guise of providing experience. A professor may exploit the admiration of her student, using him as an easily accessible sexual partner, or plagiarizing his work to advance herself professionally. A religious leader may manipulate the fear of God in her followers to build a material fortune.

An example of such dangerous actions shocked the American public in 1993 when it came to light that human beings had been innocent subjects of secret research on the effects of radiation between 1944 and 1974, some if it sponsored and funded by the United States government. Was it arrogance that existed in the designers of such research, and the political leaders who condoned it? Secretive and scientifically unethical approaches were applied to experiments with powerful, unknown chemicals. Such research should have had the blessing of an Apollo, a god who represents clarity and justice. A clear and honest approach to studying radiation might have more time-consuming, but need not have involved lying and harming human beings who could not argue their rights. Devious attitudes, which belong to the playful realm of a Trickster god like Hermes, were wrongly brought to play in the realm of the gods of science.

Trickster gods of mythology are known to bring down the arrogant, but they do not destroy the innocent; in fact, the Trickster is usually depicted as a savior of the innocent. The example of using trickery in the radiation studies underlines our society's confusion and lack of differentiation of power principles. This kind of example points to the fact that we can still naively give power to irresponsible leaders and then feel betrayed by them, just as the ego can lose all sense of priorities under the sway of archetypal movers that are beyond its control.

In our complicated world we can no longer afford to encourage our leaders to feel like superheroes as was done in simpler times and places. Imagine, at one time rulers were not allowed to set foot on the ground because it was feared it would dissipate the transcendent charge they carried from forces on high. To project power onto strong leaders gives a group a feeling of safety and control; the group members need not take the responsibility that freedom entails, but experience their power vicariously through the leader.

But today the greatest insult we can lay on a leader is that she holds herself aloof, much less aloft. The power of royal families like Britain's diminishes with each generation, as envy and resentment grow among the have-nots about the cost of the monarchy. I suspect that resentment grows in the royalty as well, about having to maintain decorum in the face of constant surveillance by the press.

In contrast, Czechoslovakia's velvet revolution evolved under the leadership of Vaclav Havel, who refused to live in the palace. After becoming president he continued to reside in his working class digs in downtown Prague. Although to his constituents he was a hero, Havel did not define himself as superior to the common man; he preferred to *be* the common man. Havel lives out a relationship to authority that seems to include respect for the hermetic as well as the heroic.

In a materialistic society where money attracts power and attention, we can always see ourselves as have-nots, relative to someone else's acquisitions. Leaders easily fail to evoke a balance of respect and envy and become targets of resentment from those who perceive themselves as have-nots. Nevertheless, envy of the powers of leadership does not seem to be provoking many to clamor for the responsibilities of leadership. Sociologist Amitai Etzioni sees that Americans have a strong sense of entitlement and a weak sense of obligation to their communities. A study has shown that many young adults would expect to be tried by a jury of peers was crucial, but the same population said they would be reluctant to serve jury duty![4] This suggests a disquieting trend toward wanting security and comfort without responsibility, setting the stage for careless but charismatic leaders to step in and fill the vacuum created by an absence of leadership. We want leaders who will not be self-serving and will speak for all, a task which has become impossible except for small interest groups. Unity has become difficult to manage, even for the small group of the family, or the marital pair. With so many philosophies, attractions, and distractions available to us, the ground shifts just as we are about to take a stand. How is commitment possible? Still, races and nations cling to their notions of firm self-identity with all the desperation of those promoting lost causes.[5]

Without foresight of the outcome, we can at least say of the present world that the collective shadow is being unfolded, or as Billy Graham put it, "Evil is getting worse!"[6] What's more, goodness is hardly getting better!

If it is hard to be a leader, and even harder to be a hero, how will we govern ourselves? Can a society survive, have viable authority, without heroes? Are we in a hero-lull, or are heroes history? Heroes bind us to the future, remind us of our passions, motivate us to struggle, inspire, raise us from lethargy, rescue us from anarchy. What will happen to the archetypal energy carried by heroes? If death is transformation of consciousness, what is afterlife for sky-heroes and where do they go to be transformed when there is no underworld? For the fabric of culture is being turned inside-out, so that what was hidden and forbidden is deliberately exposed and scrutinized.

In the absence of an underworld, perhaps a Superman's hell is to be earthbound. There is after all, no privacy. A hero cannot find a decent place to change personas without being intruded upon; Clark Kent would surely have a problem! Phone booths are few and far between; we must conduct our most intimate phone conversations in the open within earshot of every passerby. And forget anonymity. If the satellite spies or Internal Revenue Service don't uncover Superman, the advertisers' hit lists will.

But wait! Isn't the business suit the power costume of our time? With institutions pandering to "the bottom line," the purely motivated—dedicated teachers, researchers, clergypersons, medical servicers—are rarely free to work without money-baggers breathing down their necks. Perhaps we haven't heard the last of Clark Kent. After all, business, commerce, and merchants are in the realm of the Trickster Archetype, so who knows what's in store for Mr. Kent? And who knows what's in store for us if Mr. Kent turns his superpowers toward the world market. Would he retain his attitude of altruism or take the approach of looking out for Number One? Would it mean the end of hunger, or the proliferation of Kent Towers, Kent Enterprises, etc.?

If the Hero is earthbound, his vision may become lateral rather than vertical; the distance between peaks is great, but if our Hero resides in the neighborhood, he can see more details of the ordinary. Instead of conquering other universes or acquiring more power, perhaps he could apply his passion to everyday minutiae; in the psyche of the individual and collective, he could repair, teach, encourage, maybe fall in love.

Myths describe Trickster as not a mere polarization overagainst the hero; indeed, Trickster sometimes collaborates with or even becomes the folk-hero. Neither do the trickster gods typically stand in opposition to the high god as open rebels, except in the Judeo-Christian religions, which we will examine later. Rather, they play off of the dominant authority, and by their contradictions, bring issues to light and reinforce the basic structure of the society by their clarification of fundamental conflicts. As folk-hero the Trickster represents the underdog who prevails in the end. African mythology, like that of Native Americans, tells of the Hare as that cunning aspect of the creator which represents the prevailing of the small and weak in the face of great power. We can appreciate why Brer Rabbit stories were passed along through generations of American slaves who enjoyed identifying with the quick little Trickster, who outwitted all the more powerful creatures.

But the typical hero of literature and myth is, unlike Brer Rabbit, a super-

...flict, his bravery never wavers, his greed never bests him, his ...udable. His very existence calls out for a trickster who vio... ...idicules righteousness, and poses ethical questions. No matter ...ic psyche tries to repress it, in the long run, the Trickster will arise to fulfill... purpose: to further awareness and communication between all possible factions.

Hence, as the patriarchal era seems to be approaching decline, bringing unrest and universal turmoil in its wake, we can expect the Trickster to be around to take up the energy which has been withdrawn from patriarchal investments and vestments. The continual rise of commercialism, communication explosion, relativity of values, prominence of satirical comedy, high energy, fast pace, preoccupation with sexual imagery of our times characterize the Trickster rising. Whether Trickster's influence will ultimately be expended creatively or destructively depends on the awareness and intentionality of human beings, us.

PART II: WANTED: ETHICS, DEAD OR ALIVE

Trickster gods of mythology move within a divine plan which orients their continual state of flux and gives meaning to their actions. But human beings are not always situated in clear relationship to the divine. The Trickster Archetype, moving through human beings, may be positively oriented with regard to a purposive core, or may be an autonomous, meaningless force which can be destructive. In contrast, when the Hero archetype moves through a human being, it is decidedly oriented to some high god or principle; but heroes also cause destruction when their vision is too narrow or they are overwhelmed by arrogance and need for power. When we identify with the Hero, if we do not also relate well to the Trickster, chances are these two archetypes will meet in us in a troublesome way, often with the Trickster diminishing the Heroic potential. And the anti-heroic psyche is equally vulnerable; without a positive relationship to the Hero it can exhaust itself and inundate us with a reckless energy. And both Hero and Trickster can be ruthless and heartless unless related to the goddesses who love and protect life, nature, and the inner regions of the psyche.

An example of imbalance is the plight of urban youth, not just in North America, but worldwide. Goaded by images of the rich and famous, feeling unseen as individuals, having a high degree of aggressive energy with no opportunities to apply that energy in service beyond the personal, the youth of big cities resort to having power or getting high as their means of self-gratification. In archetypal terms, young city dwellers are often identified with heroic and ecstatic powers (such as the Greeks attributed to Herakles and Dionysus), unbalanced by lack of exposure to the nature goddesses and to the relativizing influence of the Trickster. When one feels treated like an object, rage ensues. When one feels unseen, being Somebody warrants foolhardy heroics; but without the perspective of a Trickster god's larger life-view, the future of such heroics is usually early death or prison.

Lucky is the adolescent who comes under the influence of an adult with a healthy dose of Trickster available in their psyche, for example, a humorous teacher, an ironic coach or cop, a playful adult relative. Exposure to Trickster through opportunities to laugh at oneself without too much shame, to role-play, to experiment with a variety of identities, to communicate with different kinds of people, relativizes youth's heroic bravado with humor and a more life-affirming perspective. Also, opportunities to experience the tranquilizing effect of nature's stillness, her soothing expanses of greens and blues, curved planes and soft textures, could balance the constant exposure to concrete, metal, sharp sounds, and harsh lines of the city which defy one to drop one's guard. And to harness the heroic energy to a broader purpose, or to find the ecstatic experience in music or mysticism or mentoring younger kids, can reorient young people creatively. Hermes, Herakles, Dionysus, Aphrodite—all are present in the inner city for inspiration or torture.

Characteristic of the Trickster gods of mythology is that they are coeternal with a high god. They precede humankind and are associated with the creation of the material world and with the creation of death. As archetypal figures they personify influences that are built into our psychological "hardware"; they are not optional psychological accessories. They do not let us forget that by nature we are instinctual, physical, desirous creatures, no matter how refined our spiritual aims might be. To deny this nature does not bring peace, but sows seeds of revolution in the psyche.

For example, a potential for enjoying excess, and not just well measured pleasure, is modeled by Hermes, the hungry infant god, who stole the cattle of his brother Apollo; before taking any of the meat for himself he offered it to all the gods in sacrifice. His theft was not an autistic act; he maintained relationship to Father Zeus and Brother Apollo, even as he committed his transgression. Also his sacrifice demonstrated that his mischievous insouciance was not born of power-seeking or arrogance, but of unbridled appetite for pleasure and love of life.

However, his love of life did not prevent him from taking the lives of the animals he needed for food. Here is an intriguing image—thievery, killing, and sacrifice—and it occurs through the god's hunger at the dawn of civilization. Jungian analyst Lopez-Pedraza writes:

> In the "Homeric Hymn to Hermes" there is an evocation of the dark nighttime of man's past. Scholarship conceives the basis of culture, i.e. religious ritual and mythological thinking, as products of the search for food. I would say that killing animals with weapons, religious ritual and mythological thinking together compose a basic and conflictive complex in humankind.[7]

Lopez-Pedraza holds that the conflict between nature and culture threatens the survival of humankind, and lies at the root of the psyche, manifesting as pathologies at the basic level of the instinct of hunger, such as eating disorders. He speaks of the propensity to excess as a "titanic component in human nature," recounting Jung's concern that excessive procreation would cause destruction by overpopulation. Lopez-Pedraza states, "We are living in times of ever increasing excess, which is unreflective."[8]

The key word here is "unreflective." Like unconscious titans we humans thoughtlessly ram through nature in our heedless pursuit of materialistic pleasures and mindless conveniences. One popular psychoanalytic view of unreflective greed was proposed by Dorothy Dinnerstein. She attributed the sense of power gained in conquering nature to the male's desire to compensate for early ambivalence toward the mother's body.[9] A rational way to understand human behavior is to notice that the repertoire of responses becomes conditioned to certain stimuli. For example, Dinnerstein sees a connection between the male's ambivalent love/hate relationship with mother as sole caretaker, and his ambivalent relationship (and displacement of hunger, need, and aggressive feelings) with Mother Earth.

This dynamic which Dinnerstein attributed to males, (i.e., the need to achieve mastery over [Mother] nature) probably exists in many individual men. However, there is also the fact of archetypal greed, part of every human being, male and female, with which we must all struggle. As such, greediness cannot be reduced to being the result of some infantile experience, but, as Lopez-Pedraza points out, is present in the pre-dawn of the human psyche. Edward Edinger refers to fundamental greed in terms of devouring monsters, Behemoth and Leviathan, as representatives of the primordial concupiscence of being, remote from human values. "Our existence is based on protoplasm—greedy, lusting, devouring matter."[10] In other words, greed is not just a reaction to parenting styles, but a universal, a fact of nature, and our human task is to recognize our greed and take an ethical position in regard to it, not deny, project, or euphemize it.

Something has happened within my lifetime to the perception of greed. The negative aspects of greed used to be stressed, and it was regarded as a powerful flaw of human nature which all but a minority of people tried to inhibit for the good of the many. Even the natural expression of greed in young children was not condoned. Now it is a badge of cleverness in children of all ages. And life today for the affluent is so rich and complex that it is hard to distinguish between having enough for survival and being greedy.[11]

DIVINE RESEARCH ON GREED

Survival on earth places us in a moral dilemma, a basic dilemma with which children grapple, and with which those who maintain contact with the child in the psyche continue to grapple throughout life.[12] When my daughter was six years old she heard a sermon about the goodness expected of us by the all-good Christ. After the service she saw the minister greeting people and challenged him about this: "You said Jesus doesn't want us to hurt each other, but why did Jesus make everything eat other things?" Obviously, to my surprise, she had given this some thought.

The minister replied, "Animals eat each other because God allows the animals to follow a natural law, but people are expected to follow a higher law." He quickly turned to someone else and left my little carnivore standing perplexed to work out alone the horror of this fundamental conflict, the conflict which preoccupied Jung from an early age. Early in life Jung felt the tension between survival mechanisms and a hypocritical niceness preached by the ministers in his family. Later he wrote: "Egotism always has the character of greed, which shows itself chiefly in three ways: the power-drive, lust, and moral laziness."[13] These aspects of survival-based egotism, he felt, rendered us unconscious of the equality of our fellow humans.

The dilemma thickens as our planet diminishes and we wonder how to reconcile our desire to survive with our compassion for other life-forms, even for our fellow humans. What kind of creator would put us in such a dilemma? It is not hard to imagine that we are playing our parts in some cosmic experiment in moral judgment. Are we victims of hostile forces, or intrepid explorers of our own darkness, the return of the repressed? One might speculate about mischievous gods enjoying our present-day scenario with sadistic relish, another might imagine the divine compassionately allowing us to mess with it until we get it right. No wonder we are fascinated by science fiction as it acknowledges such basic questions by playing with them and with possible answers.[14] Jung shows a penchant for sci-fi as he muses:

> Once more we are appalled by the incongruous attitude of the world creator toward his creatures, who to his chagrin never behave according to his expectations. It is as if someone started a bacterial culture which turned out to be a failure. He might curse his luck, but he would never seek the reason for the failure in the bacilli and want to punish them morally for it.[15]

Einstein's famous fundamental question is so human: "Is the universe friendly?"

Erik Erikson wrote that he saw in psychoanalysis and in Gandhi's spiritual philosophy a similar approach to life as an "experiment in truth."[16] If humankind is an experiment in truth, each of us is both the experimenter and the subject at once. We observe ourselves wobbling between truth, half-truths, and falsehoods in our attempts to represent our complex realities.

Being assigned such a responsibility as that experiment entails does not give most of us much feeling of power. Perhaps as our numbers increase we become more like children of a large and spiritually hungry family whose parents cannot sustain them, where greed has dominion over dignity, narcissism over cooperation. Perhaps we are relegated by mass media to an adolescent ethic. Or are we in the same shape we've always been in, but more aware—as a result of advanced communications—of our condition, our weak, vulnerable, gossipy, bloodthirsty condition?

Whether or not as subjects of divine research, a number of us are pushing every possible moral limit as if to test the stress point. Sociologists call our current condition "moral anarchy." Sociopathy is in the air.[17] Does the unraveling of the moral fiber of society harbor a rebirth at a higher level of functioning, or does it mean the end is near? Is the fadeout of the twentieth century curtains for civilization?

Progress's Shadow

The Western world is hero-oriented at the conscious level. We operate ostensibly to achieve ideals and conquer vices. The trickster is much more conscious in other parts of the world where cunning is accepted as a survival technique. Adolf Guggenbühl-Craig notes that every myth, such as our popular Myth of Progress, in which we expect to progress ever closer to a perfect world, carries a shadow. In our case, Guggenbühl-Craig proposes, the shadow myth is of anti-progress or Armageddon.[18] Clearly, eschatological predictions around 2000 A.D. abound; that date has long been linked to the end of the world. As such, it has been suggested that it serves as a source of fatalistic despair or indifference in many. Less extremist views exhort us to pay attention, to heed warnings, to remember the demise of previous cultures in order to avoid the extinction of the human race.

For ages humankind has expressed such concerns through myths and legends. In 1890 Pope Leo XIII had a vision of Christ giving Satan a free hand in the world for the next hundred years,[19] years which did see Nazism, Communism, materialism, nuclear proliferation, and some would say, Satanism, flourish. The Pope foresaw that the century would be a test of Satan's power, to which men would succumb or resist; if resistant, the vision foretold, we would learn more benevolent ways of treating each other. This vision reminds us of the wager between Yahweh and Satan which is the opening gambit of the story of Job. Though Einstein concluded, "God doesn't play dice,"[20] the Old Testament God of that story did play dice with Job's fate as the power struggle between Yahweh and Satan, fueled by possessiveness and envy, played itself out.

The psyche seems to want to experience Satan as redeemable; his redemption is the theme of many stories. The Koran tells that Satan will be forgiven on the Last Day.[21] Among Christians, an old folk legend tells that Satan was God's first-born, and that when Christ was created, Satan saw that God loved him more. Satan turned against them both, and as a result, humankind will continue to suffer until Satan comes to peace with his envy and makes amends to God.[22] It needs to be added to the legend that it takes a powerful transformation to come in contact with one's envy and one's need to surrender pride and accept frailty. For some, nothing short of a brush with death can bring about such a transformation. This transformation of envy into peaceful contentment is often imaged by the psyche (as we see in dreams, myths, and art) as contacting and connecting with the Feminine Principle, or Anima, in her aspect as Dark Goddess. Satan, then, needs to be more in touch with his Anima.

If astrology has anything to tell us, this well may be happening. The astrological prediction based on the precession of the equinoxes, which brings us in the year 2000 to the early phase of the Aquarian Age, suggests that human society will undergo lessons that will make us a more compassionate and life-affirming—in the language of archetypal psychology, more "Anima-aware"—group. The values of generativity will surpass those of competition, say astrologers. But is it too late? Marie-Louise von Franz, Jung's outstanding student and colleague, has spoken out for years about the state of decay in civilization:

> I have the impression that our culture and civilization is in a final stage, that it has entered a stage of decay. I believe either that we shall find a renewal or else that we are at an end. And this renewal I can only see in that which Jung discovered, namely in a positive contact with the creative source of the unconscious and with dreams. These are our roots.[23]

Von Franz is referring to the fact that Jung, who said that the two main features of a mature mind were reason and moral values,[24] had a vision of renewal: the renewal of each conscious person through his or her dedication to the continual struggle with the shadow. This struggle, Jung predicted, would lead to a wholeness and an integrity that would not rely on collective authority, but would grow with the capacity for ethical judgment nourished by the deepest wells of life sustaining spirit in the core of our being.

Jung's own dreams and preoccupations culminated in "a little essay" that he considered his most inspired, *Answer to Job,* written one spring while "plagued by my liver."[25] In it he confronts the contradictoriness of a God who seems to have created sin and left it to humankind to find resolution. Jung believed that the individuating person, seeking authenticity beyond the collective mind, is confronted with archetypal questions, expressions of the Self which require dialogue and emotional engagement. He or she is no longer fulfilled by complacently going through the motions of living in the small world of acquisitive comfort seeking. Through encounters with larger questions, those wrestling matches with angels and demons, come the answers to questions of integrity that suffuse life with meaning. Divinity becomes a force to be reckoned with, not an abstract Father to be honored once a week. As Edinger puts it, "God is now to be carried experientially by the individual."[26]

But how is one to find resolution, much less carry God, and how are we to find the deep springs of hope within this "positive contact with the creative source" when we are fragmented very early by a life which has never been centered? Many of us are too psychically sundered to have ever remembered the experience of touching the life-sustaining spirit directly from within. How do we achieve integrity if we are conditioned to avoid the core of being by means of dissociation, drugs, and other avoidant behaviors?

The unknown factors are: How many conscious beings must there be and how soon must they come to awareness to avert an overthrow of human consciousness by the endless sleep? The question is not whether consciousness is valuable, but rather, can it happen that enough people value consciousness to change the direction of our careening? The story of the hundredth monkey who adopts a new behavior and significantly influences the behavioral pa[...] species is cogent. What can we expect of ourselves, and how many hu[...] a hundred monkeys?

Or, to pose the question from the other end, how long does it take a group of humans to become a herd of rhinoceroses? In Ionesco's allegorical play, *Rhinoceros*, the protagonist determinedly holds onto his humanity while everyone around him, including his fiancee, opts for metamorphosing into a beast, because it is fashionable.[27] How much of our humanity will we sacrifice in order to achieve the right image?

Theoretical Ethics

Sometimes we have to put principles aside and just do what's right.
Garrison Keillor on "A Prairie Home Companion" radio show.

To illustrate one aspect of ethical complexity we have only to look briefly at our television sets. One day on the morning news an actor representing a group entitled "Coalition for Values" declared that there was a hole in the moral ozone, and that perhaps the media and music industries were "destroying a generation" by playing fast and loose with destructive imagery. In rebuttal to this charge, entertainers and artists insist that they create nothing new, but only reflect back to us what exists. They don't want the responsibility for our morality. Satan, a regular on the television show, "Saturday Night Live," (John Lovitz's character) when accused of undermining listeners' morals by composing evil lyrics for rock bands, says, "I live in hell. I write what I know." By what universals, or virtues, and for whose greater good can we judge entertainment? Regardless of the ethical theory applied to questions of artistic license and moral responsibility, there is no simple solution to this thorny subject.

Whenever morality is the subject of discourse, the focus is often on an immoral element negatively influencing the values of others (one bad apple, etc.). But here's an astounding fact: experiments in the communication of moral principles show that *one person can raise the moral consciousness of the whole group*. Psychologist Lawrence Kohlberg's research in moral development seems to demonstrate this uplifting fact.[28] We rarely entertain the possibility that Satan on "Saturday Night Live" writes what "he knows" in order to get a reaction that challenges his reality—that he is not just devil, but devil's advocate, wanting to be challenged, wanting his attitude to be transformed, wanting his moral consciousness raised. In that case, those who ignore him increase his pain by their withholding. In other words, Satan may need dialogue, not just mirroring or avoidance.

Kohlberg's six stages of moral development progressed from ethics which were survival-based, and later convention-based, then culminated in a morality of justice whereby we attain a perspective beyond our own interests and recognize the rights of others and the welfare of the whole. Kohlberg cited Mahatma Gandhi and Martin Luther King, Jr. as examples of the highest stage of moral development. The theory proved fertile and inspiring, though methods of assessment for purposes of training educators to apply the theory are problematical and controversial.

Carol Gilligan further elucidated Kohlberg's work by identifying two different cognitive styles. She found a masculine cognitive style which focused on rights and responsibilities, and a feminine cognitive style, focused on care and relatedness, which influenced the way boys and girls responded to moral dilemmas. In Kohlberg's schema the masculine style prevailed, which did not do justice to the feminine style and tended to give females the appearance of inferior moral capacity. Gilligan offered the images of a "masculine hierarchy" and a "feminine web" to illustrate her findings:

> The images of hierarchy and web, drawn from the texts of men's and women's fantasies and thoughts, convey different ways of structuring relationships and are associated with different views of morality and self. But these images create a problem in understanding because each distorts the other's representation. As the top of the hierarchy becomes the edge of the web and as the center of a network of connection becomes the middle of a hierarchical progression, each image marks as dangerous the place which the other defines as safe.
>
> Thus the images of hierarchy and web inform different modes of assertion and response: the wish to be alone at the top and the consequent fear that others will get too close; the wish to be at the center of connection and the consequent fear of being too far out on the edge. These desperate fears of being stranded and being caught give rise to different portrayals of achievement and affiliation, leading to different modes of action and different ways of assessing the consequences of choice.[29]

People whose cognitive style is masculine, oriented toward hierarchy, can feel hemmed in when at the center of a web of relationships; those whose thinking style is oriented toward relatedness, can feel isolated at the top of the ladder. These differences significantly influence the way that people perceive the ideal solutions to moral questions. It appears that morality is influenced by not only gender, but intelligence, education, and emotional stability as well. To add another dimension, let us consider that we all contain a contrasexual component which renders each of us subject to inner conflicts between our own masculine need for hierarchy and our feminine need for web.[30] In Gilligan's differentiation of gender styles is an echo of an ancient duality in the area of law, that is, the tension between justice and mercy, associated with the masculine and feminine respectively.

Although Gilligan described her schema as about "themes," not "genders," and her associations to gender are not absolute but empirical, still critics of Gilligan express wariness about implications of gender differentiations which imply biological premises. The bias against biologism stems partially from the fear of genetic engineering, a powerful tool with appalling potential for destructiveness, and partially from the fear that biologism contributes to stereotyping and unfair assumptions, i.e. men do not care about relationships or women cannot think in terms of rights and responsibilities. Contrapuntal to these fears is confidence that if we examine biological differences fairly and not with the intention of proving superiority, we will find that there are some differences between sexes, races, and species which contribute to beauty, that they balance and enhance the richness of life on earth. Rather than shrink from looking at the truth about our differences, we can learn to look with generous intent.

Gilligan's work also encountered debate from those who refused to be convinced that the need for justice and the need for care and mercy are gender correlated. Some feminists consider it dangerous to associate caring and compassion with the feminine—the danger being that society will continue to relegate women to caretaking roles exclusively.[31] In spite of the controversy provoked by their theories, Gilligan and Kohlberg have given us a valuable springboard for considering some of the ontological problems of our complex society as we aim to find moral principles, not rules, to help us govern ourselves.

The human individuation process can be seen as the development of integrity. Moral development usually proceeds with maturity, influenced greatly by intelligence and milieu. The problems presented by low intelligence are on-going; there will always be those who are incapable of the abstract thinking involved in objectifying good and evil. Unfortunately, stupid people do sometimes come into power, especially when weapons are readily available as they are now. Inevitably society will have to deal with them, and with parents who are incapable of learning to parent, and citizens who are incapable of the abstract thinking involved in understanding fundamental tenets of democracy. All the heroes in the psyche cannot eliminate stupidity and greed. But though intelligence is out of our hands (unless genetic engineering becomes accepted), we are still responsible for our milieu.

Historians, sociologists, economists, and psychologists have been examining the roots and fruits of individualism from many perspectives for some time. As I write this my anxiety about the precariousness of individualism in the previous Soviet countries, to which I am spiritually tied, disturbs me. The experiment in democratic pluralism on a worldwide scale is still in process, and the crucial questions are still out. Is it possible to maintain a society of individuals, each responsible for his own economic safety, and still sustain an ethical majority in that society who are sufficiently psychologically developed to care about the safety and well-being of others? And can those who are concerned about the well-being of others attain and survive political power without being altered by it? Can a democratic society which keeps absorbing immigrants who have no experience of democracy maintain the society's original ideals? And in the individual, can a polytheistic psyche survive without an organizing principle, or can that principle by-pass the heroic ego?

IINDIVIDUATION AND INTEGRITY

The psychological community is deeply concerned about the answers to these questions. As an analytical psychologist I am committed to bringing whatever influence I have to furthering a society which allows maximum development of the individual within a worldview that is compassionate and grounded in the reality of life on earth. While the sociologist focuses on the influences of group forces, the psychoanalyst focuses on the influences on the individual and of the individual on his milieu. Therapists observe (and I observe in my own practice) that people who are allowed the freedom to develop their abilities, who have basic survival needs and at least a minimum of need for attention met in close relationship to others, and who are encouraged to reflect on their motives, override their base greed and become generous and caring members of society.

But we also see that many small children do not receive the minimal degree of attention needed to develop emotional stability, and that disorders in thinking, perception, and impulse control result that do not respond to the usual controls, disciplinary measures, and rehabilitation efforts designed to make good citizens of them. A certain percentage of these find their way into the psychotherapist's domain, and a certain percentage of those muster the inner resources called for to respond to treatment through psychotherapy. This leaves many others whom society has to care for in alternative ways, such as through medications, varying degrees of incarceration, and welfare; they are the responsibility, the dependent "have-not" shadow of the "haves."

As for the "haves" who are concerned with psychotherapy, in spite of the ambiguity around statistical proof of the value of depth psychotherapy, experienced psychotherapists observe—and become convinced by numerous examples—that people, assuming they have food and work, become more generous and flexible, not more selfish as a result of sustained self-reflection. While we may appear self-absorbed during some stages of therapy, in the long-run we usually find in ourselves an integrity that is authentic, not merely conforming. To the general public observing singular examples of people who have had long-term psychotherapy, it is not always obvious how much immature behavior has been replaced by responsible behavior. We must know how far the person has had to come, and from what extremes of genius or pathology, extraordinary talent or obsessions, to be able to judge the results, a fact which makes scientific measures difficult to apply. An outside observer could never look into the psyche to see how many years of struggle kept one marriage, poem, child, hope from being extinguished.

As sociologists point out, therapy is one way of purchasing attention as one purchases attention from waiters, masseurs, and by owning expensive cars or sneakers or a gun.[32] Receiving a minimal amount of attention is essential to psychological well-being, and if therapy consisted only of providing that minimum, it would be of some value. But the attention of a therapist is the beginning of a process, not the purpose. Our concern as analysts is how receiving attention may enable self-reflection, and how self-reflection evolves into ethics.

Webster's dictionary essentially defines "morality" and "ethics" interchangeably. I like Erik Erikson's distinction, however, which he makes in the context of examining an ethic of non-violence:

> Non-violence, inward and outward, can become a true force only where ethics replaces moralism. And ethics, to me, is marked by an insightful assent to human values, whereas moralism is blind obedience; and ethics is transmitted with informed persuasion, rather than enforced with absolute interdicts. Whether the increasing multitudes of men can ever develop and transmit such an ethical attitude I do not know, but I do know that we are committed to it, and that the young are waiting for our support in attempting it.[33]

This statement is taken from Erikson's comparison of the spiritual truth of Satyagraha as formulated and lived by Gandhi,[34] and the psychological truth as formulated and lived by Erikson through his identification as a psychoanalyst. When Erikson says "we" are committed to the development and transmission of an ethical attitude, I believe he is speaking for psychology, and particularly psychoanalysis which attempts not to impose a set of morals on the individual, but to assist each one in finding an authentic ethical attitude.

This is not to imply that psychoanalysts or people who have been analyzed are paragons of virtue. As James Hillman repeatedly hammers home, psychoanalysis is not a hero's journey toward growth and maturity; as such it could only be repressive. Psychoanalysis is an exploring of what is, not what should be. For that reason it is in the realm of the Trickster, though there may be heroic moments and opportunities to explore one's heroism. In discovering an authentic ethical attitude, guilt loses its potency and gives way, not to dissoluteness, but to sensitivity. No need for heroic motivators to persuade or dissuade when we see our behavior and its consequences from a broader vantage point. Good therapy enables us to enlarge our perspective, to place ourselves and our condition into a larger landscape.

Analysis itself is deeply concerned with ethics but is not moralistic; indeed, it even entails cruelty in its method.[35] Every interpretation can be perceived as an act of violence, in as much as it splits an undifferentiated state with the sword of consciousness. Furthermore, the role of the patient can be seen as that of a thief, stealing what he can from the psyche of the analyst.[36]

As for results, sometimes in therapy there are vast expansions of ability or love or patience gained, but one isolated, stubborn complex continues to sabotage the personality. Unfortunately sometimes years of increasing awareness break down in a single regressive act. But when we say that analysis assists one in finding an authentic ethical attitude, we mean that the process with its attention to reflection and introspection intends to, and usually does, facilitate an ethical approach to life and to relatedness. Analysis promotes an authentic ethic, not by repressing and judging, but by considering priorities and consequences and subjecting taboos to the crucible of imagination, a process Jung called "integrating the shadow." It is in this process of coming to know the shadow that we encounter differences between archetypes in the psyche, such as Hero, Trickster, Animus and Anima.

Clowning Around in the Shadow

One tactic for approaching the shadow is through humor, an essential quality of trickster, and one often absent in the superior hero. The clown, a facet of the Trickster Archetype, provides opportunities for us to relax and, through identification with the clown's contact with primitive states, to let go of the psychic work that ego- functions require. In the Native American Hopi culture, the clown is seen as a visionary who reminds the people that our human destiny is not to become perfect, but to become spiritual creatures.[37] In the world of the clown and cartoon we temporarily abandon ego and the reality-principle for the world of the archetypal Trickster where we are not limited by time and space, and where there will be no sad consequences of our behavior. The distinction between having contact with primitive aspects of the psyche and being primitive is an important one. The distinction is not always obvious and cannot be made on appearances. Since the profound can masquerade as simple, only knowing the degree of another person's awareness of the shadow can tell you about her relationship to the primitive psyche, and about whether she is simple by choice or by compulsion. Regarding the clown's ability to repair the psychic damage done by the stress and sobriety involved in maintaining strong boundaries around the shadow, Ulanov explains:

> This magical reparation is one great source of the clown's appeal. His antics provide us with a space with which to experience our aggressive impulses to the full, without our having to be responsible for the results. Our egos can rest from the burden of the cause-and-effect sequences we know so well in our diurnal reality. At least for the moment our egos do not have to hold everything together. We can let go. We can enjoy the wreckage fully, like a child knocking over a tower of blocks or making a great mess of mud. We can enjoy our own truce in tranquillity, not needing to hold our own opposite emotions together. We can indulge vicariously in our impulses to make messes, to let everything fall down, to smash, to rip, to smear—and all without payment of guilt. No need to repair damage done by our hate, because we experience it as totally separate from and unconnected to our love. No sadness or remorse over the damage our destructive impulses may do, because no one has been hurt. In fact as well as in fantasy, it was great fun.[38]

Ulanov reminds us that a characteristic of Trickster's realm is that it is a place where outlandish antics do not cause permanent damage. And as we have noted, this is not the realm of scientists and governors, but of their friends and lighthearted companions.

In a study of Edwin Lear, who introduced the genre of nonsense poetry into nineteenth century English literature, Clifton Snider finds numerous Trickster qualities in Lear's personality and literary works. "The true spirit of all nonsense," says Snider, is "compensation for all artificial strictures, a joyous release from inhibitions."[39] A wanderer who suffered from epilepsy, depression, and loneliness, Lear shared surrealistic images in limericks which clearly bear the trickster touch:

There was an Old Man of Whitehaven,
Who danced a quadrille with a raven,
But they said, "It's absurd to encourage this bird!"
So they smashed that Old Man of Whitehaven.[40]

The Raven is an animal aspect of Trickster, and feathers are often associated with tricksters, as we see in caps and costumes of fools and jesters. A good deal becomes "a feather in one's cap." Another bird associated with Tricksters is the cock. William Willeford describes numerous examples of the fool aspect of Trickster portrayed as cock. He notes that, as the cock announces the arrival of dawn, the fool expresses the incipient consciousness still in the darkness of the unconscious.[41] It is the fool who usually carries the new consciousness of the collective when the dominant principles are on the decline.

The heroic attitude carries us away to a place of ideals so we come as close to perfection as possible. But Trickster brings out the truth through embodied, particular ways, never through abstractions that would take us away from human emotion and human physicality. Characteristic of Trickster is its shape-shifting capacity.[42] We can't predict what persona it will take. This, too, separates it from the heroic, whose task is to be reliable. Like the prince in James Lapine's play, *Into the Woods*, some of us are "raised to be charming, not dependable."

Superheroes and tricksters have valid but different functions, and lately popular culture is kinder to tricksters. One of Superman's miracles was that he always looked perfectly groomed no matter what he had been through. This marks him as obsolete today where the proper look is ungroomed, or shall we say, relaxed. The look is naturally contrived—hair treated so that it looks as if it had never been touched by a comb, clothing made to look beaten and torn. Oversized clothes in layers gives us the charm of clowns, or homeless people who must wear all they own. Comfort defines propriety; yet we torture ourselves (tousled perms, tight jeans, etc.) to appear comfortable. One way to understand the current love of grunge is to recognize it as part of the a-heroic mystique. Our costumes caricature the heroic qualities of dignity and virility. The forbidden is being differentiated and exposed as never before (literally, as women wear their underwear as overwear), a necessary step toward overcoming reactions of either repression, denial, or compulsive acting-out; those reactions kept the forbidden in its place, that is, out of mind, and in the cellars of the psyche.

In previous generations depth psychology usually encountered the problem of getting through to the repressed liveliness which had been relegated to the shadow world. Now we have a different task. It is not the instincts which are in the dark; rather, the connection of instinctual liveliness to some purpose, and the joy in living that gives life meaning are dimmed, far from consciousness, for many people.

To find the reasons for our sad alienation from our own sources of liveliness, we must look more deeply into the shadow, beyond the physical instincts, which have all been acknowledged; beyond the emotions, which have all been legitimized. In the shadow-world, Trickster is guide and psychopomp, so with her we may come through the unknown to the wellsprings of hope and life.

Shadow's Guide

Observing ethical development we find that the early adult years usually mark a transition from belief in absolute truth to an understanding of contextual relativity of truth and ethics. But some of us never attain this level of tolerance of ambiguity and capacity for objectivity. We go on evaluating in black/white mind-traps until something rivets our attention to other possibilities. One reason for the fascination with cops, crime, and dirt-dishing gossip may be that we seek out that which expands and differentiates our contact with shadow. The positive aspect of deliberate focus on unacceptable behavior is that it makes compulsive, or unconscious acting-out impossible. This is the rationale behind paradoxical methods of therapy, which will be discussed more in Chapter III. It is hard to get away with the excuse, "the devil made me do it," when we've been educated to imagine the compulsive acting-out of the repressed. We learn to understand acting-out by having it presented in such a way that enables us to reflect on it. This happens in therapy when the therapist identifies the patient's acting-out and confronts the patient about it so that they can both see beyond the behavior. It happens also when we see someone else being found acting-out, and we reflect on the meaning of it for ourselves.

For example, we learn about acting-out through the exposure of clergy who have been unable to successfully maintain repressive behavior and have acted sexually inappropriately. Through public exposure their transgressions are forced to consciousness, the consciousness that is theirs and ours simultaneously. Through public exposure we all participate in their/our transgressions. They are we. We must reexamine our sexuality, our puritan ethic, our secret longings. The sociopath within must first have its attention caught and held by being mirrored in order to come to a larger perspective of its desirousness. We watch the humiliated, "fallen" minister on TV, and we are caught, our attention snared; we must identify with this foolishness on some level, though on the conscious level we may be feeling superior. If we were immune from such transgressions, we would not be captivated, and would probably not be interested in them. But it is difficult to say who is immune and who has not been exposed, who has not yet looked into her own unconscious sociopathy.

Trickster helps us establish distance from our own and others' sociopathy, and distance is necessary for reflection. Observing the transgressions of others, like listening to trickster stories, is a homeopathic treatment of our own shadow when handled with care; we take in a small dose of the disease, not enough to overwhelm and result in hopelessness, but enough that defenses start to recognize the condition.

We must be aware, though, that there is a seductiveness in the shadow that entices; the compulsive attachment many of us have to crime and mystery stories, film noire, violent games, and fascination with the bizarre testify to that seduction. Gory stories feed our appetite for blood, but that appetite can become excessive. Seeking experiences of the shadow world runs the danger of being subsumed by it; a little poison inoculates, but a drop too much kills. Being too close to evil and too curious about it can be just as unwise as being too avoidant of the dark side. If we are going to attempt a dialogue with Satan, we had better prepare well, and have some courageous allies backing us up. In her study of the trickster in addiction, Linda Leonard gives an example of shadow seduction in Joseph Conrad's lifelong struggle with darkness. Conrad tried repeatedly to manage his fascination with "John Barleycorn" and the lifestyle it held out to him, and repeatedly found himself overcome by the power of alcohol.[43] Alcohol and drugs are tricksters, promising what they can't give, demanding confrontation and not gullible acceptance.

The siren's call to Odysseus is a metaphor for the pull towards that world of self-indulgence that traps many of us into a stagnant cul-de-sac, whether through addiction to chemical substances, video games, computers, reading, phone sex, fantasy, television, or anything else that substitutes compulsive, exclusive, and escapist behavior for being engaged with the real world. Some religions exhort us not to expose ourselves at all to the darkness of seductive substances or activities, or else to arm ourselves mightily and go in as missionary soldiers. Trickster's attitude is to explore, uncover secrets, appreciate, examine. Even though we can identify a tricky element in all seduction, it would not be a typical Trickster's intention to cause someone to become trapped in addiction; just the opposite, Trickster would be a resource for escape from the ecstatic, Dionysian self-indulgence of addiction. Here we should recall that Hermes gave Odysseus the herb of protection against the influence of beautiful Circe who turned men into piggish beasts.

Another example of being seduced into the shadow occurs when one's job depends on living out some aspect of collective evil, such as killing. This dynamic is a factor in Post Traumatic Stress Disorder, among combat military, in totalitarian groups, and exists in civilian life as well. Temple Grandin, professor of Animal Sciences at Colorado State University, observed that in slaughter houses the constant exposure to killing transforms some employees. She recommends that workers in that field of meat processing be rotated to avoid problems of overexposure to death. Some develop a hard protective attitude and start killing animals coldly and mechanically; others start to enjoy it and torment the animals more and more. Dr. Grandin notes that there is a high correlation between the way people treat animals and the way they treat the handicapped, and this is reflected in state laws. According to Grandin, "Capital punishment states are the worst animal states and the worst for the handicapped."[44]

Temple Grandin is an interesting person in her own right on the subject of moral behavior. Her life story is a fascinating description of the development of an autistic child who was able to attain a high level of functioning in society. One of her personality characteristics is difficulty in pretending, in using deviousness or dissembling of any kind. She does not understand lying and deception and is unable to employ tactics of manipulation. Failure to understand pretense is almost universal among the autistic, according to Oliver Sachs. Grandin's relationships are totally straightforward and logical. The usual social interactions are emotionally empty for her, but her capacity to relate to animals is profound and gives her keen insight into that shadow area of cruelty to others.[45]

Grandin's unique view of social life contributes to our understanding of how the pull of the shadow creates a tension, luring us to surrender. The task of remaining conscious is not effortless. I am not referring to the efforts of suppression or repression, but to the effort of exploring the psyche through reflection and imagination. We fly away from it, get lost in emotions, dissociate, numb out, become stubborn and cynical, rationalize. And if we do pursue our fantasies in a reflective manner, we may be resistant to the brutality and ruthlessness required to dismember the seductions of the primitive world. As our most prominent creation myth illustrates, knowledge is costly, and whoever would become conscious is not able to remain in paradise. Occasionally it is granted us, tax-free, by Mercurius, and comes suddenly, through a stroke of genius or a brilliant flash of wisdom. But more often awareness is hard won and requires tireless plodding over the same ground until something gives, as psychotherapists and parents all know. To come to consciousness without a gift from heaven is to persist, demand, or to commit a theft from the gods.

And then, with awareness comes the awesome responsibility to the chronically hopeless members of the psyche that we have been forced to acknowledge. The keeping in touch; bringing meals, attention, and daylight; making them comfortable—like old, senile relatives we must not forget them, these hopeless degenerates of our inner world, the unredeemable murderers, pedophiles, cannibals, idiot children of our psyche, knowing them is our only way out of our pathology, pragmatism, egotism, rationalism.

Order's Shadow

Trickster shows us that order is relative and all identity is in flux. Throughout nature organisms go through periods of breakup of their current level of organization followed by reorganization at a higher level as growth proceeds. Child psychoanalyst Michael Fordham has helped us to understand how the defenses of the infant and child relax to allow the object of a new archetypal constellation to be received, and then restructure themselves again to assimilate the new contents. He describes this as a deintegration-reintegration process. The term "deintegration" describes a purposive reduction of tension which allows an opening for the new experience of an archetypal representative, as opposed to disintegration which would imply a failure to remain intact.[46] We are looking at a psychic equivalent of shedding the old skin or cocoon. People in the process of deintegration are often described as "having a breakdown," when a long-ranged vantage point would comprehend the process as a "breakthrough" or "breakup" of an obsolete order.

Clearly the macrocosm of society is in a period of disorder. The possibility of breakdown seems very real, but a more optimistic view would hope that we are in a state of deintegration. In the microcosm of an individual personality, deintegration would signal opportunity for reorganization at a higher level of awareness. When we consider the barriers between races, religions, genders, and financial status being broken down along with the breakdown of moral standards, we see something positive possibly emerging from the chaos. This is not to imply that boundaries are not valid or desirable. We are not equally talented, industrious, intelligent, compassionate, or capable of strong leadership, and our differences contribute to the opulence of outer and inner life. But our breakdown may also be freeing us from the oppressive categorization and stereotypes that impose false limits on ourselves and promote harsh treatment of each other. Thomas Moore, in his book, *Dark Eros: The Imagination of Sadism*, develops this theme by showing that the fiction of Marquis de Sade creates the very figures that we repress and undervalue in a sentimental view of morality. Sadeian imagination recognizes that we do lust, dissemble, deceive, and to deny that we do only distances us even more from the soul. Denial of our shadow leads to a sentimentalized world, a split life weighty with the burden of maintaining impossible ideals and foiled with the incursion of repressed shadow appearing again and again as personal symptoms and social disaster. The key into Sade is a slight twist of imagination, the decision that the frenzied pursuit of right living, impossible virtues, and sentimental values is neither necessary nor an honest reflection of how we live, even in the midst of those ideals.[47]

Moore is arguing that the inclusion of the shadow side of love, and in fact, of every virtue, comprises true integrity. But admitting the dark aspects of our personalities does not mean abandoning virtue. To include the dark forces in our awareness requires care and respect for the power of shadow to seduce us into hopelessness.

PART III: SOCIOPATHY, STAMINA, AND HOPE

It is our fashion these days in psychology to attempt to look at behavior "scientifically" and to find behavior patterns based on perceived norms. Behavior patterns have been viewed for generations in descriptive terms, such as terms of moral precepts ("salt of the earth," "bad eggs"), non-judgmental contextual observations ("a family man," "a loner"), possession by divinities (Aphrodisian grace, Dionysian madness), the effect of previous existences (dharma, fa), or behavioristic reductions (reactions to a schizophrenogenic mother, chemical imbalance). Today our categories are strongly colored by psychiatric notions which influence not only the mental health professions, but courts, schools, and popular jargon. In an attempt to classify differences in the more consistent factors of character, psychiatry has identified the concept of "disordered personality." The psychiatric nosological category known as "personality disorders" includes "anti-social personality disorder" (sociopaths and psychopaths), as well as a number of other character types that fall short of society's image of a well-adjusted personality. Probably each of us is susceptible to our complexes enough to find a fit with some aspect of the personality disorders.

My standpoint on diagnoses is that they are useful only when they facilitate communication between professionals who understand the relativity and inherent danger of labeling. While the conceptualization and synthesis that goes into categorization is a useful and expedient shorthand for some circumstances, I do not find it helpful generally to think in terms of diagnoses when working with someone in therapy. More than likely, a diagnosis hampers my straight reception of what the patient is giving. What is helpful to me sometimes is to think of the diagnoses as clusters of complexes which can occur in anyone at particular times. For example, it is useful to identify the presence of a sado-masochistic field encompassing me and my patient; my own withdrawal into a schizoid position during a session; an inclination to act-out sociopathically against the therapy; a borderline state existing in one or the other; a paranoid flavor to my thinking, etc. Relationships move in and out of these fields or states that complexes create.

Sometimes a person's cluster of complexes is organized around one strong archetype, such as when the Mother, or the Father, or the Trickster, or some other archetype, is a dominant factor in the individual's behavior and the interactive field he sets in motion unconsciously around himself. For example, a middle-aged divorced man complains that he cannot seem to "get his life together." He has a great many talents, a profession which thrives in spite of his art work which takes up huge chunks of time; a relationship with a woman who can't accept his avoidance of commitment, but can't tear herself away either; children who always need more than he has to give, but who thrill with the precious, madcap time that he does spend with them. He suffers because, while his life is dominated by the capricious Trickster, he is a human being who longs for the kind of peace and security that Trickster never serves. Even though the Trickster manifests in positive ways in his personality, not destructive ones, it is exhausting when not balanced by other energies. It runs over his desire for a home, and for a relationship of unambivalent devotion. His rambunctious personality does not give his loved ones enough security for steady devotion to thrive; there is always the anxiety about whether he will be there, always something in them hanging back so as not to be too hurt when he dashes off to a new project. If the Father Archetype gave the Trickster some support in his psychic space, he might be more inclined to settle down. If the Hero Archetype were prominent along with the Trickster, he might be more decisive, or pride might result in a much darker picture, in which we might see him using his talents to promote himself at others' expense. If the Puer Archetype were strong, he might be less available to his family, or more devoted to his art, and so on.

Now, to return to the question of the diagnosis in the therapy session. Inevitably an interplay between levels of integration occurs within the therapy session, just as it does throughout life. Patient and therapist dip into early infantile, child, and adolescent states if the process is moving. Similarly, patients with fragile integration may move into highly differentiated or enlightened states, which could pass unnoticed if we are conditioned to expect less of that person. One hopes that the therapist can see and recognize the value of these enlightened states by being open to them. I am afraid that if we define or diagnose too well we may make pathology our focus and close ourselves to such recognition. It is Mercurius the Trickster who helps us to navigate these changes of integrative levels and changes of focus, to stay present, by means of his gyroscopic influence, his capacity to identify with any state.

Webster's dictionary, in its lengthy definitions of "personality" and "character," mentions morality and ethics only under "character," and common usage usually implies an ethical component to character which is not taken for granted when we speak of personality. "Character" carries a connotation of integrity, the awareness of a reliable system of guiding principles. In 1979 the American Psychiatric Association dropped the term "neurosis" from its terminology and introduced the classification "Personality Disorders" in the Diagnostic and Statistical Manual (DSM III).

Here I feel obliged to mention that this diagnostic reference book itself raises ethical issues. One of its uses is to determine eligibility for reimbursement for psychiatric services by insurance companies and government agencies. Since human behavior can rarely be understood in terms of distinct entities, the decisions about what constitutes pathology is often arbitrary. In fifteen years the definable disorders have burgeoned from 106 to 300, and cover so many personality traits that a University of Michigan survey found that at least half of the American population could be identified as suffering from a psychiatric disorder. Professors of Social Work, Stuart Kirk and Herb Kutchins claim:

> DSM-IV oversteps its bounds. Its authors seek to define how we should think about ourselves, how we should respond to stress, how much anxiety or sadness we should feel and when and how we should sleep, eat, and express ourselves sexually. Although people inevitably base these judgments on personal and social values, the psychiatric association tries to extend its professional jurisdiction over daily life by arguing that its definitions are based on science.

Kirk and Kutchins point out that political pressure from gay activists, feminists, and Vietnam vets resulted in changes in what the association presents as science. They accuse the manual of pandering to insurers, drug companies, and therapists by medicalizing social problems.[48]

There are those who would disagree and who defend the APA's diagnostic system. But whether we approve or disapprove, we recognize a phenomenon which has been observed by story-tellers and novelists long before it was a diagnosis:

the disordered personality. A common denominator of all the personality disorders is a certain limitation of vision, a faulty imagination, a lack of breadth of insight, a rigidity and constriction of standpoint. In the arena of our disorder we are subject to illusion, and our attempts to manipulate reality to conform to our illusion bring disharmony to our lives. We do not use imagination constructively to enlarge our lives and our vision. Unable to create an experience through a symbolic life of play, we become compelled to find literal expression of our illusions.

The American Psychiatric Association's "Personality Disorders" include descriptions of disorders involving conscience and ethics, (once known as "character disorders") as well as other syndromes in which ethics is not a primary focus. The principal disorder of conscience, Antisocial Personality Disorder, is an example of narrow imagery, as it tends to be very bound to the present, unable to project the imagination into the future, nor to learn from the mistakes of the past. What matters in this disorder is the tangible gratification of some momentary tension, at any cost. Ironically, this short term vantage point enables the sociopath to tolerate great discomfort and suffering. Pain is lived in the moment, and the sociopath is not anxious about whether the pain will be long-standing. A great deal of the anxiety most of us suffer comes about through projections into the future: What will happen? How will it end? How will I go on? What will others think and do? Such questions are not big in the sociopath's priorities.

Because its attention is focused on the present and on the concrete rather than the long-term or inspirational, the sociopath in us is extremely observant of our surroundings and of other people's behavior. We read cues on the faces and in the voices of our victims of manipulation, which makes us better than many psychologists at sizing up people and situations, and, like Trickster, enables us to see behind a facade. We don't see the importance of the consequences of our behavior on others, because our focus is so narrow and short. We fail to imagine what others may feel, and can only feel *when* we feel, not when we try to *imagine* feeling. Spirit does not infuse our material being, but is shackled to it, without room for interplay between the spirit-world and the pragmatic, visible world. We are not incorporating the Trickster's ability to span different worlds and world-views.

Sociability's Shadow

In countless stories and legends, trickster figures and the Trickster Gods' behavior borders on the sociopathic in its ambiguous morality, its intense awareness of the present and of the particular, and its capacity to tolerate and minimize suffering in itself and others. What is similar in Trickster and sociopathy is the abandonment of absolute values, the devotion to the moment, the diminishment of suffering. Trickster is the messenger-god who comprehends the purpose and value of every other being, god, human, and animal. He does not denounce, but separates and integrates. What distinguishes the Trickster from the sociopath is breadth of vision. Trickster is anything but short-sighted. It is precisely because he brings us to the border and dangles us over the cliffs of shadow that we become aware of what matters.

Pride and arrogance also distinguish sociopathy from Trickster. Pride is the factor which separates evil principles—for example, Satan, who wants to be bigger than God—from Trickster Gods who do not seek self-importance seriously. Trickster likes himself and his position as the non-authority. The combination of pride and tricksterism in a human being can be dangerous or criminal. The British entrepreneur/thief, Robert Maxwell (whose life was made into a popular musical), acquired fame and fortune, but stole millions from his workers' pension funds to buy a British tabloid. His shrewd business tactics were not balanced by compassion, but were inflated by hubris.

Another difference between Trickster and sociopathy is memory. Trickster's present is not exclusive of the past and future. Unlike the eternal archetype, the sociopath is a finite being, trapped momentarily in time and space. The sociopath focuses only on the immediate, but Trickster is omnipresent and oriented toward a universal purpose. An example is found in the Coyote story of the Native Americans in the Northwest.[49] This is an abbreviated version of a widely varying figure and story:

> Coyote heard about a handsome young man who wanted to marry but thought he was too good for the girls in his town. Coyote disguised himself as a beautiful girl, new in town, and seduced...the proud young man. They married and had children, but the woman would not let anyone see her children. After some time of making the man very happy, she left him and the children, who were then found to be wolf-puppies. Then every one laughed, for they realized the beautiful woman was Coyote. "This conceited young man has managed to take a man for a wife...." They had such a laugh about it that the young man left the village in shame.

Coyote, despite his primitive style, has a largeness of vision and a purposiveness which is beyond our scope to perceive, while the sociopath's wiles are strictly for the benefit of one individual, small complex. Sometimes that complex is dissociated from the rest of the personality and has no connection to any conscious principle. It acts like a trickster's penis, autonomously with no relationship to the rest of the body. Or it acts like a trickster figure with no connection to an organizing principle, no high god, no Mt. Olympus.

It is dangerous for us, limited to our human viewpoint, to identify even temporarily with Trickster. This is one reason why the stories of Tricksters are treated with such respect and care in the societies which honor them. The stories are recounted in a way that promotes imagination and discourages identification. They tell us that this particular aspect of the divine can comprehend us, can see through our lies and dishonesty, can even admit that dishonesty is part of the divine plan on which we must each take a position at some time.

Taking a position requires more effort than the sociopath can muster. In their elucidation of the dynamics of the clown archetype, Ann and Barry Ulanov describe how the clown creates a space in which the ego can rest from the task of holding opposites together.[50] In sociopathy we live in a similar, non-elastic space literally, not imaginatively with humor.

Heroes, Hermes, and Hubris

Psychologists observe that in the absence of an integrative function or organizing principle, which Jung conceptualized as a relationship to the Self, we experience extreme degrees of inner tension, registered as emptiness, terror, and self-contempt. To survive in the face of such disturbing tensions, persons (and some other animals) exhibit comforting mechanisms, such as narcissistic, arrogant, rebellious, or compulsive behaviors. At this point I would like to highlight arrogance, a prominent feature of the sociopathic personality which critically affects situations when dialogue and negotiations are needed. I have been pondering the role it plays in our global problems, as arrogant leaders have fed the public's cynicism. And the relationship between arrogance, audacity, authority, and confidence seems to be important for our times.

As a woman I have accommodated at times to the arrogance of men and have suffered and raged against the effects of arrogant adults on the feelings of children.[51] As a psychoanalyst I witness the pain of others at the hands of arrogant parents, employers, doctors, spouses. As a citizen I am frustrated by arrogance in the sociopolitical world—arrogant politicians, business developers, attorneys, medical practitioners who defy dialogue. Wherever we hope to be able to trust that issues can be discussed honestly, we feel betrayed if facts are distorted to protect the informant's arrogant image. "My product (behavior, method, etc.) has not been proven dangerous."

Still, we know that arrogance can be a helpful foil against too many blows and knocks to a fragile sense of self; also, the bluster and bluff of competitors influences who will survive, in nature as well as poker. Most grandiose and inflated behavior begins as an attempt to manage or cope as a child. Idealization fails to find an object, and is introjected. Arrogance implies a defensive exaggeration of one's superiority, whereas audacity implies a bold, or even rash expression of oneself in the face of some authority. Both imply a problem of self-confidence; arrogance appears to bolster one against inner self-doubt, and audacity against an outer threat. I have come to distinguish between arrogance in the service of the Hero and arrogance in the service of the Trickster.

Arrogance is sometimes the attribute of a hero. Wisdom-heroes typically model humility (Abraham Lincoln, Martin Luther King), while power-heroes typically model arrogance (George Patton, Muhammed Ali). In trickster stories, as we might expect, arrogance is paradoxically portrayed. The Trickster is as often the object of derision as he is the agent. When Trickster is the agent, no one is exempt from humiliation, not even the gods and the heroes. Mythologies reveal that it is the nature of the Trickster Gods to eschew power and to undo heroes.[52] Representing the underdog as he often does, the Trickster's antics could usually be described as audacious, rather than arrogant.

The arrogant are tolerated, tongue-in-cheek, within the realm of Trickster, who rules liminal experience, such as adolescence and the world of play that spans the borders of reality and magic. Playful arrogance is a delightful excursion into make-believe, carrying us to dizzying, dazzling heights of self-importance. We can enjoy ego-maniacal entertainers as long as they amuse us. We feel good by our identification with their success and power, and we are not personally affected by their self-serving quirks. Comic Roseanne's outrageous verbal abuse of anyone in her path, including her children, shocks us into laughter. Interviewed by Bill Maher on his audaciously tricksterish television show, "Politically Incorrect," Roseanne revealed that anger at injustice fueled her humor.[53] She mimics arrogance to attack the arrogant. Madonna's crass attention-seeking catches, amuses, fascinates us, as she knew it would. We appreciate the exposure of the forbidden in entertainers like this, because we don't have to try to live with and relate to their show-biz characters. But outside the realm of entertainment, arrogance is a serious problem, for when we are arrogant we are inflated and unable to listen to the truth about ourselves. Intimacy demands honesty; arrogance makes intimacy impossible. Honesty depends on negotiating a consensus of reality; inflation hinders negotiation and realism.

Usually arrogance can be linked with compensation for wounds to self-esteem. Psychologist Gerald Adler calls it "pathological certainty."[54] A woman with astute insight into her own behavior admitted to me, "I wanted him to mirror me, and when he didn't, I became arrogant and harsh." Knowing this relationship between arrogance and narcissistic wounding may change our understanding of the self-arrogating person, but not our emotional response to her. Arrogant behavior provokes an emotional response; it can cast a spell (Hitler), or seem pitiable (Saddam Hussein), depending on our vulnerability to the effects of the arrogant behavior. Parents of adolescents usually come up against arrogance as the child struggles to move into a new adjustment to the world with wavering confidence; and most parents will admit to being drawn into emotional blow-ups in reaction to that arrogance, even though they may try not to over-react. What passes for gutsy in one generation is ridiculed as arrogant in another. In our society flaunting oneself is both discouraged and rewarded; those who dare to do so are both resented and found captivating. They remind us that in each of us is a child whose need for attention is insatiable. As much as it loves attention, the child knows scorn of its neediness, and fears that scorn. And this child within can never grow up, but only waits, patiently or not, for attention.

As mediator and peace-bringer Trickster helps to create an atmosphere in the psyche that diminishes the need for exaggerations of self-superiority. The archetypal approach regards the exaggerations of complex-behavior as fundamental to the nature of psyche. As such we treat the behavior by deepening our contact with the complex, giving the archetype within the complex its due through reflection, imaginally and not concretely. Meanwhile, developmental and physiological psychology try to fathom the human factors that lend to extremes in behavior, especially when those extremes cause senseless suffering. In the case of conditions that breed arrogance and personality disorders, we know that there are genetic and environmental components interacting. Archetypes manifest in our bodies, in our histories, in our attachments, attractions, destinies. The Self cannot be known except through our relationships and concrete expressions in the material world.

A Developmental View of Disorder

In the stage of infancy when the psyche makes an enormous leap of trust, and accepts both the gratifying and frustrating aspects of life (usually represented by mother) as parts of a whole to be tolerated, a new level of psychic organization occurs. The energy needed to make that psychic leap probably comes about through a capacity to reserve energy from discharging of impulses and affects long enough to imagine their gratification. Simply said, we think that the infant sacrifices some impulsivity and learns to hold on for a bit; instead of discharging a lot of energy in a tantrum or a panic, the infant observes, listens, anticipates, and "figures out" from its memories of previous experience, that relief is on the way. The reflective instinct awakens. The archetype of the Mother with which we came into the world, was projected and now begins to be introjected. There is evidence that this has happened when the infant can "mother" or comfort itself with a thumb or a toy. Such a "transitional object" is the first observable evidence of what Jung called the "transcendent function."

This measure of trust, which ideally is part of everyone's experience, unfortunately is never actualized in some who remain unable to find the psychic stamina to make that leap of trust. In children who have not had to endure a minimal amount of frustration and separation from mother, where stamina has never been required or developed, the capacity to invest emotionally in imaginary play is seriously impaired, as is the case when frustration has been too severe.

Without psychic stamina, the world remains more simple. Good and bad are irreconciled, so that the reactions we have to a "good" person are not brought to consciousness when the person frustrates us. We do not adjust our reactions to spare the good person, because at the moment of frustration, there is no good person, and no channel for remorse. There is no usable memory for the good in that person. There is only a need and a deed; I hurt, therefore, you pay. The rights and hardships of others are inconsequential. This is the inner world of the paranoid position of the early psyche, and of the sociopath who does not invest great psychic effort into delaying gratification, reconciling contradictory feelings, or in trying to empathize with what another might be going through.

It may be hard to comprehend how a person who displays sociopathic behavior could lack stamina. Typically these are energetic, physical people. However, in the area of restraining action and imagining the future, there is an absence of stamina, a weakness. Research is inconclusive as to why this is so. Neurological, hormonal, and behavioral theories are advanced, but none is conclusive. Twin and adopted child studies suggest a genetic component. At one time the XYY genotype was associated with sociopathy, especially extreme aggressivity, but that theory has failed to hold up. Other neurological factors have been considered, which might account for a kind of neurological aphasia seen in the lack of emotional depth in antisocial people; some postulate neurotransmitter problems.[55] With the development of new technologies that allow scientists to localize and look at the structure and function of the brain, psychologists have found support for the theory that violent murderers' brains differ from those of control subjects in the degree of activity in the area of the prefrontal-cortex.[56]

We must be careful lest we reduce behavior to known biological factors while ignoring the complexity of learning and values on physiology. Jan Volavka, author of *Neurobiology of Violence*, warns against research that neglects the moral sense, a protective factor which prevents development of violent behavior.[57] Also, Nobel prize winning psychologist Roger Sperry transcends the reductionist view of physiology and integrates consciousness and higher values into the scientific picture. Sperry, noted for his research on the role of the brain hemispheres and mediative *corpus callosum*, predicts a hopeful new paradigm in psychological thinking:

> In the old view everything was determined from below upward. In the new view, however, things are determined reciprocally. A train of thought, for example, determines what is going on in the brain's neural nets as much as the other way around. The reciprocal upward and downward controls are not just feedback nor are they in conflict, because the two are entirely different in nature. The higher supervene, not intervene, on the lower.[58]

Sperry goes on to emphasize that reductionism fails to adequately include the causal effects exerted by patterns in different micro-macro structures. Values and chemicals are mutually influential.

Whether or not we have the physiological sophistication to explain it, developmentalists hold that inconsistent parenting during the crucial stage of trust and separation in infancy can contribute to the lack of psychic stamina. The infant must receive attention in order to be able to pay attention, and attention is fundamental to reflection. Regardless of the origin, it goes without saying that this failure to develop, or this regression to a lower level of development at times of fatigue or toxicity, is neither deliberate nor deserving of blame, even though we are obliged to restrain and prevent our sociopathic element from harming others. One of the circumstances that curbs development of superego, aesthetic awareness, commitment to principle, conscience—whatever we call that sensibility to some ethic—and that furthers sociopathic behavior, is an environment where little hope for future gratification is seen, where one gets when the getting's good, or forever goes without. Such a perception of the state of affairs may be completely distorted, but our parents, our own delusions, or the influence of the mob can convince us that the future is dismal, nothing to count on. Authority figures, too severe or ineffective, do not inspire identification.

Family therapist Ivan Boszormenyi-Nagy uses the phrase "destructive-entitlement" to describe the alternative to dialogue used by children who have no trust in a world that seems only exploitative to them. The dismal future is faced with a sense of alienation, a vacuum where there ought to be a hearth. The psyche may tolerate a sociopathic complex existing alongside a Hestian love of hearth and home. That is, within one person's psyche may be two disparate complexes or sub-personalities, one being sociopathic, another being devoted to domestic tranquillity, like a hit man who goes back to Mom for home-cooking, or a gangster family man whose devoted wife does not care to know what her man does for a living; but without intimacy and honest dialogue between the two, there is no authentic ethical position—the psyche remains split. Without hope there is no reason to look forward, and with no memory for the past, there is no space for guilt or reflection on one's actions. In our sociopathic state of immediacy there is no space/time where guilt or need for sacrifice can come into us.

Another kind of orientation to sociopathy occurs under very different conditions. The child does form a bond of trust, does develop a set of principles, does identify with some authority figure, but that figure teaches sociopathic values. The child's personality structure is intact, but emulates a sociopath, and is conditioned to antisocial behavior. These different sources of sociopathy demand different approaches by society and by therapists to the problems they present. On one hand we have victims of neglect and abuse, on the other receptors of a gangster mentality encouraged by adults whose experience, no matter how delusional or maladaptive, is perpetuated. The latter is more likely to be successfully immoral because his sociopathy is congruent with his ideals.

There was a time in my very early training when analysts believed that the personality disorders (then called "character disorders") were untreatable. This was because few of us analysts were conscious of the character disorder in ourselves. We were products of a frame of reference based on hierarchical thinking which placed the analyst in one category of mental healthiness and the patient in another. Later it was shown through embarrassing exposures that analysts, too, were subject to substance abuse, dishonesty, irresponsible treatment of others, and other effects of fragmented integrity. Through exposure of our transgressions we became aware of what it meant to be disordered in character and became open to learning how to treat such disorders.

The *American Psychological Association Monitor* of January, 1994, carries the first page headline: "Sexual Deviancy a Disorder, not an Evil: Psychologist finds Dahmer's compulsion reinforce value of help for sexual abusers."[59] Jeffrey Dahmer, the serial killer whose cannibalistic compulsions and mutilations of young male victims horrified hardened crime investigators, is an example of murderous offenders who are now, theoretically, considered treatable and not hopelessly degenerate. Dahmer's cannibalistic compulsions became overt when, as a lonely, isolated adolescent, he resorted to fantasies of controlling others as a way of keeping them from leaving him. Most sexual offenders have a history of being victimized as children, which makes early identification of these children crucial in preventing further violence. It does not mean that personal history ever explains their behavior. The majority of abused or deprived children do not become criminals, and thus far, psychologists have no sure way of explaining why one man uses his trickiness to enrich his life, and another to poison it.

Neither can the presence of a particular archetypal pattern in a person's psyche be preordained by human reason. There are multiple factors involved in becoming a sociopath, and in rehabilitating one. It is impossible to predict who can be redeemed. Without intervention in childhood or adolescence—when in many cases, including Dahmer's, the deviancy is still at the fantasy stage—treatment must labor at dealing with compulsive enactment of the impulses. If we can intervene earlier and treat a fantasy, we may forestall the literalization and enactment of the fantasy; otherwise we then must hope to reverse the process, exchanging the compulsion with the expression of the compulsive content through fantasy. We try to establish a symbolic resolution of the desire feeding the impulse.

Substituting a symbol for concrete gratification of an impulse is conditional, depending on many factors, especially the neurological makeup of the subject and capacity for learning new behavior. Only with childish optimism would we hope to rehabilitate a significant number of adult sociopaths. With children, the outcome looks only slightly more promising, and requires early detection and effort to change not only the child's behavior but his milieu. The diagnosis that usually covers children who, without intervention, run the risk of becoming sociopaths is "conduct disorder." These children are described as showing a pattern of violating basic rights of others and age-appropriate societal norms. We can see already that defining "societal norms" will make this diagnosis problematic. In any case, physical aggression and cruelty toward others, including animals, lack of concern for property rights, truancy, running away from home, lack of empathy, restlessness, and lack of guilt and remorse are common features. Self-esteem, frustration tolerance, and capacity to contain anger are low. The behavior that comprises conduct disorder goes beyond the transgressions of rules and mores that are part of every child's development at some times, for the pattern is persistent. The disorder is often treatable, but demands cooperation between the therapist, parents, school authorities, and community agencies involved in the child's care—no small order.

Additionally, the parents need to be amenable to learning new behavior, and not unreasonable, not hardened to interference in the name of help, not inured to authority, not too afraid of being seen, not psychotic or drug-dependent. Unfortunately, those who work with children observe that conduct disorder is increasing while safe, secure environments for children are harder to come by.

Advocating a research approach to understanding the strengths of sociopaths, Brantley and Sutker suggest we may learn to encourage their prosocial behavior, and additionally come to discover the mechanisms by which sociopaths manage fear under trying circumstances.[60] Sociopathic strategies may have important therapeutic implications for those immobilized by anxiety, who could use some strategies for distancing from their fears. The panic disorders and the sociopaths are related through some factor which is missing or suppressed in the one and exaggerated in the other. Though treating sociopathy may sound like a job for Superman, it is not. Superman may be needed to hold hopeless sociopathy, but skills other than brute strength are needed to transform redeemable sociopathy.

THE STAMINA TO HOPE

When we boil it down, the problem of weak ego-stamina is a failure to hope, which rests on imagination. To me, a most moving section of the Holocaust Museum in Washington, DC, is the part devoted to the resistance movement, valiant attempts by individuals to pit themselves against Nazism. They acted on hope, which Henri Desroche likens to the Hindu rope trick:

> It is as though human beings—personalities and/or collectivities—who are burdened by the weight of necessities, found something like the rope to be a message, an announcement, a revelation, a gospel. Whether they believe this rope to have come from elsewhere…or from within themselves is of no consequence. In both cases it is a rope that they throw in the air, in other words, into space, into the clouds, into the sky. To the observer it seems there is nothing to keep it up except for the impalpable and inconsistent worlds of fantasy, wanderings, and absurdity. And yet this rope is anchored. It holds. And when humans grab hold of it and pull themselves up, it takes the strain, it maintains its rigidity.[61]

Hope is not necessarily rational; perhaps it is delusional. It is the capacity to imagine possibilities which allows hope, and hope which allows courage. Even without heroes to model it, courage is possible, and necessary to make us complete human beings. If examples of lack of integrity seem to outnumber acts of courage, those courageous acts are powerful. Gorbachev; Sadat; Rabin and Arafat in that momentous and painfully hesitant handshake of 1994—leaders whose courage made possible some giant leaps toward cooperation between generations of warring peoples; their actions, and those of statesmen from other UN countries who mediated their talks, are as much the work of the well-integrated Trickster gods of communication and boundaries as is our cynicism and satire. Heroic teachers continue to exhibit hope in the face of deteriorating teaching conditions. Large acts of courage by seemingly "little" people can be recounted by those who have witnessed disaster areas. Four brave people, unknown to each other, rescued Reginald Denny during the Los Angeles riots of 1991, and said they were just doing what they considered an ordinary act of compassion. Strangers dive into icy waters and fire-storms, to rescue strangers. This is not sentimentalism. Even when an archetype such as the Hero submerges into the collective unconscious, it continues to actualize in individual psyches. The heroic, if not acknowledged in a larger, formalized image or mythic figure, exists in individual acts of courage which bring hope to the disillusioned. This is courage on the human level, not a high-blown ideology of some larger than life superior hero. And it is a kind of heroism which incorporates Trickster's capacity for objectivity and shrewdness, as well as compassion and the courage to touch the untouchable. Perhaps it is the grounded Hero.

CONCLUSION

There are at least three possible attitudes toward the ethical confusion that questions of survival have imposed on our current civilization. One attitude is to have faith in a given system of rules and principles, another is to detach oneself from the problem, and a third is to commit oneself to a continual process of dialogue and examination of principles.

The first approach is to adopt a position of having the answers through complete faith in a doctrine of moral behavior which one accepts without doubt or conflict. Achieving such faith, and surrendering one's decision-making functions to it, is a comforting existence as long as one is not confronted with disbelief. In order for such a position to be effective, it must be accepted universally. Therefore, when one holds such doubt-free positions, one must repress any aspect of psyche that questions. Also one must hope to impose them on others, or convince others of adopting them. Erikson sought out Gandhi as an exemplar of ethical awareness; but another idealization crumbled when Erikson discovered that Ghandi failed to acknowledge the relativity of his truth. Erikson held that Ghandi, by imposing his beliefs on others, violated his professed ethic of non-violence. Ghandi was gifted in his ability to stand on high moral ground with regard to his enemies, but his brutal wielding of his truth did violence to the integrity of those in his family and immediate web of care. His outer non-violent stance politically was in contrast to a violent approach to those in his personal life.[62] A version of Ghandi's attitude dominates those who insist that revelation by God is the only source of truth, and who find revelation only in their holy book and not in ongoing discourse that attempts to relate the book to the voices of its followers—whether that book be the Bible or Koran or the collected works of Jung.

A second attitude toward ethics is to feel desolute as driftwood, and to abandon any attempt to hold an ethical standpoint, especially when agreement seems impossible. This "anything goes" attitude often underlies an apparently complacent exterior, an attitude found among some in poverty, and also when one scratches through the veneer of wealth and status which is not applied to, or shared with, the good of all. It is found in the lassitude of the spiritually empty and the desperation of the spiritually deprived, both of whom have lost hope.

Such flaccid spirit would warrant pity, except that spiritless people often express their attitudes in a public way that has a special appeal to children whose values are being formed. For instance, the creator of some extremely grisly and violent video games containing scenes of sadistic torture and mass murders, claimed that he had no responsibility for its effect on its child-market audience. Indifferent to the larger needs of society and to the consequences of his public sadism, he held that responsibility lay fully with the viewer, regardless of age. In *The Psychotic Core*, Michael Eigen discusses the effects of repeated trauma on the psyche: "One loses one's sensitivity to catastrophe and no longer experiences its increasing horrors. It may be possible for a culture to do this on a grand scale."[63]

A popular defense of the creators of amusements like video games is that parents have the responsibility to determine what their children watch; meanwhile, the complexity of modern life is such that the most conscientious of parents cannot control the barrage of information to which children are subjected. At least in his outer self-display, this video game author seemed to close the window or cover the mirror at that point, unable or unwilling to look further into his behavior (the "evil eye- blink," in contrast to the "evil eye"). It seems that he had gotten so far out in his video world, that he could not go home again, if home is where the heart is.

A third attitude toward ethics is one of commitment to ongoing reflection, questioning, self-examination and dialogue, of willingness to tolerate ambiguity, uncertainty, while not relinquishing the struggle to know right from wrong at each and every choicepoint. Such an attitude, like a democratic government, is not as safe or as efficient as a totalitarian attitude. It requires that we have a positive relationship to the Trickster, in other words, that we be filled with spirit, the Holy Spirit, the spirit Mercurius, the Holy Messenger. Mercurius identifies with no other archetype, but is the one who is able to relate to all and communicate with all without being beholden to take the part of one over another. As messenger he does not guarantee that the recipient is ready or psychologically equipped to take in the message, in which case the message will default.

Having no preconceived answers, this attitude invites us to wrestle with moral questions and enjoy the excitement of looking for clues throughout the universe. That universe includes the inner world of deliberation as well as divine inspiration, and the outer world of observation and analysis of natural law as best we can determine it. It requires some capacity to think about life in the broad sweep, and not only for one's individual gains. It requires a great deal of trust in the future (the Self) and an openness, a relaxation of stricture to allow some new archetypal organization to emerge. It requires enormous amounts of compassion and tolerance for one's own inadequacies and for the faults of others.[64]

Men, women, and children of the third group need to look at how the ethical positions we take reflect the interests of all people. Democracies have worked effectively when there was a large majority who held like values. This is not likely to be the case in the near future. Until now, public ethics was an arena which many groups of people did not enter. For instance, women, though they have typically been the power behind the moral atmosphere within the family, did not enter into public debate in positions of power until recently. Men in public life often reflect the values reinforced by their mothers or wives; however, generally the larger issues of societies have been decided by men and in the interests of the power of male authorities. It is essential to our dialogue now that we add overtly the voices of women to the discussion of how we will survive, for women and children make up a majority of the species, and this majority no longer feels subservient to male authority.

In order to open the dialogue about survival to women as well as men, we may find it helpful to think about the fact that the Trickster is typically portrayed cross-culturally as masculine, regardless of the fact that women are stereotyped as intuitive, mercurial, antihierarchical, and in fact have been surviving for centuries by means of trickster skills. If this is a period which Trickster dominates, what does that mean for the feminine? I refer to the feminine principle as it manifests in the personalities of men and women, for we know that males can carry the feminine principle into the world (Ghandi), and women in their public and private roles can be moved principally by masculine values and traditions (Shannon Faulkner, who omitted all references to gender in her application to an all male military college and was inadvertently accepted). Where is the feminine principle in the Trickster? This has not been obvious, in spite of the fact that Tricksters are considered to be androgynous.

Trickster always invites us to look beyond the obvious. Could this be the nature of a new archetypal organization for which we as a society are preparing? I believe we are on the edge of a new manifestation of the Trickster whose feminine side is more conscious and constructively influential.

In trickster fashion, let us begin by turning back, a return to the ancient paean of Homer to the complementary god and goddess, Hermes and Hestia. Hermes was coupled with several women, mortal and immortal. With Aphrodite, or in some versions the goddess Cythera, he produced an offspring, Hermaphrodite; with a nymph, an offspring, Pan. He is said to have lain with Brimo, and the nubile Chione, and with Hecate, and some early aspect of Artemis, with whom he begot Eros.[65] But Homer places Hermes and Hestia in conjunction, and in terms of complementarity, these two are ideally matched. Together they represent the sacred spaces, inner and outer, and the attitudes of containment and expansion. Homer says (referring to Hermes as Argeiphontes):

> Hestia, you who have received the highest honor, to have your seat forever in the enormous houses of all the gods and all the men who walk the earth, it is a beautiful gift you have received, it is a beautiful honor. Without you, mankind would have no feasts, since no one could begin the first and last drink of honey-like wine without an offering to Hestia.
>
> And you too, Argeiphontes, son of Zeus and Maia, messenger of the gods with your gold wand, giver of good things, be good to me, protect me along with the venerable and dear Hestia.
>
> Come, both of you inhabit this beautiful house with mutual feelings of friendship. You accompany good works with intelligence and youth.
>
> Hello, daughter of Cronus, you too, Hermes, with your gold wand. As for me, I will remember you in another song.[66]

Hestia, goddess of the hearth, and Hermes, the trickster god: For me they provide the perfect guides in analysis, the one spanning and connecting all complexes and levels of awareness, the other keeping the work close to the center and grounded in warmth of authentic human relatedness. Attachment and separation, Gilligan tells us, "anchor the cycle of human life, describing the biology of human reproduction and the psychology of human development."[67] Holding the patient's material with the devotion of Hestia in the spirit of Mercurius is my experience of doing analysis.

As for the issue of transformation of sociopathy, it appears that with sociopaths and other personality disorders this divine dyad is particularly helpful. We need the mesmerizing fire of Hestia to hold the attention of the very labile spirits of those whose psychic connections are so tentative. The personality disorder needs to be "held to the fire," and we need the quick mercurial energy of Hermes to keep pace with the wily, mobile, and fragmented moods of these personalities. The highly structured, unbending, authoritarian persona of the orthodox psychoanalyst that was prevalent a generation ago was no match for the personality disorders. Flexibility is not a trait to be found in the typical patriarchal therapist, who operates under the superman myth.

Modest Hestia and irreverent Hermes represent very different archetypal patterns from those of the heroic Greek divinities, such as Herakles. Herakles, the strongest man on earth, considered himself equal to the gods, who called on him when deeds of superhuman courage were needed. His rash reliance on brute strength at the expense of foresight reminds us of the worst aspects of today's heroic approach to problem-solving; he would have been willing to destroy the sun or the sea if they got in his way, an attitude we find now in regard to solving environmental problems on a very short-term basis. Like Herakles, we would destroy another species rather than create new ways of helping people earn a living. Yet Herakles could show genuine sorrow and desire to expiate his wrongdoing when shown his folly. Like the worst representatives of our heroic patriarchy, in madness he destroyed his feminine soul. This he brought about by killing his first wife and children, an act that he so deeply regretted later that he did his renowned Herculean penances.

Herakles' relationship to the feminine is fraught with ambivalence, passion, and misfortune. One legend tells that Herakles, murdered by Typhon, the last and most evil child of Gaea, recovered life through the smell of the quail. In death, Herakles seems to have contacted his feminine sensitivity to be so affected by an odor. Heroes often have to reach extremes in order to contact their feminine nature. The gentle little quail, a symbol of the feminine principle, rescued the great hero from death;[68] but at a later time it was the feminine in the form of his wife who inadvertently almost caused his death. A shirt that was meant to be a love potion and protection against the seduction of another woman, instead caused him terrible torture; his distraught wife committed suicide when her gift backfired so cruelly. Eventually, in pain and despair, Herakles arranged a huge funeral pyre to destroy himself, and was taken to Mt. Olympus, never to be seen again on earth.

Edith Hamilton speaks of the "miracle of Greek mythology" which created a humanized world and made gods in man's image, in contrast to the terrifying pre-Greek, inhuman, colossal, and bestial deities. Greek deities were good, attractive personages who at times were petty and cruel, but never incomprehensibly irrational and mysterious, as were the sphinxes and inhuman monsters of earlier cultures. Hamilton considers Herakles an allegory for Greece itself. "He fought the monsters and freed the earth from them, just as Greece freed the earth from the monstrous idea of the unhuman supreme over the human."[69]

Herakles, the Superman of Mt. Olympus, removed himself from earth when his work was done. Homer's poem to Herakles is pertinent.

> At first he wandered over earth and the inexpressible sea, and suffered. He struggled hard, and he did many fantastic things, really extraordinary tasks! Now on the other hand he lives on the beautiful top of snowy Olympus, and he loves it.[70]

Perhaps the grounded superman in each of us can expect to complete his humiliating suffering in earth-hell (where, like Herakles, he may contact the quail, his feminine principle), and then, to subside into a well deserved rest, as we wish for the patriarchy. In a peaceful place of repose we might put our dreams of conquering nature to rest, and assimilate and reflect on our heroic experiences. Earthwise then, we could take this time to refocus our attention. But refocusing implies a period of clouded vision.

I suggest that we are presently suffering from cloudy vision. We have little capacity for long-range sight; consequently, we no longer crane our necks toward the heavens asking, "Is it a bird? Is it a plane?" In fact, except for astronomers and a small number of UFO watchers, we hardly look up at all. We don't expect to find answers by looking up. We look mostly into the mirror, and the mirror of the camera, scrutinizing our own reflections.

CHAPTER II

THROUGH LENS AND LOOKING GLASS

A Native American creation story tells that in the beginning, Earth was a little mother in darkness. Grandfather Sun talked with her and told her of her splendor. Since she could not see, but could only feel, she asked Grandfather Sun to shine his light on her so that she could see herself. He refused, for he knew that if she could see herself in her full luxuriant beauty, she would become vain and difficult and impossible to satisfy. But she cajoled and badgered him until he finally gave in, and the first morning was created as light came to Earth and illuminated her magnificence. Then Little Earth Mother said, "It's too bright! Take it away! It's too bright!"[1]

Our little mother, in contrast to Narcissus, had the mother-wit to take effulgence in moderation, and thus survived for a world that now enjoys a balance of light and dark. But the story reminds us that the importance of seeing and being seen is such that it moves even the celestial forces. This fact is repeated each time a human being is created, for anyone who cares for an infant knows the power of eye-contact. Parents find that gazing at the face of their baby can be more fascinating than looking at a movie or at a precious work of art. The boundaries between subject and object blur; who enjoys more the looking and the being seen, parent or child? Surely the child needs the parent's attention for survival, but parenting is not an altogether altruistic task. The parent needs and enjoys attention from the child as well.

Reflection and Survival

Nature insures the attraction of mutual attention. Research suggests that babies relate to the eyes of their caretakers before they are able to distinguish any other features. The degree of pleasure infants meet in this early eye-contact is a factor in how readily or how anxiously they later respond to more complex facial configurations. The first experiences of seeing and being seen have an important influence on how a person will perceive and relate to others, how comfortably he or she will be socialized. Such deep instinctual processes echo both personal and archetypal influences.

On the personal level, being mirrored and admired leads to a feeling of fullness and well-being. The baby who knows this experience is fortunate. But some parents' eyes convey more anxiety, irritability, or disgust to the receptive baby who interjects and emotionally reverberates to the feelings it receives. The impact of early trauma associated with seeing and being seen may make itself felt in lifelong tension in the upper face, identified by the psychoanalyst, Wilhelm Reich, as eye-blocking, or armor. Eye-blocking may contribute to physical problems of vision, or to psychological problems associated with looking or being looked-at which vary in intensity from mild anxiety to hallucinations. In their milder aspects the effects of eye-armoring can be decreased through body therapy or other systematic programs of exercises which combine physical and psychological opening experiences, such as yoga taught by a master, or method-acting with an enlightened drama coach. In the case of severe blocking and psychological impairment, body therapy must include intense psychotherapeutic work to mitigate years of defensive muscular and psychological armoring.[2]

But there is meaning to the act of "looking" which extends beyond our personal destinies. How we perceive ourselves as regarded by transpersonal forces significantly colors the human experience. For example, to imagine being sized up by the shrewd eye of a trickster god creates a quite different effect than that of being scrutinized by a stern judgmental god, or basking in the loving gaze of a benevolent mother goddess, or participating in a cosmic process of continual creation in which personal identity is a temporary illusion and there is no One to watch Anyone. On the archetypal level seeing and being-seen are symbolic of all knowing. How we are seen by our gods or absence of gods determines how we are known, and how we are known influences who we think we are.

The fundamental act of consciousness implies a separation between the seeing subject and the seen object. Creation myths portray this archetypal experience as the act of separating the primordial oneness into two; for instance, in some myths that moment of knowing is described as the separation of light out of darkness, or the separation of the One into the Great Mother and Great Father, the appearance of the World Parents.[3] From another reference point, this act of separation marks the entrance of Maya, the beginning of illusion. The eye and the mirror are symbolic of such fundamental psychological processes as coming-to-consciousness and developing a sense of two-ness that allows reflection and self-consciousness. The focusing qualities of both lens and mirror allow heat and light to be gathered to one central point, where combustion can create a transformation. Psychological combustion is implied as well in the moment of knowing; when subject and object are split by the focused attention of knowing, a psychological energy-releasing transformation occurs, comparable to the energy released when a dry leaf bursts into flame, or in the splitting of an atom. Until the realization of "the other" is possible, we live in blind fusion.

Throughout cultures we find the survival value and the power of being seen projected onto god-images, as in the Yaqui creation story above, and in references to the eye of god, or to multi-eyed gods and goddesses which are found in myth and iconography worldwide. North Americans may be especially familiar with the woven wool Ojo de Dios in the Southwest. Being watched conjures up notions of being special—whether of being cared for on the one hand, or of being spied upon or devoured on the other. Schizophrenia produces the persecutory eye of paranoia, while mystics have given us imagery of a loving and nurturing eye of god, as in the drawings of Hildegard of Bingen and the poetic language of Meister Eckhart ("In limpid souls God beholds his image; he rests in them and they in him.").[4]

In addition to its association with coming to consciousness, the nurturant eye is also associated with generativity and fertility, and as such it is incorporated into images of genitalia. We know, through psychodynamic material such as dreams and free associations, that the eye can be a carrier of displaced sexual energy, which may endow vision with extraordinary importance or render it vulnerable to psychogenic symptoms; and if the eye and the genitals are integrated in pleasure, voyeurism deliciously enhances sexual excitement.[5]

As the eye serves as a supplementary sexual organ, so the genitals are organs of a kind of "sight." Native American trickster stories are full of examples of penises that "know" things of which the rest of the body is unaware; breasts have been compared to eyes that convey important erotic information, and women often think of their way of knowing being located in the pelvis.[6] In fertility rituals of ancient Egypt, women representing the goddess were paraded on barques down the Nile exposing their genitals to insure the abundant growth of crops. Continuing this theme, Edward Edinger refers to Jung's childhood dream of the eye in a subterranean phallus as analogous to the eye of the snake-symbol of power the Pharaohs wore on their foreheads to ward off evil.[7]

Putting the eyes out can be a sacrifice of sexual desire, but also a sacrifice meant to attain the capacity to look inward. The ancients mythologized the universal tendency to compare heavenly bodies with eyes. The Eyes of Ra, the sun god, and the Eye of Horus, are met frequently in Egyptian art in the symbol of eternity, the udjat. The eye of the sun fertilizes, sustains, and protects life, or scorches and destroys. We look to the stars as eyes of night which seem to watch over us. Multiple eyes can be interpreted as dissociative states, as in fragmented ego states when one feels pursued by hateful figures; or they can be scintillae, sparks of divine consciousness strewn through the unconscious universe. Then, too, the single eye can be a symbol of omniscience, as in the Egyptian and Masonic symbol of the eye of God in the triangle; or, the single eye can be a symbol of obsession, as in the Greek Cyclops, or evil-eye of the Celts. The third eye, of Buddha, or Nemesis, for example, transcends the material advantages of seeing and being seen. It symbolizes the chakra which is the link between the natural world and the supernatural realm, and it reminds us of our need for spiritual illumination. Shiva's third eye usually looks inward, but periodically it looks out, burning everything it sees and warning mere earthly creatures of their relative powerlessness. The third eye reflects the dual aspects of cosmic heat: the extroverted heat of desire, and the introverted heat of asceticism. And the moon can be felt as terrifyingly cold, the "great venomous mirror of nature"[8] which paralyzes the naïve male.

In ancient Greek art Justice is depicted as a woman blindfolded, while Nemesis, the personification of Righteous Anger on Mt. Olympus, is a woman with eyes open, including her third eye. Ethicist Mary Daly contrasts the social awareness of Nemesis, enraged by injustice, with the kind of blind male justice that is concerned with upholding rules while ignoring social injustice, poverty, racism, sexism, etc.[9] And it was Nemesis who heard the prayer of a scorned lover of Narcissus. In pity for all those whom Narcissus rejected, Nemesis played the trickster and caused Narcissus to see his reflection in the water and to become himself the pining, perpetually unfulfilled victim of self-love. In trickster-fashion Nemesis uncovered the true condition behind Narcissus's inability to evolve into relationship with another: his extreme self-absorption.

The myth of Nemesis and Narcissus illustrates the psychological importance of righteous anger in penetrating the narcissistic defenses. The prickliness of narcissism tends to keep others on the defensive, so that the habitual narcissist often gets away with abominable behavior while provoking guilt in others about hurting him. Rarely does he get back a dose of his own rage, but when it does happen it may have a profound impact. A most transforming experience for the narcissist is to become angry at his own behavior, as can happen if his self-absorption results in tragedy.

MIRRORS, DREAMS, AND TRUTH

The psychological fact is that mirrors, like eyes, carry great power. They are tools which aid us in establishing objectivity and the capacity to reflect. In contrast to the absorbing-mirror of Narcissus, the mirror-shield essential to Athena distanced humans from the primitive world and enabled the objective world of culture and art to be substituted for *prima materia*. Her mirror enabled humans to move beyond self-absorption and to see on the larger, transcendent scale of aesthetics. This brings us to one of the crucial questions of our era: will we move beyond our current selfish-absorption as a race, and transform our narcissism into a generative purpose? With this question watching over our shoulders, let us continue to explore the archetypal underpinnings of seeing and knowing.

A Native American belief is that a mirror has medicine that looks at you and works to empower you.[10] In folklore and myths the mirror expresses a preoccupation with truth, and purports to provide us a glimpse of the true state of the soul. The Virgin Mary in her title, Mirror of Justice, reflects the patriarchal creator to his creatures.[11] At the other extreme, when the mirror is turned against Medusa, she must incorporate her own horror, and it immobilizes her. Which brings us to what I believe is another crucial psychological fact for our times: evil is presumably destroyed by having to face the horrible reality of itself. We continue to ponder this presumption.

When loved ones die we generally assume that their good outweighs their evil. Consequently, we have customs to aid the soul in arriving at its celestial destination. For example, a mirror is hung in suspension above a tomb so that the soul is attracted upward to begin its ascent toward heaven. Mirrors in the home of the recently departed are covered so that the soul is not delayed on its journey by becoming absorbed in its image, for when a person finds his reflection in a pool or mirror, his soul is said to be called out of its spiritual state and actualized into matter.

Dreams are an analyst's favorite tool in the search for psychological truth because, like mirrors, they reflect back to us our unconscious preoccupations. Dreams are our eyes into the inner world. Dreams and mirrors are tricksters in as much as they expose dualities, pose riddles, such as, "What is the reality?" or "Who is the fool?" Often the fool, uninhibited by conventional blinders, sees too many possibilities. He may not see the clean-cut way that things should be.

Polite society perceives him as having a "boundary problem." William Willeford discusses the self-division of the fool with its many images of doubling, from the jester's wand with its self-replicated head at one end, to the numerous duos of popular comedy. Willeford points out that the mirror-image of the fool or trickster presents surprises which goad one to serious self-reflection. In his example of Holbein's illustrations to Erasmus' Praise of Folly, a fool looks into a mirror with serious intent to discover himself, and the image in the mirror sticks out its tongue in response.[12] Tricksters blur the distinction between reality and reflection, thereby provoking us to look more deeply and ask more thoughtful questions. Willeford also illustrates his point with the female joker of a Tarot deck whose mirror reflects an image that not only functions independently of its subject, but reflects the audience as well as the woman-joker herself. In the double presented by the Trickster, there is always more than one bargains for. The seeker looks for reflection of what she knows, but receives instead a shocking expansion of her consciousness.

Willeford reminds us that the fool stands at the edge of each of two ways of seeing: the first, like drama, holds a mirror up to nature to show us what is; the second, like the mirror of St. Paul through which we see darkly, concerns our relations to what lies beyond natural understanding. The Trickster's influence guides us to these borders in terms of our human drama, and then with wiser knowing of the reality of the psyche, into a realm that exists beyond our material world.

Like Trickster, the analyst at times functions as a mirror in which the patient faces his own soul indirectly, until such a time when he can know the soul and be known directly. Current narcissistic preoccupation with reflection, I suggest, is related to the urgency we feel collectively to learn the truth about our human nature, to see beyond the superficial preoccupation with literal "having," in order to attain a deeper knowing and being.

Whoever Knows God has an Effect on Him

In the words of this section title, quoted from *Answer to Job,* Jung wrote of Yahweh's need for reflection, theorizing that, as with parent and child, the need for mirroring is a two-way dynamic between the creator and the creation. This concept, at once primitive and profound, Jung amplified throughout his life, and it permeates his psychology, his approach to patients and their treatment, and his approach to the ills of the soul. The seeds of this philosophical concept were sown early in Jung's life when an obsessive, scatological thought drove him to explore the issue of being seen and seeing; the autonomous fantasy of God destroying the cathedral with a large turd released from the heavenly throne caused Jung great anxiety (as described in detail in his autobiography). Being seen by God as a thinker of sinful, blasphemous thoughts was one part of Jung's struggle; but seeing God in His dark aspect was the more troublesome part for the young son of a minister to try to comprehend. Finally, the transformative part of his struggle was the realization that there was no one in Jung's environment of holy men with whom he could expose such unconventional ideas in order to discuss them. Those who suffer alone can empathize with Jung's anguish. He carried the pain of his problem, and the added pain of not having it mirrored by another human being.

The presence of a reflective other in our times of darkness brings a bit of light and comfort, even if—indeed, especially if—that other does not feel obligated to do anything at all. After a period of carrying his troublesome awareness alone, Jung came to the resolution of his distress: his God saw him and his thoughts, having had created both, and therefore could contain both with forgiveness and grace.[13]

As a youngster Jung had been exposed only to a god-image that was judgmental in its omniscience, and like many of us today, he was never introduced to the image of God as compassionate trickster, or nurturing woman. Characteristic of the Trickster Gods is that they are all-seeing without judgment; it is another, often the high god, who evaluates what is seen. For example, the all-seeing Hermes saw his parents, Zeus and the nymph Maia, copulating at his conception, and enjoyed the scene without moral judgment. One of his first acts as a babe was to improvise a risqué song about that primal scene—we might say he was born singing an X-rated cradle song! To see both God-aspects, the high god and the Trickster in concert of continual creation, as Jung came to do on his own as a result of his suffering, opens one to an entirely new relationship with God.

In contrast to Hermes' non-judgmental curiosity, Hera's curiosity and spying is motivated by intense passion and desire. She desperately desires intimacy and refuses to live without it, no matter who must suffer for her efforts. The difference in attitudes brings clashes between these two. Hermes, born with nonjudgmental knowledge of his parents' transgression, is referred to by Homer as "Argeiphontes," meaning slayer of Argus, the hundred-eyed monster which Hera had guard her rival, Io. The Trickster's capacity to remain free, untrapped by passions such as jealousy, the "green-eyed monster," allowed him to overcome Argus, the embodiment of jealousy and the symbol of Hera's dark matriarchal powers. In response to Zeus's plea and Io's pain, Hermes patiently displaying typical tricksterish facilities, put all of Argus's eyes to sleep with the music of his pipe of reeds and his enchanting stories, and then killed him.

In this example Hermes models a way of dealing with inner monsters, such as the negative mother complex which can destroy our self-esteem, or the critical judge, which can demolish our relationships and our creativity. Jungian analyst Gary Astrachan's interpretation of this myth notes that in freeing Io, who is the object of Hera's persecution, Hermes demonstrates a psychological solution to madness. Hermes frees the soul (Io) from overwhelming guilt and from the madness of obsessiveness and paranoia. The schizophrenic has to be enabled to free his aggression, to make conscious his hostility against envious psychic introjects. Astrachan points out that Hermes, like no other god, gives us through this dark side, a model for relationship between the opposite poles of sociopathy and paranoia, both extreme disturbances of conscience. We will come back to this idea in chapter three.

Astrachan also notes that Argus is transformed as well; he was rewarded by Hera for his loyalty by being turned into a peacock. The peacock is alchemy's symbol of unity and signifies the culmination of the alchemical work in the integration of all states of consciousness (eyes) into one magnificent plume. True to the paradoxical nature of these things, the peacock was also considered the bird of Hermes which conferred immortality on all who ate it.[14]

An important phase of psychological development is learning to confront monstrousness, no matter how ugly and fearful monsters may appear to be. Once able to look the monster in the face, we next learn discernment and strategy. We learn there are times when direct opposition is futile or will exacerbate the problem. When the eye is too powerful, we don't invite it to look at us more intensely. We hope to distract or appease the gazer long enough to gain the upper hand. But it is crucial that we do not learn to evade by strategy before the first step of direct confrontation has been experienced; otherwise true courage is aborted. Both these steps, the courage to confront evil and the capacity to discern the cleverest way to overcome evil, are important experiences particularly of adolescence, though they may be faced at any age.

Adolescence with its triangles, mixed loyalties, betrayals, and identity clashes, prepares us for the vicissitudes of committed love. If we do not acquire the courage to confront our monsters, we end up dancing with them repetitively. Like Zeus and Hera, couples who will not talk about jealousy in a forthright way can spend years indirectly entertaining the green-eyed monster, persisting in honoring him with their attention, as they alternate blows and deceits. Scenarios of jealous passion are power-food on which the monster grows fatter and fatter. Though these scenarios make good opera, Hermes does not enter into such contests; instead, he distracts and soothes the monster, convinces him that he need not remain vigilant, then deals him a fatal blow. With the intrapsychic monster out of the way, we can face how we think and feel about each other without monstrous distortions.

The Argus myth presents a paradigm for those who suffer from fiendish passions. By meditating on this story of Hermes, we learn that it is possible to soothe and still this inner monster who is such a source of pain when taken literally. First, we must sit with the fiend, becoming intimate with its ugly skin and foul odor until we know well how it works in us. When we can place our evil precisely enough to predict its moves, then we deal the capturing blow. (I prefer capture, since we never know when we might need a handy fiend; the captured complex may work in our behalf.)

Whoever knows God has an effect on him; and might we add, whoever knows Evil has an effect on him?

Trickster as a Messenger of God's Plan

As for Hermes, he must stand trial for murdering Argus. As a form of purification, the gods threw stones at him and by this means freed themselves from blame of association with the crime. A heap of stones became a symbol for Hermes ever after, as at the crossroads passersby added a stone to the heap to absolve themselves of guilt.[15] Hermes assumes a scapegoat position by taking the blame for an act which was welcomed by many, although perhaps not by Hera. He is seen in this instance as a Christ-like figure who carries the burden of guilt. Transferring the ancient account into contemporary perspective, we can conclude that as stone-throwers (blamers) we are not hermetic, but when we assume and contain responsibility for evil, that is, when we admit our errors and wrongdoing, we are close to Hermes.

Carrying awareness of responsibility and final judgment, Trickster accompanies us on our last journey. As the Egyptian Thoth, he presides over funeral rites in his role as divine scribe. The inventor of writing, he sees and records the deeds of the dead person before they are put on the scales against Mayet, spirit of world order, sometimes represented as an ostrich "feather of truth." Here is the paradox of Trickster, the God of Liars, as he cooperates with the Goddess of Truth at the final judgment. The two are counterparts who each promote the connectedness of the natural order. The irony of this image allows us to admire the sophistication of Egyptian mythology, which, contrasted with a god-image of a single judgmental Father, should make us wonder. If happenings on earth are taken to be images of the divine world translated into finite matter, then our models of ethics and justice seem incongruously imperfect and unfair, favoring the wealthy and the politically powerful as they do. Given the clumsy, lumbering nature of most modern legal systems, it is hard to imagine them as a reflection of a god who will judge with the sensitivity to nuance implied by the "feather of truth."

In ancient Egyptian society, however, a much more complex, multifaceted god-image was reflected in human society. Robert D. Pelton also researched the trickster figures of four West African societies and offers profound insights into the "mythic irony and sacred delight" of the Trickster gods.[16] Pelton's exposition of the mythology of the Fon society reveals a complex set of relationships within the divine beings with regard to being seen: Mawu-Lisa, the high god, is androgynous. The feminine aspect, Mawu, predominates. Of Mawu's seven sons, each of six is given dominion over some aspect of creation (animals, plants, etc.) with a special language for each dominion. The youngest, Legba, she spoils and keeps close to her, but he is given the task of visiting all the others' kingdoms and reporting back to her. Typical of all tricksters, he is her linguist, translating from each brother's language back to her language. As her mediator, all gods and humans must address themselves to Legba in order to approach the high god.

Consequently, Legba is the agent of Fa, god of divination, who sees one's fate. ("Fa" also refers to one's individual destiny.) The Fon society's intricate delineation of personhood, destiny, and soul with its many aspects—for example, its ancestry, guardians, shadow, sentience—precedes psychoanalysis' twentieth century attempt to describe intrapersonal and interpersonal dynamics. The Fon's schema is an example of the philosophical sophistication that so-called "primitive" people demonstrate to outsiders who are able to penetrate their world and be receptive to its meaning. For the Fon, each person is a unique interrelationship of many cosmic forces. When harmony reigns, destiny is hidden; but when discord arises in one's life, one seeks one's "fa" in order to find direction. In such a worldview, one progresses in awareness through discord and pain, not through complacency, a view with which psychoanalysts agree. Legba is honored as the god who can reveal, but also modify destiny. Therefore, it is he, the Trickster god, who assists humans in negotiating the negative or evil forces of destiny as well as the benevolent.

Pelton recounts the myths which express the Fon understanding of Legba's role as mediator between the divine plans and the everyday life of humankind. In one of these myths, Mawu sets a mysterious primordial being, Ghadu, atop a palm tree to observe the earth, sea and sky. Ghadu had sixteen eyes which she could not open herself. Every morning Legba asked which eyes she wished to have opened. To prevent others from overhearing her reply, she put into his hand the number of palm nuts which corresponded to the number of eyes she wanted opened. As Legba opened her eyes, he too looked about to see what was happening so he could report back to Mawu.[17] Still, chaos reigned on earth and Legba urged Mawu to send Ghadu to teach humans the language of their parents so that they would know how to behave. Instead of sending Ghadu, Mawu sent the three sons of Ghadu to rule earth, sea, and sky, and gave Ghadu the keys of the future: a house with sixteen doors, one for each of her eyes. When men wanted to know the future they would play the palm nuts as divination objects. This would open an eye of Ghadu and the corresponding door to the future. The three sons showed men how to use the palm nuts to find their souls. Mawu gave soul to each one of us, but a person can know her soul only by knowing which eyes Ghadu opens to name it.[18]

Ghadu's stasis contrasts with Legba's mobility. When she closes her eyes, only he can open them. She can observe from her treetop perch and see into the future, but it is Legba who is able to survey, report, and actively bring about actual harmony. The male-female complementarity of this image permeates many African myths, and in this one the feminine's dark stillness is complemented by the masculine's active openness. As in many animal societies, masculinity is associated with exhibitionism and exposure, femininity with the covert and inconspicuous. The feminine grounds and centers the creative activity of the masculine. The myth continues:

One day Legba and Ghadu came to visit earth. They slept together, but during the night Legba sneaked away to lie with Ghadu's daughter, Minona. Ghadu was furious and back to heaven they went to bring the case before Mawu, who ordered Legba in punishment to forever be sexually aroused and forever unfulfilled. This was nothing new to Legba, who began to play sexually with Ghadu. When Mawu reproached him he reminded her that it was she who had ordered him to be sexually insatiable. (This reflection of Legba's guilt back to Mawu is reminiscent of Jung's childhood resolution of his conflict with sin by including God's responsibility in the struggle.) Ghadu's palm tree was now transformed to the erect penis of Legba. Thus Phallos was honored by being given a prominent place in the continued generativity of creation. Pelton says:

> To identify so humorously the *axis mundi* with the erect male organ is to show how truly the language of life is human as well as heavenly. Thus, through Legba, men and women are able to know the inwardness of their social

identities and the outward shapes and courses of their secret selves. As he knows the movements of Mawu herself, so he has mastery of all human passages, inner and outer, and insures their completion. He is always the master of successful intercourse.[19]

According to this African mythology, it is the mother goddess, Mawu, who is behind Legba's mastery:

> Mawu, the creator, makes Legba what he is; Mawu sets him in action; Mawu bestows Fa through him; Mawu enables Fa itself to be a source of transformation and change; Mawu empowers Legba to be the special agent of the consecration of the people to her and the daily revealer of the fundamental patterns of human life. Throughout its whole range, Fon life is a crystallization of the exchange between male outside and female inside. It is patrilineal yet maternally guided, ruled (traditionally) by a king with male ministers and inwardly controlled by Mawu and a female court, shaped in the daylight by Lisa, Gu, and the pantheons of male divinities and within each house subject to Minona, the goddess of the home, in the arch of the heavens and in the depths of both earth and ocean upheld and formed by Da, the serpentine force within both male ejaculate and female placenta.[20]

In contrast to patriarchal theologies, this West African theology shows concern for balancing energies of male-female, open-secret, dark-light.

THE SEEN, THE UNSEEN, AND THE CAMERA

The importance of balancing what is seen and what is hidden, and what is masculine and feminine, is implied in these West African stories; by contrast, in Milan Kundera's contemporary novel, *Immortality*, the opposite, that is, the imbalance of what is exposed versus hidden, is the focus. Agnes, Kundera's female protagonist, is appalled to hear that "a consumer-protection organization had proposed that in future all [surgical] operations should be filmed and the films permanently filed." Agnes longed for solitude and imagined that "in the end one single stare will be instituted that will not leave us for a moment, will follow us in the street, in the woods, at the doctor's, on the operating table, in bed; pictures of our life, down to the last detail, will be filed away to be used at any time, in court proceedings or in the interest of public curiosity."[21]

Agnes speaks for that part of psyche that seeks darkness and quiet sanctuaries of the soul, and that deplores the constant invasions of privacy that modern life demands. Such invasion is *de riguer* in totalitarian governments, but in democratic societies consumerism brings its own versions. Invasions of privacy in "free" societies may be large-scaled and obvious, such as the networking of surveillance systems, credit bureaus, police records, and tax collectors; or more trivial but still disquieting, like the fact that state departments of motor vehicles make millions of dollars by selling their lists of motorists and their statistics to advertising firms. Or like the more personal disquietude of the couple in California who facilitated the arrest of a voyeur by videotaping the voyeur videotaping them. Agnes flees to Switzerland, a place known for self-containment and introversion. (Her ironic end I leave to Kundera to report.)

While some of us are Agnesian, or Hestian, about guarding our privacy, others are utterly fascinated by watching ourselves, and watching ourselves watching ourselves, and watching ourselves being watched. An acquaintance tells me that it is very important to be noticed, even if the attention is negative. "Make an impression, even a bad impression, rather than no impression," is his motto. This attitude moves those who choose talk shows as confessionals for airing their business. It is not unusual to find a group of people videotaping themselves and then watching the video of themselves, reliving the event even before dispersing, before memory becomes a factor. Such dominating preoccupation with being seen suggests a fear of being ignored or of being invisible. Recalling our earlier discussion about the need to be mirrored in infancy, it may be that my friend's insistence on making an impression is related to his being orphaned at an early age. And true, visibility is a commodity not easily maintained in our large, impersonal, ethnically flattened modern life. It is the paradoxical nature of individualism to want attention, but to never get enough. Survival is not enough for today's hopefuls; lacking spiritual convictions, we reach for concrete immortality, being remembered. On film, at least, our image might live forever.

The very fundamental survival value of being seen is accentuated by the camera, especially by the movie and television camera. The power of the camera is that it bypasses our rational minds and affects us directly emotionally; it enters the unconscious, pulling us with it and enveloping us in its moods, especially intensified by the technique of the close-up. In the facial close-up that isolates and amplifies every nuance of expression, we enjoy a magical participation in the actor's experience. The fundamental experience of gazing into the face, and particularly the eyes of another, with all the power that that action holds, is indulged by the camera's close-up. No other art form allows quite as magnetic an identification with another person.[22]

Kundera has Agnes's husband, Paul, present the viewpoint of the imagologues on the subject of being seen: a person is nothing but his image:

> It's naive to believe that our image is only an illusion that conceals our selves, as the one true essence independent of the eyes of the world. The imagologues have revealed with cynical radicalism that the reverse is true: our self is a mere illusion, ungraspable, indescribable, misty, while the only reality, all too easily graspable and describable, is our image in the eyes of others. And the worst thing about it is you are not its master. First you try to paint it yourself, then you want to influence and control it, but in vain; a single malicious phrase is enough to change you forever into a depressingly simple caricature.[23]

This description of the personality through Paul's eyes represents an extreme attitude towards being-seen based on a totally extroverted orientation. He recognizes that self-identity is complex, that we are not unified and clear as ego-psychology once led us to believe, but are multi-dimensional organizations of tensions and facets, sometimes rather loosely held together by a common skin. It is understandable that this recognition might bring with it a certain disillusionment, an apathy, even a disdain for attempting to seek personality integration. Integrity begins to seem naive or pretentious when human nature is unveiled to be such a hapless bundle of contradictions with no one very capable at the center. Kundera, through the tension between his characters, reminds us of basic questions: do we have any substance as individual entities? Do we have a soul, and does it survive beyond this finite world? Kundera provokes us to think about the hope for immortality in its relationship to being seen, and, as artists do, he makes us more aware of the complexities of human nature, in this case, specifically, our narcissism.

Perhaps the less one feels appreciated as an essential being in the here-and-now, the more one longs to be recognized by posterity. And the less one hopes for a resurrection after death, the more one is concerned with living through one's earthly image that can be projected into the future. The idea of a core-of-being connected with a source beyond our own consciousness seems too idealistic or wishful from the contemporary cynical vantage point that we explored in the previous chapter. It might be posited that there is a Legba spanning the various contents of our being and providing some framework for the fragments, but, we wonder, is there, could there possibly be, and do we even need, a Mawu behind it all?

For Jung, the answer was affirmative: not only is there a feminine Mawu, but also a container for all the deities imaginable. The Self—beyond the individual ego, even beyond the polytheistic dimension with its anthropomorphic glimpse of purposive archetypal forces—Jung conceptualized as creative source, drive toward completion, and container of all differences. The individual, by connecting intimately with the Self, whether Self is imaged as container, energy, or center, realizes a source of meaning and integrity beyond one's personal life. (By capitalizing Self we will distinguish the supposed container from the self as psychologists use it to mean an organizing faculty within the conscious realm.)

Reflections on Reflection

We might conceptualize the individual as being in tension between the pull of the persona, the outer image which is largely dependent on the reaction of others, and the pull towards an autonomous private experience. On each end of this tension a reflector is necessary if the experience is to become conscious; that is, we need recognition by others to come to notice how we appear to others, and we need to feel seen or heard by someone if our inner life is to become more than a series of passing images. The reflector on either end of this public-private spectrum may be a tangible personal contact or an imaginal archetypal contact. For instance, perception can range from being seen by neighbors or space aliens to being observed by a supreme being. The inner life can be mirrored by mother, guardian angel, or a cosmic source. Public life may be lived for the purpose of individual glory or as a part of a communal process; private life may be experienced as an autistic phenomenon that ends with death, or participation in a larger consciousness. The sense of participation with something beyond our personal interests is what Jung meant by being intimately connected with the Self.

Knowing who and what we are is a lifetime pursuit and the lines of definition keep moving. But it is also possible to move beyond collective images and opinions, and to throw an anchor or rope into the Self, so as to tolerate more comfortably the discrepancies among our many self-images. For some, a strong faith in a divine being is accepted without question and provides that anchor; it is as if the Self throws the anchor and the receiving person need not search within for a source. For others beset with questions and incongruent experiences, effort is required to find and activate the anchoring experience. It is the effort of self-reflection.

An example is demonstrated by a patient who sought to deal with her self-discrepancies through self-reflection. A well-respected, accomplished professional woman, she allowed herself to reflect on and to share with me a desperate need to be seen. This resulted in a period of distress that we both felt as interminable.

When the slightest lapse of attention toward her occurred on my part, she would become bereft and murderously rageful. By tracking each terrible experience of my supposed indifference or hostility toward her, she lived through a great deal of anguish about her substantiated neglect as an infant. She was forced to admit that, in spite of her successful persona, she had been in long-standing pain, which had left its scars of discomfort about being seen that damaged all her close relationships. During this arduous therapy and without any coaxing from me, she spontaneously followed an intuition and began a ritual of meditating in the presence of an image of a madonna with child. The eyes of the madonna, which she now feels are eyes of empathy and compassion, became symbolic of the eventual acceptance of her tragic infancy. Her contact with the archetypal mother represented by the eyes of the madonna became her anchor in the Self.

Through that connection with the Great Mother, she did not dispose of her loathsome anguish and fearsome memories, but was able to relativize and forgive my human failures, and also those of her parents. I speak now of authentic forgiveness which is hard won, not merely a deliberated change of words or intentions. It is important that she followed her intuition in finding her way to the Mother, for if I had been the one to suggest meditation or some other process, it would not have given her the power of listening to her own soul's way.

This case touches on assumptions that we have been circling: we are very dependent on others for our self-image as babies. With good luck we establish a strong sense of self in early childhood; but in adolescence just that sense of self is subject to reexamination and revision, and we are again exquisitely vulnerable to outside opinion. Usually around the beginning of young adulthood, the philosophical mind blooms to the potential of establishing some distance from our emotions and of reflecting more objectively on ourselves. Then it becomes possible to grasp that no one else can define ourselves either, that we are not only whom we seem nor whom others deem worthy. No, we are more, and we have some degree of choice as to where we place our source of values. We have come through the place of unconscious participation to self-differentiation, and then from self-preoccupation to conscious participation in the world. But though such self-definition is possible, obviously many of us do not grasp it.

Throughout this developmental process leading to the capacity for self-reflection, the body plays a paramount role. Though we don't know what the psychological awareness of the infant is like, we do know that, as Little Earth Mother in the Yacqui creation story does, we experience ourselves through our kinesthetic and auditory senses first *in utero*. Later, we depend on others to reflect back to us visual data about our image. As babies we know nothing about our appearance except as it is reflected by others. In modern times it is difficult to imagine what self-perception is like without visual cues obtained through mirrors and cameras. (Perhaps studies of the blind, of which I am not familiar, could be of interest here.) Both mirror and camera have become indispensable artifacts of modern life, artifacts which have made us very dependent upon our outer images. Does this preoccupation with persona hinder or help us in our capacity for self- reflection? Patricia Berry tells us, "to develop the echo in one's narcissism one must achieve a certain painful distance in and by which this echo can sound."[24] Does the echo we find in the literal mirror benefit psychological self-reflection? We know that a realistic body-image is an asset to self-understanding, but at what point does one's physical image become unnecessarily distracting?

The ability to attach and detach from objects—whether the object be mother, a drug, our body-image, an ego-state, money, lover, etc.—rests on self-knowing. Only with that knowledge, and that ability, can one dare to come close in intimacy, and know that distance is still possible when one needs it. In order to create such distance as Berry suggests, and enable a deeper self-awareness in an unreflective, reactionary person, psychotherapists sometimes play back to them the sound of that person's own voice, or the visual image of themselves through video cameras or mirrors. This is therapeutic because it is more than merely observing one's physical self; it is done in an atmosphere (modeled by the therapist) of psychological as well as physical self-reflection. Because the therapist models emotional distancing, the information can be relativized and considered in perspective along with other personality factors.

Just as one's image can be self-absorbing, it can also make us more aware of our relative place in the larger society; becoming more realistic in our perceptions of ourselves, we begin to see our place in a community as a container to which we have some responsibility. Psychotherapy has been accused of paying too little attention to this dimension.[25]

As we examine this faculty of self-reflection, it does not become simpler. In fact, more questions and complications come to mind. Seeing the ins and outs of others so continually through the eye of the camera seems to have complicated our capacity for self-reflection even more. Consider how the camera has contributed to an insatiable curiosity about our own possibilities and a questioning about physical boundaries. We burst with self-images and bridle under any limitations. The old adage, "Boys will be boys" is obsolete; boys will be boys, and will also be girls, if they like, while girls demand the right to be boys, or another color, size, shape, or to have another family other than the one into which they have been born. The only thing that no one seems to be clamoring to be is old; yet old and young clamor to be seen. A twenty-year old basketball star is congratulated for publishing his autobiography which is reviewed on national television news. No one seems to question the irony of writing about life from the perspective of twenty years. But he has a precedent in some of his elders who clamor to be seen in obsessive detail as they chronicle their lives in autobiographies that include several volumes.

Modern society, like its favorite toy, the camera, seems obsessed with nosiness. And, as is typical of tricksters in numerous folk stories, we seem to be exploring and nosing into everyone else's life, every fixed standard, every border, sniffing like puppies at every new scent, every possibility. Just exactly how greedy can we be before something stops us? How outrageous in dress or behavior, how sadistic, violent, vengeful, bizarre, iconoclastic, devious, perverted? Don't tell us what we should be, let us find out for ourselves by trying it all, and in one lifetime. It's not that we look for information in past patterns; few of us want to be bogged down by looking at history. That would mean taking our eyes off the camera-mirror of the now. A comic describes his egocentricity: "It's not like I don't care about others…it's like, 'There are others?!'"

Why this exaggerated need for attention, for exploring the ultimate in exhibitionism, in narcissism, in self-indulgence? Is it simply a response to the ubiquitous camera, or is the popularity of the camera an effect of something deeper? What will be the effect of a generation or more of narcissists on the collective psyche? Will we become more skillful at psychological self-reflection as a result of seeing our physical image repeatedly, or comparing our physical image with that of others?

Returning to Kundera's couple, Paul claims that the more people are indifferent to politics and the interests of others, the more obsessed they become with their own faces, their individualism; but Agnes feels that concern with being public means that an individual no longer belongs to himself, but is the property of others. She notes that the eye of God has been replaced by a camera; the eye of one has become the eye of all.[26] The subject of self-reflection and its complications through camera and mirror leads us further into the nature of narcissism.

The Matter of Narcissism

Narcissism as a phase of healthy development, or as a personality characteristic, or as a temporary regressive state, all of which can be seen as defensive reactions to threats to the integrity of the self, is distinguished by psychologists from the

Narcissistic Personality Disorder. Narcissistic Personality, identified and diagnosed as a disorder by the American Psychiatric Association which publishes the diagnostic standards in *The Diagnostic and Statistical Manual,* was not officially recorded until the 1970s. Yet clinicians now identify many of this personality type, and when we consider that a relatively small percentage of Narcissistic Personalities enter the clinician's office, we see even more clearly that the prevalence of the disorder is noteworthy. In the narcissistic attitude, we don't think anything is wrong with us, and don't choose psychotherapy unless trapped in a situation where our self-image is threatened.

In agreement that exaggerated narcissism is on the rise, clinicians nevertheless think differently about the causal factors of this condition, which not everyone in the general public would consider a "disorder." There is never "the" cause, as we once used to hope to find—an obsessive mother, a non-empathic or absent father, an early humiliation or abandonment, parents who exploit a child to gratify their own insatiable narcissism; these things happen to many who do not develop an observable disorder. Some theories focus on the milieu of the child's early experiences; others focus on the innate characteristics of the person which set him up for particular internal experiences; still others focus on the imbalance of archetypal influences which can occur at any time for reasons unknown.

Developmental theorists believe that something goes awry in the first year and a half of the narcissist's life, when the crucial aspects of being-seen make themselves felt. The usual stage of infantile omnipotence—to which we seem to be entitled for a while on earth when we impress others as little grounded angels—is not satisfactorily resolved. Some fault of circumstances or attachment brings traumatic feelings, or prevents further development of a flexible sense of identity. The personality is dominated by a grandiose infant whose self-esteem soars one minute and plummets the next, whose hunger for attention is painful and insatiable, who suffers from unsatisfied feelings of entitlement just as her loved ones suffer from her egocentricity, and who finds it hard to take her eyes off of the enthralling mirror long enough to turn her attention inward. The narcissistic problem is more complex than a child "spoiled" with attention; more likely, says developmental theory, something is amiss or inconsistent in the attention given to the child at an age when she needs so desperately to be assured of making an impression.

While developmentalists trace narcissistic troubles back to the first two years of life, archetypal theorists generally avoid assumptions about historical events during infancy. James Hillman writes: "Our history is secondary or contingent...the image in the heart is primary and essential.... I am not caused by my history—my parents, my childhood and development. These are mirrors in which I may catch glimpses of my image."[27] Some archetypal analysts regard the narcissist, whether man or woman, as out of touch with a grounded feminine aspect of personality, and/or consumed in the archetype of the Divine Child. The emphasis on exhibitionism implies an absence of a stable, inner, earthy anima source who can provide and sustain maternal comfort, support and self-esteem, who can nurture the creative spark of the archetypal child within, and who can inspire relatedness. Lacking contact with such an inner comforter, we are drawn outward in a continual compulsive search for the missing security, or that which some societies call the lost soul. In that lost state we fluctuate between extremes of elevated self-love and desperate self-contempt.

The capacity for attachment and detachment that we spoke of earlier is troubled in all the personality disorders, in which attachment is associated with fusion, and detachment with abandonment. This is certainly the case in the narcissist, and in our whole culture which suffers from loss of soul, reflected in the personal histories of many individuals. The high incidence of narcissism today suggests that we must look beyond the handling of the individual child to see the larger cultural issues involved in this phenomenon.

Whatever the origins of this personality type, in some cases the effects of nature seem to be prominent in such a personality: extremely high energy level and creativity; a predisposition to self-preoccupation, perhaps enhanced by special talents and dominating interests; charismatic physical or mental qualities creating a commanding presence. In other cases the effects of nurture predominate: a special role in the family; the projection of special significance onto the child by others; a hard struggle to gain attention from distracted or absent parents, and so on. As narcissists we learn only too well to play to our audience. In fact, we learn our role in some imagined life-drama so well that we completely forget who we really are and how we really feel. The anguish of the narcissistic character appears to be a need for attention, but more accurately it is a sense of loss of soul, of being split apart from one's authenticity for various reasons, a common reason being the fear of attack and abandonment because of the envious feelings of others (whether real or imagined). Without the ballast of a consistent feeling of self-worth, we narcissists are exquisitely sensitive to what others see and feel about us; we fly high in identification with the gods, and drop into suicidal despair as a result of a crooked glance from some supposed observer.

For example, a man with narcissistic problems reported that as a boy he was made to hide his excellent grades and report cards from his brother who was not well-endowed intellectually. In learning to lie about the person he was, the good student became very confused about his intelligence, which he regarded as a liability, not an asset. No Jacob, he could not enjoy his advantages over his brother, but had to pretend Esau was his equal. He accommodated to the world as his parents thought it should be, and lost himself.

Narcissists adopt an image for purposes of adaptation at the expense of the authentic self. The therapeutic possibility of reaching through the layers of pretense and adaptive behavior to touch authentic experiences sets up intense anxiety in the narcissist, who usually bolts at the discomfort. Our narcissistic adaptation hides and protects the central sense of identity from the control and envy of important others, while appearing to appease them. Since the maintenance of the narcissistic state is complex and preverbal, and authenticity has to be pieced together bit by bit, transformation is not quick or easy. No matter which approach to treating the narcissist is followed by the clinician, the first obstacle to a therapeutic relationship is trust. Superficial trust is established quickly with narcissists. Experts at charm, narcissists can drive a therapist out into left field for quite a while by convincing him that the therapist is the long-awaited Great Hope, and no one else has ever understood the patient as well. The spotlight is powerful in the narcissist, and dazzles whomever it shines upon, whether it be therapist, friend, or lover.

But this will not last, if therapy takes hold. There will inevitably be a black period of betrayal when the spotlight goes out, or moves to someone else, before authentic trust is established. Whatever original situation obtained in which the problematic adaptation flourished, the patient attempts to recreate in his close relationships, including the therapy relationship. When the re-creation of the past adaptation fails, as it must for individuation to proceed, the narcissist feels compelled to flee. Just when the therapist sees progress, the narcissist begins to feel too anxious to continue. The security of the miserable but long-standing false self protects the patient from possible fusion and abandonment. Sometimes the therapist treating the narcissist feels at the mercy of whim, like a fan of a vaudeville actor who is always playing to a new audience. Or perhaps the therapist feels like the woman who allows her lonesome cowboy to come and go, seeing his alienation but also that he always leaves his boots under her couch. Schwartz-Salant points out that "the formation and stabilization of the transference-countertransference process is for the narcissistic personality analogous to the suitor test in fairy tales."[28] As in the opera *Turandot*, every suitor of the raging and grandiose princess is beheaded, until one appears with heroic amounts of love, courage, and persistent loyalty to appease the fury she carries about the rape of her ancestor.

Because of the narcissist's tendency to back away from intimacy, a cue to the presence of the narcissistic dynamic in a friend or lover is the experience of there being no opportunity to rest in the relationship. Whenever we are feeling securely held and are ready to sink back into intimacy, the narcissist detaches. Naturally treatment is lengthy and risky, often painful for the patient and for his/her imperfect mirror, the therapist, who "can never get it right." The narcissist seeks an inner truth, but the search is frantic, compulsive, and bound to fail; the therapist knows she is not the answer or the truth, but hopes to establish a connection with the narcissist, at least enough of a connection so that the patient can cast an anchor of hope into the Self. When that happens there is a process of separation from the false self, ensuing confusion, despair, and reintegration organized around a new "core" of personality.

As narcissists we want to have control over what others see of us. This is disastrous in intimate relationships. Intimates want disclosure and closeness; the narcissist has to evade, to keep the true and vulnerable self hidden. As with all character disorders, vision is distorted by some protective constriction. The narcissist cannot see well at a distance or peripherally. As we have noted before, the Trickster Archetype may be called into play by the narcissist's concern with secreting the hidden self; but because the disorder curtails vision and imagination, the Trickster does not function constructively. Being so concerned at keeping the false image intact, the narcissist cannot risk looking away or getting lost in paying attention to another, unless the other provides a mirror in which she hopes/dreads to catch a glimpse of the Self. The adaptive ego checks to see that its idealized (false) image is intact; while the authentic self hopes to locate its source, the Self, or integrating principle. The narcissist maintains vigilance to protect the adaptive shell at all costs.

But the narcissistic defense also prevents us from asking crucial questions and taking in essential information, and so in spite of all our watching, we fail to see important data. All efforts are made to keep the false image what it should be, and so we, in our narcissistic complex, are often shocked when we are rejected or fired from an attachment or job in which we believed ourselves to be indispensable.

Trickster, Narcissism, and the Search for Soul

Since what "seems to be" has higher priority than what "is" in narcissism, Trickster is always evoked by the narcissistic complex. Pelton says the Trickster "pokes at, plays with, delights in, and shatters what seems to be until it becomes what is."²⁹ Trickster tells it like it is, for communication is uppermost, how-it-is is uppermost, how it seems to be or should be is meant to be shattered. This puts the Trickster at the center of the narcissistic dynamics, paradoxically as the antagonist of the narcissistic defenses, yet simultaneously as the only one who can truly understand and accept them. For there is a paradoxical aspect of the narcissist's preoccupation with the mirror, and it is this: if we can ever find the Self in the image, we can be free! If we can find the Self, separate and emerge from it, know its Otherness, we can relate to it rather than identify with it. We can have the mirror inside, have it speak to us, hold us, wait for us, instead of having to be so omnipotently self-protective. We could let go, and know.

In the Trickster something wants to show us "how it is," not only by pointing to our shadiest qualities, but holding them up to the sun's gaze for the greatest possible multitudes to see. Trickster doesn't hold up only our conventionally positive traits; she brings the shadowy, unattractive, and shameful elements into the sunlight of collective consciousness too. And that is what appears to be happening in a tricksterish way as our society becomes more enamored of seeing itself. In our current preoccupation with exposure we have taken the old first lines of the primer which for many of us was the introduction to collective life, "See Dick, See Jane," and exaggerated it to enormous proportions. Jane and Dick's every tear, dream, and orgasm is enlarged for the super-screen in the sky. Yet we are finite, and limited to seeing only a few things at a time. What is missing from this picture? What nuances are overlooked, what shades lurking out of range of the camera's eye, what small secrets of the soul slipping through the cracks? What data are we, in our narcissistic society, refusing to take in? And what is it we are looking for as we scrutinize our own reflection?

Schwartz-Salant, by noting the similarity between Trickster and narcissism, suggests that what is being looked for and overlooked is the relationship to the feminine and its capacity for reflection:

> Narcissism is a trickster, leading one to all kinds of inflation and self-importance with nothing in the end to show for it.... Generally, narcissistic character structures are involved with individuation much as Mercurius is.... They represent both the urge toward individuation and the drive toward the regressive fusion of ego and Self. Narcissistic character structures can lead to *a birth of the feminine or to the repression of this realm of being and body with its own spirit and consciousness.* As well, they can lead to a capacity for reflection, or to its continual suppression under the dominance of a grandiose-exhibitionistic power drive.³⁰ (Italics-DM.)

Mythical Narcissus gives us an image of one whose longing for connection to his own soul is so great that it overrides all other concerns. Similarly the narcissistic character is preoccupied with seeking the truth of herself, and to care for anything or anyone else at this stage of her development would only divert her from her primary task: that of finding the soul she hid protectively so long ago that she does not remember that it is hidden, but feels compelled to retrieve it from the mirror. Here we meet ourselves today, bereft and thoroughly preoccupied with retrieving what we know not. Taking our cues from the narcissistic personality, we can surmise that modern society's urge toward self-absorption means that we are seeking the truth of ourselves. We must find the Self in the mirror in order to separate from it and to relate to it instead of improperly identifying with its power. Our relationship to the feminine inner world is out of balance. As a narcissistic society we can assume that we are probably skewed toward too much masculinity; we identify with power and extroversion, as we project into our god-images. We search the mirror for our missing soul parts which will bring us closer to completion and help us to experience affection without fusion.

In the West African Ashanti theology there is a balance of male and female powers, as we have seen is also true in the Fon. Ashanti goddess Asase Yaa is equal in power to the male god Nyame. She is neither his wife nor his creation, but the likelihood is that "each has a hidden aspect somehow reflecting the chief characteristics of the other."[31] The social order of the earthly society reflects this double divinity: the King has a Queen Mother who shares his rule, and each chief and subchief each shares power with a Queen Mother. "The Queen Mother is to the King as Asase Yaa is to Nyame: the resource out of which the source of life draws life and renews life."[32]

It is practically impossible for us, so long steeped in Western tradition, to imagine a psychological foundation that is informed by an early teaching of the masculine and feminine nature of God, and that can assign true value to the psyche and to introversion. More often our way is to tolerate the inner life only if it proves pragmatic or attention getting in some way. Our extroverted values bias us toward seeing other cultures as less successful if their technology and levels of material comfort are less advanced than our own. Like a narcissistic personality who disdains the experience of others, a narcissistic society tends to overlook the wisdom and information conveyed by the philosophies, arts, and music of other cultures, which are often much more sophisticated and differentiated than its own. In our society we tend to overlook the closeness that some other cultures have with animals and children, and with nature herself, connections which are often far more advanced than our own, stressing as they do cooperation with nature rather than conquering.

Cut-off as we have been from our feminine soul as a culture, we express our condition through our narcissistic adaptation, vacillating between fears of fusion and abandonment. Although there may seem to be a developing reverence for "The Goddess," there are still women and men mutilating their bodies and souls to fit into a masculine image of how we should be. Relatively few of us are at peace with who and how we are. In psychology our bias shows in the experience of the ego in terms of what I think of as "yang functions," functions of doing, actively participating in, even "overcoming" both outer and inner worlds. Yet we know from experience and from numerous examples in universal stories that it is sometimes adaptive to do nothing but contemplate or wait, to live what is.

Because of our bias toward extroversion, and in spite of Jung's explorations of the need for balance, introverted behavior is still often pathologized and regarded as weak ego-functioning, when it may be exactly what is needed in order to mediate the unconscious. This bias towards extraversion was abetted by Freud's view of the unconscious as Id which was seen as something to be mastered by Ego. It is less so under Jung's influence which bids us to respect the information from the unconscious as a valuable source of survival data, data which can balance our over-weighted conscious vantage point. I like to think of the ego-functions as representing the yin-yang principles, able to be active or passive, assertive or reflective, as called for by the circumstances.

With an androgynous view of the ego functions, with regard to the resolution of the narcissistic adaptation, the acceptance of the yin-ego opens one to retrieving the lost element of soul that is being sought in the mirror. We have images for this which indicate the importance of Trickster in the process: for example, Hermes bringing the abducted feminine, Persephone, back to the upperworld; Hermes rescuing the Divine Child, Dionysus, when he was born of Zeus and had to be taken from Hera's sight to be cared for by nymphs; Biblical nomadic wise-men throwing the plotting king off track to allow the escape of the Divine Child, Jesus. These images of the recovery of the lost soul,(represented by the feminine, or by the archetype of renewal and creativity, the Divine Child), with the help of the shrewd and caring Trickster, all imply that there is a central organizing principle by which the fragments are related in their process of continual flux. The notion of a center need not imply stasis, but rather a purposive order as opposed to unrelated random events.

Longing for Center

These stories of rescuing the abducted soul connect us with the Trickster's function of reuniting what has been severed. At other times, it is Trickster's function to sever in order to promote awareness of the unifying principle. For example, in the Fon mythology, the center is Mawu-Lisa, the Mother/Father god. Mawu wants her sons to be together in harmony. But such a peaceful state would provide no differentiation in the world. Trickster fosters quarrels between them, and then mediates between them to guarantee the delineation of all forces while preventing a dominance of one over the other. As Pelton poetically says:

> Legba's very deception of (Mawu) shows how she has willed the humanity of the cosmos, for his actions reveal that the features of divine power that seem so inimical to man—its acceptance of, permission for, or creation of divine and human conflict—are those which make human life possible. Legba is the agent of heaven, but also the friend of earth, because he, like Ananse, domesticates conflict, which the Fon know to have a life-creating purpose. He helps Mawu to bring the human world into being by focusing and refining the divine power.... The place where men live is far enough from the divine center so that men are free, yet close enough, above all in the very intimacy of the social structure, to guarantee that this structure will not spin down into nothingness, but in its spinning to be renewed. Legba moves from divine center to human periphery and back to enable each always to find its full manifestation in the other.[33]

The Trickster behind our society's current narcissism may be insuring that we differentiate what about us continues to seek contact with the divine center. Yet we seem so much farther from the center than the Greeks or the Fon felt themselves to be, and our social structure is so much less intimate, that we border on despair of making contact. Our abstract notions of God pull us like kites toward spiritual freedom. The problem is, a kite or balloon-spirit, fleeing from the messiness of nature, signifies a schizoid attitude about its own body. It is not only nature that is messy, but our thinking becomes messy when we try to integrate intimations of the soul's immortality with the clearly demonstrable mortality of the body, soul's temple.

Each theological system has its way of trying to solve the question of dauntless spirit in deteriorating flesh. What a variety of solutions we have manufactured, each a reassuring, creative vision of possibility! Even the nihilistic death-as-finality is reassuring to some. For those who cannot find shelter in theology, physics is reassuring. For instance, holograms could give a glimpse of possibilities of eternal individualism, or quantum theory could suggest that the notion of individual soul is a temporary delusion resulting from our primitive notions of space and time. For the time being, the image of a risen and glorified body raises more questions than it answers for us mortals. But the images of bodiless spirit or of reincarnated spirit in a different body is puzzling as well. Surely anything is possible in the realm of physics and the tremendum beyond the perimeters of mind. A spirit with free choice of molecular structure ranging from very dense (as in earth matter) to very refined (as in ethereal being) is one way of imagining a custom-made eternal life. Another image is of a rearrangement of our facets or mini-selves in new contexts within different organizing principles. Mortality is our beautiful and terrible mystery.

In any case, while embodied, we need to hold our kite-spirit with a firm footing in Mother Earth. Our cosmic image need not be skewed to the Yang principle, but could also be in touch with Yin and oriented to nature. Trickster, present in all energetic forms, may help us to ground ourselves in the remembrance that all our questions reflect our meager degree of enlightenment. Trickster tells us that our consciousness is but a firefly to the cosmic light, and our light years but an eye-blink to eternity. In the absence of clear answers to our humble questions, Mercurius bids us, "Rest in the belief that frees hope, whatever that may be for you." In the same spirit is this poem by Derek Walcott:

LOVE AFTER LOVE

The day will come
when, with elation,
you will greet yourself arriving
at your own door, in your own mirror,
and each will smile at the other's welcome,
and say, sit here. Eat.
You will love again the stranger who was yourself.
Give wine. Give bread. Give back your heart
to itself, to the stranger who has loved you
all your life, whom you ignored
for another, who knows you by heart.
Take down the love letters from the bookshelf,
the photographs, the desperate notes,
peel your own image from the mirror.
Sit. Feast on your life.[34]

CHAPTER III

SCRUPLES AND SOUL DOCTORS

Among the Ashanti people of Africa, the spider-trickster, Ananse, is cherished for his cleverness and gleeful insubordination to the High God, Nyame. Nyame's partner, the Queen Mother, Asase Yaa, seems to appreciate contradiction as Ananse does. Anthropologist Robert Pelton tells us that Ananse focuses the clarity of Nyame, draws forth from Asase her hidden powers, and functions as the intermediary of creative interchange which brings the continuation of new life.[1] At night Ashanti children gather in a circle to hear "spider-Ananse stories."

> The scene is an image of social life, in which babies are born at the center of a people, but as they grow they move outward toward adulthood, old age, and death. At the heart of the circle is the storyteller, often a woman who is for the moment both the chief elder and the Prime Infant, the witness to what the people know and can become. In this old man or woman, the edge of the circle is brought back into its heart, and the movement outward and the movement inward are shown to be movements of metamorphosis, ontological passages.[2]

Spider-Ananse is the dynamo between this movement, weaving inner and outer. In his merry way, Ananse also brings contradiction, jealousy, and, in the following story, even disease to earth:

> He (Ananse) tells Nyame that he will bring him a beautiful maiden if Nyame will give him, to kill and eat, the sheep that Nyame sacrifices to himself on Saturday. After eating it, Ananse discovers a village filled with women, all of

whom he marries. A hunter reports that Ananse has fed the sheep to the women and married them. Nyame becomes envious, so he claims all the women for himself except one who is sick. She asks Ananse to bathe her, collects the water in a gourd, and becomes beautiful. Again the hunter reports to Nyame that Ananse has made a fool of him by keeping the most beautiful woman for himself, and so Nyame takes her too. Ananse then invents an insulting song about her, and in vexation begins to dance with his sons. The crow reports this to the High God, who now wants the dance as well, but Ananse will only perform the dance in Nyame's harem. Nyame and his wives dance with Ananse, but the one who had been sick will not dance until Nyame forces her. Ananse strikes her with the gourd, and the diseases are scattered everywhere.[3]

This is a confusing story of a god who collects diseases, then releases them into the world of humans, along with a creative dance, juxtaposing disease and disorder with creativity. Pelton analyzes this story in depth. Here I will let the story do its own work, as I wish only to underline that the Trickster moves between chaos and order, between power and impotence, between sickness and health. He is the agent of the powerful central principle, the Self, as that power manifests in human existence. As such an agent, Trickster enables us to look at the problem of human suffering with compassion and from different perspectives, including the perspective of various levels of consciousness.

The Search for Meaning in Suffering

The Ananse story is confounding, just as the mystery of disease and suffering confounds us humans on the quest for meaning. Through the ages, the Book of Job continues to speak to that sense of mystery. Still, when we are confronted with pain it is as if we are without a history of experience to draw upon, and must each discover anew how to take it. And nowhere in our society do we find more passionate controversy about moral issues than in the field of medicine, especially medicine as it pertains to both ends of the life cycle: who has a right to be born, and who has a right to die? So deeply lie the answers about what is medically good or evil, that people are willing to be killed and to kill for their beliefs when faced with the questions.

We are grappling with ethical questions raised by the possibility of cloning human embryos, of grafting animal parts onto humans, of creating "designer babies" with the genetic characteristics we prefer, of designing pleasant personalities by means of cosmetic pharmacology, of impregnating post-menopausal women and even men. Abortion or euthanasia, each at a final boundary of the life-spectrum involving questions of pain, freedom of choice, and quality of life, create conundrums of ethics that seem insoluble. Here more than ever we need guidance from the divine, but each human faction believes its opinion is sanctioned by the divine. The guidance of Trickster/Mercurius enables us to look at a problem from all angles and levels of being, free from fanaticism, to hear the needs of others and to communicate our own needs effectively.

I met with a friend to offer my condolences after his mother passed away, and he told me this wonderful trickster story:

> His mother had been living in a nursing home for years, gradually deteriorating physically and mentally, until finally she stopped taking in food and water. The family acknowledged her body's decision to die and they were at peace with that. They advised the medical staff to keep her comfortable without heroic measures to prolong life. The nursing staff agreed, but her physician refused to let her become dehydrated. Every time he saw her looking as if she might be dehydrating, he ordered an intravenous feeding and brought her around for another few days. On his last visit he was pleased to see her rallying, with good moisture and color in her face. But soon after he left she drifted peacefully to death without interventions. What the doctor didn't know was that the nursing staff had prepared her for his visit with a bit of lip gloss and blush, just enough so that the Angel of Life would pass her by and let her go quietly to sleep.

The Hippocratic oath was originally made to Apollo, the god of scientific medicine, under whose auspices this physician was functioning. But the nurses were following Hermes, the god of holistic medicine, the guide of souls, of journeys, and cunning wisdom. Hermes and his assistants among the nursing staff in this instance, helped their patient along her natural journey, even though it took some bluffing and blush to do so.

TRICKSTER, SHAMAN, HEALER

Some maintain that Hermes is the god of shamanistic medicine, although one authority on shamanism, Mircea Eliade, attributes the role to Apollo and says that the figure of Hermes Psychopompos "is far too complex to be reduced to a 'shamanic' guide to the underworld."[4] In African mythologies the Trickster mimics and satirizes even the seriousness of the shaman. He does so, not to overthrow the priesthood, but to show the underbelly of everything, including himself. Even though a shaman may serve the high god rather than the trickster god, both gods are intimately involved in healing, and both carry responsibility for disease, according to the story of Ananse above. In the case of Greek mythology, both Trickster-Hermes and High God-Apollo carry the caduceus. Homer tell us that Hermes' caduceus, the golden wand, was acquired by Hermes from Apollo in exchange for the tortoise-lyre; later the caduceus changed hands again from Hermes to Apollo's son, Asclepius. Ginette Paris notes that the passing of the wand from Hermes to Asclepius signified the bridging between the ancient ways of healing through magic, represented by Hermes, to the new scientific attitude and consequently the secularization of medicine, represented by Asclepius.[5]

For both healers the caduceus, with entwined serpents around the staff of life, symbolizes the union of opposites, the creation of order out of chaos. Apollo and Hermes share those symbols, Apollo underlying order and Hermes underlying chaos. But for a journey which has no clear destination—the journey of life, the journey to death, and the journey of psychotherapy, for example—Hermes, the non-authoritarian god who enjoys equally the company of the good and the wicked, is our guide.

In the healing arts, the worlds of Hermes, Apollo, Dionysus, and Poseidon overlap and merge at times, bringing common elements to what first seemed to be distinct entities. Magical, shamanic, and healing aspects endow all these shape-shifting gods, and though, strictly speaking, magicians are not shamans are not healers are not psychopomps are not visionaries, the terms are not mutually exclusive, but nebulous. Misty boundaries in these areas do lead to confusion, especially if we try to categorize, pin them down logically, or analyze the efficacy of any one archetype in the matter of healing.

Consider, for example, how suggestion, placebo, transference phenomena, and psychic healing blend medicine and shamanism. How often it happens that we can't say what agent was crucial in a recovery from illness! An example of ambiguity in medicine is the field of body therapy today; therapists whose focus is on identifying unconscious complexes in the body posture and muscle tension, and those who consider themselves psychic healers, manipulating energy fields which may or may not be tangible, both call themselves body therapists. For the former, the patient actively participates in the therapy in an effort to alter aspects of her physiological expressions of psyche; for the latter the patient is passive, in fact, need not even be physically present, as the healer exercises power over the patient's energy distribution. No clear identities have been defined by the profession—and what a task it would be to attempt to create such definition when body therapists may combine both methods, and many other methods that fall somewhere between the two I have described.

Most psychotherapists would agree that their work falls under the influence of different archetypes at different times, but, as Jung proposed, the Trickster guides the total process, for the reasons we have been examining here. He is the guide of the therapist who considers therapy an adventure. An experienced therapist once told me that he was burnt out from seeing people hour after hour, day after day. He said he could place every patient into one of six categories and could predict what would happen in each case on the basis of previous experience with the categories. No wonder he was bored! He was not welcoming Mercurius into his office, much less amplifying the mercurial energy when he saw it in patients' lives. He was missing the spirit of adventure that gives each patient's story its meaning and uniqueness.

For bored therapists, Lopez-Pedraza's writing should be required reading. He calls Hermes the therapist's inner companion in the solitude of his daily practice; through Hermes, therapy "is turned into a psychic creative work, where the therapist can begin to love his practice in the same way an artist loves his art."[6]

Freeing the Double-Bind

Trickster's presence in therapy enables us to see through situations without distortion or prejudice. She cares nothing for dignity and is the perfect antidote to the kind of inflation that dogs those whose work involves transference: therapists, medics, clergy, attorneys, teachers, entertainers, etc. She does not endure constriction, whether it be being bound by walls or rules of logic or theoretical constructs or expectations of reliability; however, she does demand interaction and is detained by authentic confrontation and dealing, never by repression, submission, attempts to overrule, or sentimentality. She can't be captured in a sado-masochistic dilemma. She demands authenticity, and, living in the moment, resists the emotional entanglements that drive Dionysians to madness, because she remembers that everything is temporary, even our most enduring loves and hates.

Nietzsche introduced the dualism of the Apollonian and Dionysian attitudes into modern cultural history, and the creative anthropologist Kerényi added the Hermetic attitude as a third configuration.[7] Neither rational and heroic like Apollo, nor swept away in ecstasy and wild abandon like Dionysus, Hermes is the appropriate antidote when we are able to see only the options of being orderly or wild; he becomes a refuge for those who need to become unbound from impasse. He is the grand escape from the double-bind, lord of the objective-ego, symbol of liminality, spirit of the Transcendent Function.[8] Unlike Eros, whose flights lead to bonds with others, the flights of Hermes lead to freedom and possibilities. Kerényi contends that Eros is a limited and idealistic, but less clever son of Hermes. We will take up this statement again later.

In the morning of his first day of life Hermes sang the history of the gods beginning with his muse, Mnemosyne, Goddess of Memory. She is his fate; Hermes the escape artist, and those who travel with him, cannot escape from memory. This means there is no chance of losing oneself, of not seeing, no defense of denial to draw upon. The curse and blessing of Hermes is to see too much. The blessing of good memory as an asset for therapy notwithstanding, Hermes/Mercurius cannot be given exclusive rights to the therapy session, nor does he want them. Many archetypal influences move through the therapy-in-process, and Mercurius observes and responds to them all.

As for the application of these mythical themes which color psychotherapy, let us look at a few approaches which share certain tricksterish qualities. In the field of psychotherapy there have always been bold, creative therapists who lived close to the Trickster and gained the reputation of being godlike. One was John Rosen who, in the days before anti-psychotic medicines were developed, was reputed to cure schizophrenics quickly through his amazingly courageous and penetrating interventions, for example, arguing with a paranoid's delusions by claiming that he (Rosen) was Christ. Ronald Laing also approached schizophrenia in a creative spirit that has been identified as tricksterish,[9] and his confrontation of orthodox psychiatry's narrow view of mental illness is well known. Fritz Perls was another such personality, mercilessly confronting, mocking, and intimate. Milton Erickson manipulated not just the unconscious patterns in his patients, but their very lives as well, arranging for things to happen to them outside the therapy. The primary feature of Erickson's "Strategic Therapy" is that it puts the responsibility on the therapist to plan a strategy for solving the patient's problems. The therapist sets the goals, and the emphasis is on results, not method.

The approaches of psychotherapists like the ones named above seem to be highly successful in some cases. While they can illustrate some tricksterish interventions, they are not necessarily guided by the adventurous spirit of Mercurius. We have to know more about the attitude of the therapist to judge that. Sometimes the approaches are contrived, rather than hermetic, and depend on powerful personalities (Jung called them "Mana personalities") who deliberately maneuver the patient's unconscious processes in the belief that their beneficent intentions give patients needed experiences and promote the best for them. Such therapists argue that all medicine relies on an imbalance of power, and even analysis involves the therapist bringing his personality to influence the patient.

A certain amount of legend and idealization accompanies these exceptionally gifted therapists. We tend not to hear about their failures. Perls, the father of Gestalt Therapy, demonstrated a genius which inspired the practice of psychotherapy in extremely constructive directions. Like Jung, he saw the power of the autonomous complexes and taught people to become more in touch with them by personifying the complexes. At the same time, the history of Esalen, where Perls was noted for his dramatic group work, is peppered with fallout from Perls' bombastic attacks on the defenses of people who looked to him as a guru.

Sometimes therapists justify godlike interventions as a step on the way to the patients' finding their own wisdom. Manipulation is resorted to as an expedient way of penetrating a rigidity, either within the intrapsychic communication system of the patient—such as a too rigid boundary between complexes, or in the interpersonal communication system—such as a family impasse. Rigid barriers to awareness, the therapist might argue, can only be penetrated indirectly, can only have change slipped into them without overt contact with a maladaptive defense system. For example, by hypnosis we can penetrate the barrier between conscious and unconscious, by-passing defenses that even the patient doesn't want to uphold consciously. The subject's body will respond to the will of the hypnotist when the conscious mind of the subject cannot get through. Erickson even reports enabling a flat-chested woman to develop breasts through hypnosis.

Unwittingly crossing barriers between conscious and unconscious occurs constantly in common social interaction. In any relationship, including the therapeutic, we may find ourselves doing some version of condescending manipulation when we safeguard or support a person's resistance to change instead of directly confronting the defensive behavior. We may so manipulate to avoid a contest, or in order to protect some fragile area of the psyche of the other. For example, we agree with a child that her scribbling looks like the cat it's supposed to be, and we don't point out that, from our perspective, cat's have something between the head and tail. We don't push our opinions on armed guards, delusional patients, a child in a temper tantrum, and any cases in which people caught in complexes are inaccessible to reason. At such times we all commit lies of omission.

Gregory Bateson called attention to communication in terms of different levels of consciousness which can conflict in paradoxical ways, i.e., the double-bind, the classic example of the ancients being the Cretan paradox, "All Cretans are liars". The Greeks appreciated paradox as an aid to transcending human knowing and coming to experience God.[10] But to the uninitiated, a diet of paradox is disturbing. In a longitudinal study of disturbed families during the fifties and sixties, Bateson and others found such dual messages to be an identifiable form of communication between schizophrenics and their parents. An example of the double-bind posed by a parent might be, "I don't want you to live your own life because I love you too much." Therapists, in good trickster fashion, adopted the same style of communication with families as a way of shaking loose entrenched symptoms. The therapist might direct the patient to have the symptom, or perform the objectionable behavior deliberately, creating a paradoxical conflict between the part of the patient that wishes to comply, and the part that rebels.

Jay Haley took Bateson's model to its limit by considering the power component to be the dominant factor in human relatedness. Strategic therapists insist that they are not interested in the exploitative aspects of power, but only in its benevolent aspects. Chloe Madanes, who softened the power plays by asking the patient to *pretend* to have the symptom, points out that to have the power is to have the opportunity to care for, reform, comfort, and guide the other person. Conning the patient or the family in the interest of opening vistas or undoing double-binds is certainly the realm of Hermes, and, when inspired by an image of health and connected to the human heart, can be a constructive process. The pretend and play that Madanes describes may put the problem under a new lens, may magnify or telescope it into a different perspective.[11]

The dark side of manipulation is that no human being has the perfect insight of a trickster god. We are in great danger emulating an archetype. Even though patients want to give, and do give, therapists enormous power, accepting the role is not the therapist's task; reflecting on it with the patient is. I have seen individuals and families irreparably damaged by power maneuvers on the part of therapists. Paradoxing, hypnosis, manipulation of mind or body, energy therapy, even storytelling and other enchantments can be non-therapeutic, or worse, and any therapist who uses them had better have had very thorough analysis and quality supervision. Therapists also need to be very clear about the difference between recognizing archetypal material and acting it out. Being seen as the perfect mother, father, wise one, lover, or persecutor is heady stuff; subtly, the projection may do its magic and little by little we, the receivers, find it creeping into our self-image and our posture. Therapists have an obligation to stay keenly aware of these projections so as not to act on them unknowingly.

As the universality of Trickster stories illustrates, there is archetypal power in storytelling, an awe-full vehicle for unconscious control. We see patients who spend years working to free themselves from the binds of early stories that were told in their families—stories, for example, about the disastrous effects of sexual exploration, or of leaving the nest. Brainwashed with such stories, people may remain emotionally crippled for life. Similarly, even therapists can divert their patients with stories meant to motivate; for example, stories that hold up heroic, ego-enhancing ideals only prolong the uncovering of shadow when they evade the dark tendrils of envy and greed which are yearning towards daylight. There may be times when such diversions are beneficial; for example, with children who have been battered we may prefer to help them suppress their pain and provide support and hope. But keeping arrogance out of a decision to treat an adult as a child, even at that adult's invitation, is a job for Mercurius.

The noted family therapist Salvador Minuchin warned that his approach could be translated wrongly into mechanical meddling with families.[12] Seasoned therapists see the positive and negative aspects of even the simplest interventions, for instance, in greeting the patient. What greeting is appropriate to further the patient's work and psychological momentum—serious? chatty? touchy? quiet? What greeting best respects the patient's feelings? Some analysts hold to a strict routine of minimal greeting so that nothing can be read into the vagaries of small changes in facial expressions, tone of voice, and other gestures of reaction to the patient's arrival. Others try to let the moment determine the response, trusting their antennae for the facilitative point of contact.

The existential family therapist, Carl Whitaker, is noted for an approach that I would describe as "evolved hermetic": he disclosed himself to the patient or family in ways so humble and foolish that the others were encouraged to react creatively. One of my fond memories of Whitaker is hearing him describe a moment of enlightenment when he first realized that his wife was beautiful at the moment when she was quite angry at him. At that instant, in the midst of a domestic quarrel, Mercurius graced him with a sudden detachment from the usual egoic reaction and forever changed his marriage. His retelling the story forever enhanced my relationships as well, as he modeled a kind of trickster's distance that allows some new, creative response to enter.

Albert Ellis, the father of Rational Emotive Therapy, writes:

> When my clients persist in refusing to acknowledge how disturbed they really are and I see that my efforts to help them do so are not working, I take the practical, and admittedly dishonest, tack of pretending that I go along with them and work to help them with whatever emotional or other problems they will acknowledge. This particularly is true when I am seeing clients who have, in my opinion, limited likelihood of changing.... I take the

middle ground of being as honest as feasible instead of being as honest as possible...I try to be authentic to myself as a therapist.... Truth and honesty are good and ethical most of the time because they usually abet human growth and happiness. But absolute or perfect therapeutic honesty can sometimes be iatrogenic—and hence not exactly ethical.[13]

Psychodynamic therapist Darrell Dawson, representing another angle on the issue of therapeutic manipulation, writes:

> Many theoretical approaches over many years blithely advanced entrapment procedures for drawing out feelings from patients, or symptom removal by falsely prescribing what they intend to eliminate. This kind of lying may be OK. for some therapists doing short-term problem solving, but for me my mandate came to be, "Treat, but never trick." Too many people have been lied to all their lives. Therapy may represent their first honest human experience. The issue of providing trustworthiness became the bedrock for my entire career—the most singular guiding principle.

Dawson sums up his philosophy in the words of Dr. Seuss:

> I said what I said and I meant what I meant. An elephant's faithful one-hundred percent![14]

Doctors of Darkness

Therapists are still learning about the nuances of transference-countertransference. On the side of the patient we have the pitfalls of "transference-cures" which provide an imitation of integrity for as long as the idealization of the therapist or therapy is sustained. On the side of the therapist, in exploring her countertransference to its depths a therapist contacts the underbelly of therapy. The therapist may, for example, find a certain degree of sadism in the process. Thomas Moore says, "the therapist notices the innocence of a patient, exposes it, inspects it, probes it, and in a sense applauds the uncomfortable feelings that accompany analysis."[15] To deny the inherent cruelty of such a method is to bring a false rosy glow to the consulting room.

Sometimes only a therapist's dream can reveal to her how deeply she is affected by a patient's material. Dreams, physical reactions, fantasies, lapses of attention, unusual degrees of concern, all inform us of the countertransference attachment. We continually learn from the examples of previous generations of therapists in this area of a profession which is both art and science. Like a tribe held together by enduring intuitive principles, dreams of wholeness, intimations of integrity, therapists slowly build upon information passed along through lore and oral tradition, in addition to academic research. To call upon one without the other, to work only as if therapy were art, or science, is to risk falling into autistic charlatanism on the one hand, or bloodless scientism on the other.

Jung was seen as a trickster according to some observers, though I don't know if that description was based on his powerful personality outside of the consulting room or on his actual work in therapy. Still, I interpret the message that he left through his psychology to indicate that he generally rejected manipulation and working by deliberate unconscious influence, with the understanding that we never can control the latter but must attempt to work with it constructively and with the patient's greatest possible awareness.

The emphasis of Jung's legacy as I understand it is on providing conditions which aid the other in contacting his or her inner wisdom in whatever form it presents itself; furthermore, the contact with the source of wisdom takes precedence over preconceived goals or ideals of normalcy and health. We often find as the work proceeds that the goal patients arrive with and the goal the therapist may imagine in the beginning of the process are not lasting or meaningful goals. The current fascination of business offices and agencies with "treatment goals" reflects ignorance of the true nature of the psychotherapeutic process. Instead it exposes a shallow intent and manipulative attitude toward patients.

The use of tricky interventions assumes that the therapist knows more about what is best for the patient than the patient's unconscious knows. When we feel that way, therapists are looking at a big red sign that says "DANGER ZONE." The danger is identifying with the Self, or with any archetype, and playing into the patient's archetypal projections. Jungian analyst Peter Mudd likens this situation—when we take on the godlike qualities ascribed to us in transference projections—to the myth of Semele who insisted on seeing Zeus in his full glory. Jealous Hera put this crazy idea into her head. Zeus tried to dissuade Semele, but had already promised her anything and had to go through with his promise—a typical masculine ethical decision upholding a rule, and split-off from the feminine values which would have considered the relative pain to all parties and to their relationships. Semele was allowed to view Zeus in his total transpersonal power and was obliterated instantly in the fiery energy of the divine presence.

Mudd points out that the same theme occurs in the movie, *Raiders of the Lost Ark*, but Indiana Jones avoids the inflation of watching as the ark is uncovered, and escapes the fate of the others who are caught up in enhancing their egos through the power of the ark. In the same vein, if therapists, inflated by the transference energies, play god without transforming the divine energy through humble human bodies and personalities, they symbolically blast the patient and the therapy into smithereens. As therapists we may feel we are being creative, bringing something new to the patient, but we are scorching to the patient's fragile or tentative inventiveness.[16]

To carry the analogy further, we might contrast an atmosphere of "Zeus-like" therapy versus "Hermes-like" therapy. Zeus has no direct contact with mortals, but protects them by presenting himself in disguise. His reason for being with mortals is usually to gratify himself, to dally with the extravagance of diversity. On the other hand, it is Hermes' divine business to interact with mortals through messages from the upper and under worlds. He inspires therapists to find a way— perhaps through carefully chosen story, example, or metaphor—to help patients place their feet on the path, eventually to find signposts that aid them on their journey, without a care about the dignity or image of the therapist.

While it is not my intention to be preachy, this shadowy area of therapeutic power is difficult to speak about without falling into moralism or inflation, which is why we must speak more about it. The lack of discussion on this topic has led to unconscious patient-abuse and power problems; talking and imaging is our way out of possession by it. Lopez-Pedraza describes power as "the most extreme aspect of the non-image, where instead of imagination there is only a barren wasteland."[17] He reminds us that Hermes deals with being cornered, but is not concerned with power. The hermetic therapist intends to help the patient escape from psychological bindings without overpowering the patient, and without doing violence to the patient's psychological structure.

THE IMAGINAL TRICKSTER

Active-imagination is a psychotherapeutic method that catches the spirit of Mercurius, since imagination is his realm. Methods which dismember the personality, such as compartmentalizing and dialoguing with the personification of a complex, remind us of the trickster stories in which he detaches from his anus or penis and converses with it. In active-imagination we detach from a complex and dialogue in some medium with a representative symbol of the complex.

The cautiousness with which Jungian analysts are trained to approach active-imagination techniques could avert some of the distress arising from the "false memories" phenomenon. A therapist, if too eager to pursue his hunches, is capable of suggesting ideas which the patient, believing the ideas to be part of her actual history, may incorporate through suggestion. Therapists have been accused of planting ideas of abuse into highly suggestible patients. The danger of infecting the patient with one's own complexes is stressed in Jungian analytic training. Only the most arrogant therapist practices without having had personal psychotherapy and without periodic supervision. By teaching a patient to dialogue with inner figures, the analyst supports the fact that the patient, not the therapist, and not even the unconscious complex itself, is in charge of his or her psyche.

Understand that the inner figures are not thought up by the therapist, but are taken from the patient's dreams and fantasies. In doing active-imagination, patients are cautioned to dialogue only with beings and objects who cannot be contacted in life. Messages from the unconscious are never blindly followed without being subjected to thoughtful considerations of their meaning and consequences by an observing ego. Analysts are taught to be firmly respectful toward unconscious contents, and to provide the function of exerting restraint towards unconscious processes if the patient approaches the unconscious too impulsively. The patient comes to see that, because active-imagination is never done with the image of a living person in the patient's personal life, the dialogue pertains only to the archetypal realm, and must be translated carefully by the patient alone into the meaning for his or her personal life.

This cautious approach to unconscious complexes is exceedingly different from directive, manipulative, or solely cognitive therapies. Not only does it color the way early trauma and abuse are dealt with, but it significantly affects the pharmacological approach of biological materialism. In approaching psychotherapy as a journey guided by the Self, and not the therapist's or society's view of what is healing, medication becomes a tool most beneficial when kept to a minimum, in order to allow maximum communication and the free flow of imagination. Directive therapies stress the quickest possible achievement of adjustment at the expense of fulfillment of more holistic personality potentials. Coping well and being independent are not always the immediate goal of the Self. A person may need to experience being totally dependent and cared for by others in order to heal; or he may need to be withdrawn and reclusive at times to get his inner work done, and may need to welcome his own freakishnish, darkness, and death.[18]

Can drugs help with this inner work? Research into the effect of drugs on brain chemistry is essential for knowledge, but drugs prescribed clinically are no substitute for learning to experience and deal with suffering through ways that human beings have always recognized as soul-searching. The drug to improve self-confidence, to encourage extravertive behavior, to suppress anxiety, to custom-make a socially acceptable personality, are examples of the quick-fix attitude that prevails in modern medicine. The values of quiet reflection on the meaning of one's pain, of symbolic imagery which touches one personally, of expression of feelings through art, of dialogue with one's demons, of curiosity about one's conflicts and their history, are diminished in the excitement of finding a physiological antidote for emotion or conflict.

What is never acknowledged as important by advocates of the biochemical approach is that there is no discrete separation between psyche and soma. Not only do drugs influence body-chemistry, but our thoughts, deliberations, intentions, prayers, hopes, and illusions influence body-chemistry. It is possible for humans to learn to accept, resolve, and transcend, not all, but much of what appears to be biologically determining. For example, in looking at treatment of depression in young people, drawing from animal studies, some subscribe to the theory that one should begin medications at the first sign of depression so that the depressive reaction becomes less likely to be rekindled in the future. This is logical but does not recognize that early treatment of depression by long-term psychotherapy can prevent recurrence of debilitating depression with less violence to the physiology of the patient.

Psychotherapy does take longer, however, than anti-depressants and anti-anxiety drugs. Considering the problems of side-effects and long-term damage with drugs, and the problems of lengthy and frustrating treatment by psychotherapy, it is hard to say which is more trouble for both patient and doctor. But the value of psychotherapy is that the patient learns to use the depression to track its sources, and to find gratifying attitudes, lifestyles, and forms of self-expression without negating the meaning of the depressive sources. Drug companies claim that medication for depression and personality disorders is economical; I say, looking into the future for the human soul, we cannot afford it. I do appreciate the advances in chemical treatment of the psychoses; however, while psychoses usually respond well to some drug treatment, many psychoses are overdosed and under-heard. And although short-term medication can, in some cases, help a patient accept psychotherapy, for the personality disorders, over-medication has become the rule.

There was a time when psychotherapists did not expect to make a lot of money, relative to other medical specialists. Now depth psychologists are in the minority among mental health professionals as more interested in finding what is essential in the patient's soul life than in having a busy practice and a high rate of "cures." When curiosity became replaced by an interest in large profits, psychotherapy became subject to tricks, gimmicks, and "feel good" prescriptions. Many therapists promote feeling good without a notion of the soul's reasons for its distress, and this is encouraged by a culture which doesn't want to bother with struggle, even fruitful struggle.

It is frightening to me to see how many people seek help for human expressions of aliveness, such as grief reactions to loss, overt expressions of anger, feelings of jealousy or frustration or stress. And it is especially frightening because I know that many therapists would give medication or even hospitalize these healthy people when an intensive period of attention and being listened to would accomplish much more. This is especially true of those people who are described as Borderline Personality Disorder, and who are troublesome to most therapists.

TRICKSTER AND THE BORDERLINE

One of the characteristics of the Borderline Personality Disorder is the tendency to detach from parts of the personality, as Trickster does, but the splitting is unconsciously determined, not contained by the deliberate process of active-imagination mediated by the ego. In our borderline complexes we are exciting to be with because of a high level of intensity and fluctuation, and distressing because of our inability to find a central hearth for regrouping and assessing priorities.

Jungian analyst Nathan Schwartz-Salant describes the anxiety that arises in therapists who witness the unwitting fragmentation of the borderline patient, and the consequent temptation for the therapist to reduce his own anxiety by overwhelming the patient.[19] Schwartz-Salant is referring to overwhelming the patient with information, interpretations, comments about the therapist's ego-state, etc.; I would add overwhelming with medications. The Trickster is the dominant archetype in the borderline personality, which should remind the therapist just to accompany the borderline on his sinuous journey, and not get sucked into trying to direct him in some straightforward mode. The strong trickster influence within the borderline personality often cannot function positively; in the interest of deflating and protecting the vulnerable, loving self from grandiosity, envy, and abandonment, it overreaches, making the borderline's journey too self-punitive—a string of crises instead of a joyful adventure.

Jungian analyst Alfred Plaut reports a case history of a borderline patient whose behavior and character bear striking parallels to episodes in the Winnebago Trickster myth. Plaut writes: "I used to feel that he was tearing me up. What I was giving him he had to refuse. What he was trying to steal I knew would not satisfy him, was in fact further poisoning him by further increasing his persecutory anxiety."[20]

Plaut theorized that the early ego structure consists of fragments localized in physiological erogenous zones, and a detached central state, which in his patient was too weak to withstand the power of the zonal components. In practical terms, the patient was addicted to oral and anal experiences which dominated his life and relationships. My conceptualization of the process of psychotherapy that Plaut enacted, and that all therapists essentially must enact with the borderline patient, is of the analyst upholding images of the positive Trickster and functioning as an organizing principle while containing the patient's destructive emulation of the ungrounded, negative Trickster.

Plaut's observations are consistent with those of Michael Fordham. Fordham hypothesizes that in the child, before there is a centralized ego-structure, the progression of archetypal images is in reverse order from that seen in the process of individuation. Rather than progressing from persona to shadow to anima/animus to mana personality to Self, the child's psyche moves from absorption in the Self to mana to anima/animus to shadow to persona. The emergence of the anima as a grounding and centering force in the analysis of Plaut's patient came after considerable work with the early ego-self differentiation occurred.

Schwartz-Salant describes borderlines as stuck between the mythic world and the world of everyday reality, as a result of leaving the mythic realm before the maternal bonding was secure. This is why the union with the anima is crucial to the success of therapy. In his commentary on the Trickster Archetype, Jung said that these cases of problems constellated by the shadow are answered on the plane of the anima, that is, through a feminine mode of relatedness. The authentic relationship with the therapist is the key. Between two worlds, as are the borderlines described by Schwartz-Salant, we are Hermes' children, but unable to take advantage of the creative energies of the archetype in any consistent way. We are like citizens who feel like oppressed children, and look to the government for help or curse the government for lack of help, and cannot feel that the government is us, or people like us. There is an absence of connection with the powerful source, and we need whatever helps us make that connection, whether it be Mother, Holy Spirit, Mawu, Prana, Art, Environmentalism, etc.

Both Schwartz-Salant and Plaut call to our attention the fact that a characteristic of certain borderline personalities is the ability to comprehend and enjoy archetypal imagery without it making the slightest difference in their lives. Yet another kind of borderline cannot relate at all to the non-physical or imaginal.

Both remain detached from the archetypal, mythic world, because of the fear that the fragile ego structure will be obliterated in the union with the archetypal, as Semele was when united with Zeus.

Since most positive emotional experiences include archetypal fantasies of union, most positive emotional experiences threaten the borderline with fantasies of destruction. This means that while we in our borderline state seek union, and yearn for closeness, we avoid and reject connective experiences as threats to ego autonomy. Consequently we, and our therapists or others in relationship with us, are left paradoxically longing for contact which is undermined at every opportunity by us. It does no good to interpret to us in our borderline states that we reject everything positive, for that only makes us feel more of a failure and does not speak to the heart of the problem, our terror.

In treating the borderline, therapists must find the parts of themselves that are inadequate, inferior, desperate, rageful, and afraid of abandonment—not what we are "supposed" to be by all stereotypes of the healthy therapist: cool, patient, and always in control. Not only in therapy, but in society in general, the "characters," the character disorders, and the adolescents will keep pushing the limits to trick us out of what we should be and into what we are.

The Therapeutic Trickster

Trickster can be found in unlikely places in the therapy interaction. He can hide behind naiveté, behind the evading of responsibility, or behind hostility toward questions. In the naive patient a hidden cunning may defy anyone to try to enlighten him. Or the patient may appear to be trying to answer a question, but covertly there is a resentment of the question as an invasion, and a determination to evade responding. Withholding responses to questions is a tricky area for therapists, and I refer to both understanding one's own withholding as well as that of the patient. When is it in the best interest of the patient to withhold? Patients evade to protect their vulnerable feelings; analysts learn to withhold in order to give the archetype behind the question an invitation to show its face. But slavishly following this precept is to miss opportunities for emotional contact which may be more important in the moment. Then the question becomes, who needs emotional contact, patient or therapist?

At times when the therapist is needy the question of whose needs are being met becomes the most tricky. People in need or in transition are especially attracted to Trickster who rules the liminal. In marginality we are vulnerable to being conned and of conning ourselves. Also, when outside the establishment, we are likely to confront those in power by means of deception. Consequently, we belong to Trickster whenever we go through important life passages, such as the leap to trust in infancy where we totter on the brink of paranoia; such as in adolescence, when we must appease, evade, and free ourselves from the binding parental complexes; in going off to college, in mid-life, in experiencing loss, such as separation and divorce or death of a loved one. At such times the memory of Mercurius and all that he represents can help keep before us the image that the grief or disorientation we feel is a process that must not be aborted, but which can be allowed to come to a natural conclusion with reflection and containment.

Adolescents, being in such a state of transition, generally respond positively to overt tricksterism on the part of the therapist, but are hostile to covert manipulation. If adolescents feel conned or condescended to, you've lost them. On the other hand, if an adolescent accepts you as an authentic guide, she is hungry for all the advice and direction you can give, especially if she is convinced that you understand what it means to live on the edge. Knowing how important it is to adolescents to maintain a defensive guardedness, my considered bias is towards extravagantly giving of oneself and withholding little with children and adolescents, even though they may refrain from overtly indicating that they notice or care.

The Trickster is very therapeutic for children, who thrive on magic, surprise, and the trickster stories of all cultures which concern our connection to our animal nature. When I asked a little boy if he'd like to hear a story from the *Knights of the Round Table,* he said "Could we read *Brer Rabbit?*" He wasn't interested in my promoting his heroic qualities; for the moment he wanted to survive by means of pleasure. Trickster's ribald enjoyment of his own oral, anal, and phallic impulses is very reassuring for children. Like Baubo, Brer Rabbit teaches us that the spiritual cannot be separated from the physical, that even flatulence is sacred and powerful enough to slay enemies.

Being able to openly confront the impulses is reassuring for the child, and also the addict, in all of us. Eating disorders and addictions occur when we can view our impulses only in terms of unbridled indulgence (Dionysus) or ascetic discipline (Apollo). Trickster mediates between those two polarities and helps us find a healthier moderation by his acceptance and tolerance for all the impulses, the animalistic and the spiritual. A survey reported by ABC News on centenarians found that some common denominators in these long-lived people were optimism, the refusal to take themselves too seriously, and the absence of dietary systems. Sounds like a healthy dose of Trickster to me!

All the Trickster gods manifest great gusto for instinctual pleasures, a lust for life. They evince great appetites for food, they relish all things scatological, are perpetually sexually excited. Coyote hid his penis in a clump of nettles, after which it was forever insatiably itchy. When the spiritual connection to the instincts is missing or diminished, that is, when we cannot consciously recognize and respect our desires as an expression of a divine center within us, eating or defecating or sex or any physical pleasure can become godlike, numinous and overly powerful. One feels a need to do more than contain the pleasurable activity as a natural function which will go through a cyclical pattern of tumescence and detumescence; anxiously one attempts to ritualize or confine the activity with a system to be rigidly observed. As the Trickster communicates with all the other gods and worlds, he communicates with all the instincts, and wants each to have its say. In such an attitude there is little anxiety about appetites which are subject to the ebb and flow of some central source of life and nature.

But when the relationship to the instincts is unbalanced, one function—drinking, eating, gambling, masturbating, etc.—carries an overload of archetypal energy and may become unmanageable. The desire functions autonomously, not in harmony with the central life-source; it assumes too much power in the personality, is felt as demonic.

For example, the Trickster Archetype can have a chaotic effect on the personality if it functions purely randomly and not grounded by a positive relationship to the Self (high god) or the Feminine principle (Anima). The demon could look like an addictive or self-indulgent union of Hermes and Dionysus with no centering principle, or an arrogant, power-hungry union of Hermes and Apollo, or any number of other combinations. However, in mythologies which have persisted in human history, Trickster gods are always related to the center which defines their functions, even as they challenge the central principle. Similarly, the presence of a trickster which is related to the central principle in the psyche can be especially helpful when one instinctual need is disturbingly emphatic and dominating in the personality.

Trickster as Mediator

We may be able to reconnect to the instincts by recognizing the presence of the Trickster in our dreams or unconscious behavior reflecting an attempt to break free from an inhibiting yoke. As noted in Chapter II, Trickster stories often depict him as a rescuer of the innocent. He can help us rescue those parts of ourselves which need to be born into consciousness, or are being submerged by some dominant instinctual force.

Trickster is also the messenger between worlds in the treatment of psychosomatic illnesses. In uncovering the message in the symptom, the therapist must be able to negotiate between the worlds of the patient's soul; between conscious and unconscious; and between animal, human, and spirit. As Paris points out, the therapist must be able to recognize, with the help of the God of Liars, the lie in the patient, whether in the form of defensiveness or unconscious withdrawal. As Hermes put the monster Argus to sleep with diversion tactics, so the therapist does:

> ...with the patient whose problem is psychosomatic. He puts the problem to sleep (lowering defense mechanisms) in order to root it out; he charms the monster in order to kill it. This is one of Hermes' favorite tactics, avoiding any direct attack, but vanquishing Argus nevertheless. Today we need him more than ever, because psychological pain in its many disguises has become an enormous monster that eats away at our very substance. Scientific medicine is of no use in the treatment of these Argus pains.[21]

What Paris recognizes is that the unacknowledged Trickster in the prominent symptoms of today's patients requires the acknowledged Trickster in the psyche of the therapist in order to neutralize those symptoms.

Every disorder can be experienced as benefiting from the influence of the conscious Trickster. For example, Multiple Personality Disorder naturally needs a good relationship with Trickster to be able to see through and accept all the fragments and the possibility of fitting them all together, and to attract Mnemosyne, the muse of memory. A key dynamic in this disorder is dissociation from early memories, memories which must be allowed to emerge and be put into conscious perspective. The autonomous complexes also need contact with a strong centering principle, as all personality disorders do. We might say that a Hestia is needed to keep a fire going while the soul finds it way home.

Ironically, in its very motion, the Trickster lends us stability; she does so by reminding us when we are in the grip of one god, that there are other possibilities. Adolescents, not realizing this, commit suicide. Others, forgetting this, commit suicide. Killing oneself is the ultimate degree of lack of vision, unless it includes a vision of an afterlife that appears more agreeable than anything else we can imagine. Evaluating the notions of afterlife of another person takes us beyond the borders of convention and normalcy.

There is good reason to refrain from evaluating another's beliefs regarding spiritual life. If we listen to our bodies the reasons are obvious. Our communication systems, which ultimately depend on physiological transmissions, are relatively immature and unevenly developed. Billions of brain cell are unused, and we know little about how energy is exchanged between individuals through hormonal, respiratory, thermodynamic systems, etc. Although the Trickster Archetype is both an airy, mental force and a somatic, instinctual force, and although the Trickster God is able to span these realms with facility, few of us mortals have such well-refined connections between the lower and upper chakras. Most of us have some blocking or imbalance along our own energy transmission systems which interfere with the perfect communications we would like to have with other people. The eye-blocking, mentioned in Chapter II, is one example of how communicative energy can be trapped in the body and can make communication difficult. Blocking in the diaphragm separates the visceral urges from the intentionality of the rational mind and from the heart's preferences. Tension and blocking anywhere in the body prevents a smoothly flowing system of "receive-respond with truth."

It takes a very well developed relationship with trickster energy to employ its methods with heart; we must take care not to be caught in the crude lasciviousness of the lower chakras, nor in the heady-flightiness of the upper chakras, nor in a godlike way believe that we can ignore the boundaries necessary for human society to function comfortably. According to Native American beliefs, the medicine man's power is not in himself, but in his ability to suspend presence in the world and be open and watchful. The anglo mind's preoccupation with looking for cause and effect is considered to be a form of blindness.

The Reverent Boundary

The images we hold strongly influence our behavior, and the images of the therapist determine whether he approaches his work out of a power complex, or out of respect for the Trickster Archetype as guide of therapists. Native Americans are so respectful in their handling of the Trickster myths that they maintain strict regulations for telling them. Coyote myths, for example, must be told only after the first killing frost, and before the first thunderstorm, and must be orally transmitted with at least two others present who know the story. Each must be told by a given person only once each season, and must be told in a prescribed way. This cautiousness applies to the Winnebago Trickster myths, the Ashanti spider-stories, and so on, across cultures. Trickster is dangerous because he reminds us that the boundaries *can* be crossed, not that they should be by mankind. She takes us right to the border or cliff's edge and says, "Look!" Like the profane behavior of the clowns at some Native American religious ceremonies, or the Fool's Masses in medieval cathedrals, one function of the Trickster is to reinforce the existent moral structure by highlighting and contrast. Yet, if we do transgress, we know that Trickster will understand and come to our aid.

Consider the transgressive interventions of Baubo, the primitive goddess who resembles Trickster in her gross behavior and bawdy humor. Only she, with her dirty jokes, was able to bring a smile to poor Demeter's face while the mother goddess was grieving for her lost Persephone. Baubo's action gives us something to think about in terms of pornography and outrageous humor in times of darkness.[22] The caution and careful ritualization of the Trickster stories by African and Native American societies, however, reminds us that this is a powerful archetype, and we must be respectful in imploring it to accompany us. Baubo could say to Demeter, "Lighten up!" and get away with it; she was, in essence, reminding Demeter that there is a sacred space where one is free of emotional attachments, even free of death's domain.

A woman who was going through a long, painful, spiritual crisis prayed for relief. Like Job, she had had several losses and her body was showing the brunt of her distress by being ill. After her prayer she dreamed that she was filled with great spiritual and sexual energy which pulsated through her body, then beyond herself throughout the world at large, culminating in a vision that burst forth through heavenly blue light to reveal John Belushi in diaphanous robes and boxer shorts, laughing uproariously! How can one respond to such an answer to a prayer? Only with a laugh and a dance. On the subject of Nothingness, Pelton gives us the Trickster's response: "I do not know what nothing is, but when I touched it, it caught me and filled me with joy!"[23]

Now, the unconscious and the Goddess can get away with this use of humor in times of grief, but most ordinary mortals cannot. Baubo's intervention transformed Demeter's complex. But to suggest to a person who is suffering that it is possible to distance himself from the situation is usually received as a careless, nonempathic, or hostile response. An awareness of Baubo, who implies seeing through and touching the abyss without emotional attachment, must often be sustained by the therapist without overt attention to that awareness required of the patient.

A patient who is very perplexed and anguished by his instability says, "Therapy is immoral, isn't it?" Yes, in the sense that I'm only concerned about what values are authentic for you; no, in the sense that your integration as a person depends on finding your authentic values; yes, in the sense that I will not be a priestess for any religion; no, in the sense that no one can be a subject of psychotherapy who will not struggle with right and wrong. As the patient and I try to explore this issue and talk it through, I realize that I am very much in the realm of a god and goddess who have experienced every kind of humiliation and profanity and can relate to us in our sinfulness without undermining or devaluing our sincerity.

CHAPTER IV

TRICKSTER WOMAN

Use not much the company of her that is a dancer, and hearken not to her, lest thou perish by the force of her charms.

(Eccl 9:4, Old Test.)

I should only believe in a God that would know how to dance.

(Friedrich Nietzsche, *Thus Spake Zarathustra*)

It is said that in times of transition when shapes are shifting, we have to be able to dance. Now we are in transition, and we have a tension between those who would dance, and those who would hold still and hope to keep old forms in place.

A chasm separates those who feel dance to be the most profound form of worship and those who look upon dance as evil. Can that split ever be mended? It separates us humans into practically different species. Dance evokes admiration of the body through the awesome beauty of contrasting postures in motion, the primal pulse in rhythmic response, the poignancy of emotion expressed in gesture; yet, because it is primal, physical, and compelling, it may lead to lusty thoughts and selfish actions. Lust, and any art which promotes lust, is still a capital sin in the opinion of many; who can deny that lust creates terrible problems of crime, unwanted pregnancies, overpopulation, neglect of more important matters, and compulsive self-preoccupation? Moreover, lust is not love, and only complicates and twists our loving relationships. But, from another point of view, love, lust, and the spell of beauty, are divine gifts, not Satanic temptations. Surely we would be wiser to learn to manage these gifts harmoniously than to try futilely to outlaw them.

In some cultures there is no dispute because the very gods model lust as well as love. Trickster gods and goddesses approve heartily of lust. In ancient Egypt, for example, Isis's desire for Osiris was so powerful that she was able to couple with him and conceive a child even though his body had been mutilated and his sex organ had vanished. In Isis, we find such harmonious intercourse between lust and love that it is hard to imagine those two feeling states in conflict. And Themis, second wife of Zeus, was worshipped with sexualized devotedness which transformed lust into an experience of loving connectedness with all being. She was a feminine equivalent of Hermes in her roles as mediator and relativizer[1].

In our complicated culture, where pagan and puritan values clash, and so many combinations of love and sexuality are possible, a harmonious interrelationship of lust and love cannot be taken for granted. What usually is taken for granted is that it is woman's responsibility to clarify and guard both. Therefore, when things go awry in the realm of Eros, or in the expression of lust, collective opinion usually places woman at the root of the problem. Why has woman come to acquire such heavy responsibility? Perhaps examining descriptions of the myths of other times can improve our understanding of twentieth century woman's relationship to the lusty Trickster and the love gods and goddesses.

"Erotic" today implies sexuality, but Eros fostered many more kinds of bondings than just sexual attraction. Let us return to Kerényi's observation (cited in Chapter III):

> Looked at from the world of Hermetic possibilities, Eros, despite his comprehensive nature, appears limited—a somewhat more idealistic and less cleverly turned-out, dumber son of Hermes.[2]

The limitation of Eros which Kerényi is amplifying is from Hesiod's description of Eros's failure to respect insight and rationality. Kerényi gleans a sense of Eros's style of intelligence from ancient descriptions.

> He (Eros) brings wonderful memory, the luminous understanding of the spirit, but not the cold, calculating cleverness of Hermes.[3]

Eros is particularly irrational in what Kerényi calls his "profusion of the erotic." The timeless description of Eros as failing to respect rationality is agreeable to anyone who has ever loved foolishly; Eros can overpower reason, and his ways do not always seem clever from our mortal point of view.

Nevertheless, the positive face of Eros shines out of the tribute to the god which Jung wrote at the end of his life as he sorted out the essence of his work. I recommend that we read or re-read the powerful passage from Jung's autobiography, from which this small portion is taken. Jung is speaking of man's dependence on the mystery that is Eros:

Love is his light and his darkness, whose end he cannot see.... Man can try to name love, showering upon it all the names at his command, and still he will involve himself in endless self-deceptions. If he possesses a grain of wisdom, he will lay down his arms and name the unknown by the more unknown...that is, by the name of God. That is a confession of his subjection, his imperfection, and his dependence; but at the same time a testimony to his freedom to choose between truth and error.[4]

It is significant that while Jung considered Mercurius to be god of the individuation process, he ended his autobiography, at the sunset of his own personal individuation, with this offering to the god of love, an affirmation of the power of relationship. To me Jung's offering to Eros implies that, to have meaning, the personal development of any individual must be housed in the context of relatedness to others, which includes all facets of human connection, only one of which is sexual attraction.

Does the relationship between cunning, lusty Trickster, and Eros, god of loving connectedness, have anything to teach us about the archetypal underpinnings of our sexual and loving relationships today? And in an age when love seems muddled and difficult to sustain, what do myths tell us about woman's responsibility to relatedness, to tricksterish lust, to the erotic? In this connection it seems significant that the Trickster gods are very close to the goddesses; the intimate connection between Trickster and the goddesses, particularly the nature goddesses, shows in many different mythologies. For example, although accounts by Greek writers differ as to whether Eros was the child of Hermes and Artemis, or Hermes and Aphrodite, the intimate bond between Eros, Hermes, and several goddesses is obvious.

Kerényi even proposes the possibility that the origin of a male's appearance in matriarchal Greek mythology was the emergence of Hermes from the primordial triune Goddess. Strange as it may seem to us from our patriarchal imbeddedness, Hermes as the first male to appear as an adjunct to the triple goddess would have been imagined as a tender shoot, in Kerényi's words, "an impersonal masculinity, almost a toy."[5] This would place the Trickster god in the beginning of creation as complement to the creative feminine. Kerényi's image of Hermes emerging as a fourth figure to complete the triune goddess, posits an era whose image of the deity was the contrasexual mirror-opposite of the Christian configuration in heaven; the Greeks perceived Mother, Daughter, and Wise Woman Spirit, with a hermetic masculine emerging from the unconscious—in contrast to our Father,

Son, and masculine Holy Spirit, and what I believe is, in our present time, a rising hermetic feminine.

As the ancients may have begun to incorporate a budding phallic energy into their matriarchal consciousness, so I imagine now this compelling, vitally energetic, womanly figure rising, not in ascent above the earth, not to distance herself from dense matter, but rising from the depths of nature into the conscious world.

Images of a powerful "natural woman" are common in dreams of today's women and men. One currently frequent manifestation of the rising feminine in the psyche is the mermaid, rising from the ocean depths; she occurs often in dreams and art of today. Others are the Black Madonna, rising from buried crypts in the large cathedrals; the tree-spirit, who ascends from roots deep in the earth and inhabits the tree inherently or in the form of a tree-serpent; the wild woman, roaming with animals on the edge of civilization—wolves, dolphins, owls, tigers; and the volcanic-spirit, spewing forth its puissance in volcanoes and earthquakes as protest to being raped.

But, although intimations of the emergent goddess seem to be on the increase, our present culture is still far from envisioning a feminine aspect to the divine image. As for a goddess who incorporates trickster qualities, we must imagine and infer in order to envision a goddess who is as well delineated as the Trickster gods. You may have noticed that when I use the feminine pronoun "she" instead of "he" or "it," to substitute for "Trickster," you feel jarred, as if something is strange about situating a Trickster goddess in the divine schema. Yet, we have seen that the tricksters of myth and folklore are typically androgynous figures.

Whether we envision the Trickster in his masculine or her feminine form, the relationship of Trickster to the gods and goddesses of love is complex, as Kerényi's reference to Eros suggests. Love is demonstrated more in the fruits of Trickster's labor, his rescuing and mediating, than it is in overt expression and bonding behavior. The children of Hermes—Eros, Hermaphrodite, Priapus, and Pan—are all aspects of love gods. Unlike Eros, tricksters do not form a couple for any length of time, are not motivated by a need for security, and seem to enjoy the freedom of spontaneity. Jean Shinoda Bolen, in her illustrations of masculine archetypes, describes Hermes as the "bachelor god," and the feminine archetypes represented by Hestia, Aphrodite, and Artemis, all Hermes' associates, as "virgin goddesses" who do not depend on a partner as a significant aspect of their identities.[6] Hecate would also be in that group.

Because of our conditioning by patriarchal forms, the presence of independent, unpartnered women is not welcomed unconditionally in our culture. Trickster as an independent, wily force is treated with caution in all cultures who honor him, and it seems that women who represent trickster qualities are looked upon even more warily than male tricksters. For many people today, the virgin goddesses described by Bolen would be regarded as threats rather than divine advocates.

Woman-Threat

Until recently, free-spirited women were generally seen as dangerous to the stability of society, and still often are considered dangerous by many people. Unpartnered idealistic and heroic women whose personas are not associated with sexual energy, are less likely to be perceived as threats (Mother Teresa, Madame Curie), but they also are not necessarily comfortably assimilated by a community; many women will confirm that experience has taught them that being strong is not acceptable. Women with strong trickster qualities, which always include some antiauthoritarian attitudes and usually lively sexuality as well, seem to raise the defenses of males and females.

There are several possible reasons for the wariness shown towards free-spirited women. One is that women with a pronounced trickster component may arouse fantasies of promiscuity and excess that imply danger to the collective. They are too reminiscent of Nature herself in her wild, extravagant scattering of expansive libidinal energy. The desire for a secure, steady mate and lifestyle may create a tension around such women, a tension that women often feel within their own psyches in the form of conflict and ambivalence about values and morals, as well as in attitudes of society. This same tension in men appears to be more easily tolerated, both in their own capacity to rationalize any incongruence they may have between promiscuity and reliability, and in the way that incongruence is accepted by the collective (i.e. polygamous man, monogamous woman—O.K.; polygamous woman, monogamous man—not O.K.). Historian Karen Armstrong notes the irony that a that a religion which has God become flesh and share our humanity should ostracize women in hatred and fear of loathsome sexuality! She refers to early church patriarchs:

> The letters of Jerome teem with loathing of the female which occasionally sounds deranged. Tertullen had castigated women as evil temptresses, an eternal danger to mankind...(and) Augustine is clearly puzzled that God should have made the female sex at all."[7]

Were these evil temptresses, or projections of a neglected anima?

The unattached sexual woman arouses anxiety, even if she is lesbian or a crone and not necessarily a threat to the security of heterosexual marriage and family life. Witches have not been burned publicly recently, but one can find numerous real-life and imaginal dramas in which the sexually hungry woman is ridiculed and denigrated, for she evokes a fear that is scantily clothed in hostility, especially if she is older.[8]

Beidelman describes the ambivalence men show toward widows and old women in the Karugu people of East Africa; living alone the women represent a subversion of male authority. They are considered dangerous, deceptive, and greedy, devouring of children, yet powerful because of their close association with the supernatural.[9]

Fear of females appears to be even murkier than either the threat of her independence or her sexual appetites imply. Perhaps such fear cannot be understood rationally, anymore than we can explain why a female talk-show "expert" objects to a 55 year-old woman being artificially impregnated because "she would look ridiculous taking her five-year old to kindergarten," as if such a superficial concern should be part of the equation. Such shallow fabrications only confirm the fact that biases exist and are accompanied often by strong emotions, as part of the Hermes-Eros mystique.

Intrigued by the mystique, many have tendered hypotheses to explain the threat women ostensibly pose. For example, Dorothy Dinnerstein points out that Simone de Beauvoir, Margaret Mead, and H. R. Harp all held that the male's awe, fear, and often disgust, toward all things mysterious and different from himself, are concentrated in the female's fertile body. Dinnerstein argues, from a Freudian psychoanalytic framework, that fear and contempt of woman stems from the power given women as sole caretakers during the first stage of life. Dinnerstein explains:

> The dirty goddess is dirty…(because) the positive side of what she embodies—our old joy in the flesh and the capacity we still have to feel the kind of contact with life that the flesh originally carried—has been largely suppressed…it is also in large degree denied and discounted.[10]

Woman's very existence may challenge man's suppression of the natural lusty feelings toward mother's body that he once enjoyed, then learned was unacceptable. Author and Jungian analyst Thomas Moore locates the issue even earlier in an individual's psychological history, beyond infantile physical pleasure and into the area of archetypal receptivity:

> One often gets the impression that the female presence in itself contaminates, as though it were a lethal power. It is a lethal power, this anima that is carried by women. Its deep moods, its swirling clouds of feeling and fantasy, its invitation to the deep stillness of deathly inactivity and contemplation threaten the male spirit of action and understanding.[11]

Thus, free-spirited woman threatens us with honest carnal joy, with spontaneity and lack of structure, with the possibility that we might be still and contemplative instead of busy and productive, with the possibility of being fulfilled without doing and achieving. Moore's hypothesis reminds me that in doing therapy I find that being still seems dangerous to many people, who are very uncomfortable with silence and who cannot dare to give themselves unstructured time except in very clearly delineated vacation interludes. Stillness, rather than being cherished as an opportunity to reflect, feel, and wonder, is instead fraught with dangerous associations to being lazy, dumb, and underachieving. Yet everything that is so alarming about being-still can be reframed as asset in either woman or tricksters.

And then, although the stillness and depth of feeling of woman is threatening, some men are frightened by a woman's being active. A patient describes the paralysis that comes over him when a woman is animated by strong opinions and feelings, which he calls "bossy": "First something inside says, 'No.' Then I become immobilized and depressed and can't speak, and this makes them (women) crazier."

TRICKSTER-THREAT

Apparently woman threatens the masculine need for predictability and order, as does Trickster. The Trickster is enough of a threat to understanding in its masculine aspect, without bringing the "lethal power" of the feminine into the picture. Africans who worship the male trickster gods, such as Legba, Ananse, and Eshu, take these gods' free-spiritedness warily. They are careful not to invite them into their homes. Shrines to these gods are placed at the threshold, just as shrines to Hermes in ancient Greece were placed outdoors at the crossroads so that hungry journeyers could swipe from the offerings in the spirit of the God of Thieves. Neither was the risk of free access to the inner home offered contradictory Trickster in ancient Greece. The home was the territory devoted to Hestia, virgin goddess of the hearth, and the complement to Hermes.

Trickster is depicted sometimes as two-faced, literally seeing in two directions at once. If we try to confine him to the home and hearth there is bound to be discord, for he needs to be able to see the open road and is not a positive force when confined to a limited role in a limited space. His nature is to be unstable, an agent of change. The open road is a very important image of freedom; but as we have seen in examining the personality disorders, equally important is for a human being to be able to find an inner image of a safe center in which to take rest and refuge.

The same dynamics apply to psychotherapy, in that we try to create a safe and comfortable place where psyche feels at home. We need the Trickster's ability to see through situations without prejudice, to keep the psychic energy moving, but at the same time the therapist must be able to find a safe center, a secure base from which the process can move, a place of focus, a hearth. James Hillman, in a discussion of analysis as Hestian ritual, says:

> As we move ever more into a Hermes hypertrophy—modems, CD-Roms, cellular phones, satellites, 300 cable channels, call-waiting, virtual realities—I can be connected everywhere "outside" and will require ever more desperately the centering circular force of Hestia to keep from evaporating into space. In other words, in this age of excessive Hermes, classical Jungian inward analysis as a ritual observation of Hestia may be more necessary than ever before.[12]

As Hillman suggests, Trickster implies motion and connection, placing the god in a dual relationship to masculine and feminine values. His relationship to Hestia is complementary, but not adversarial, and he appears to be exempt from any fear or hostility around things feminine. There is a scene from the life of the gods as told by Homer which gives an interesting insight into Hermes' relationship to the Goddess of Love, and also to his relationship to what Jung calls "the feeling function." I refer to the bedroom scene in which Aphrodite and Ares are snared in the act of adultery by her husband, Hephaestus, who fashioned a metal net to trap them in bed. Jealousy is accepted as a fundamental emotion in mythology; there is no pretentious attempt to convince us that it is childish or pathological (although Argus materializes when jealousy is given monstrous amounts of attention). In this case, Hephaestus's jealousy seems to be considered within bounds, and all the gods and goddesses are called to see the guilty lovers.

In his book *Hermes and His Children*, Lopez-Pedraza brilliantly analyzes this scene and the reactions of the gods. He points out that all the gods are caught (in ways appropriate to their own psychologies) in various reactions elicited by the scenario. Only Hermes is not caught by it, but can freely enjoy it and even push the sexual fantasy further, imagining himself enjoying being coupled with Aphrodite. Interested readers will want to follow up on Lopez-Pedraza'a analysis in detail and its implications for therapists. However, on one point I question Lopez-Pedraza's conclusions; he attributes Poseidon's discomfort with the event to prudishness. Since I don't experience the Poseidon archetype as inhibited, I wonder if it might be Poseidon's watery sensitivity to feeling that incites him to empathize with the compromised lovers and to want them to be released from their embarrassment immediately.[13] But tricksters take embarrassment lightly as just a small fact of life, and Hermes, though certainly aware of the feelings of the lovers, would not be inhibited by that awareness, but would minimalize the significance of the embarrassment, indeed, of the whole event.

Trickster and the Feeling Function

Hermes greets Hephaestus' surprise party with equanimity and humor; other deities, through identification and empathy, show more intense feelings. Hermes is known for his friendliness and cunning, Eros for his relatedness. Where does the Trickster stand on love? Tricksters are not regarded as having the most overt feeling function; feeling may be introverted, or their inferior function. A less-dominant feeling function is to Hermes' advantage in his roles as mediator, rescuer, and manipulator of tortoises, cattle, monsters, and gods. In a close encounter requiring strategy, a strong feeling function can be a liability, a reality which can be attested to by sergeants, surgeons, spies, and others.

For good or bad, hermetic energy distances one from feeling. An interesting example of this is the paradoxical relationship of one aspect of Trickster, the clown, to the feeling function. In this context, the observations of Ann and Barry Ulanov are very helpful:

> The clown shows us images of feeling and of emotional and behavioral reactions associated with feeling, but his defended feeling is never delivered into personal experience. The clown stays far away in the archetypal world, and will not cross into the world of personal ego-existence. He shows us rubrics of emotion that could become feeling if they were personally accepted. But clowning is a rugged defense; the feeling is not accepted. What the clown displays is unlived feeling, feeling not yet available or arrived, potential feeling not yet collected—affect in shadow, unrealized.[14]

Emotional distance as attributed here to the clown is not typical of the feminine. Given the old (supposed) gender separation between thinking and feeling, it may have been difficult to identify a goddess with quite the same equanimity, or perhaps, emotional casualness, that Trickster implies. Although we may remember Baubo's atypical response to Demeter's grief, we note that not one of the goddesses came to gawk at Aphrodite's plight as she lay trapped by

Hephaestus in *flagrante delicto*. They would not intrude on such a delicate scene. But, the feminine aspect of trickster's androgyny seems to be weak in the feeling area, so Hermes was there to applaud the tricks. We have clues that there may be something that makes the feminine in men and women wary of too much mercurial energy, something that tells us intuitively that, with Hermes around, we must take particular care to guard the hearth. It seems important to keep the fires burning in the heart of things, if we are to take Hermes wisely. That position close to the heart is so universally attributed to the feminine, that it warrants being brought out and accentuated whenever Trickster is around. Ann and Barry Ulanov speak of the woman possessed by the clown energy:

> Clown-women are notable for their wit, their beguiling gestures, their far-ranging use of humor. They are greatly appealing as well as entertaining companions. But that's just it—companions, not intimates, not lovers. Caught in the clown role, they use their clowning to deflect penetration. Other people's feeling does not reach through to their own, and theirs remains invisible to others.…She does not receive the information she needs from the animus; instead it is conscripted into the clowning defense against feeling.… She is as a result lonely, poignant, maddening.[15]

Ulanov is speaking of cases in which an aspect of the Trickster has overwhelmed a woman's ego and caused unnatural things to happen, as occurs whenever we identify with, instead of engage with, an archetype. Only when we can recognize the Trickster, see its effects in our lives, and argue with it, can it enrich us in constructive ways. If a woman is taken over by a clown or trickster animus, it is because she doesn't know how to engage such an animus from an ego standpoint, and, being distant from her emotions, cannot respond with strong feelings to counter the animus position. Women who have seen only masculine models of successful ego-functioning and engagement, (most of us), are at a disadvantage when they try to present their authentic feminine instincts in the presence of such animus figures.

Still, an ability to engage and incorporate the androgynous hermetic energy is an asset to a woman. She may be intimidating to those who expect women to be passive, but by no means does her tricksterism imply that she is out of touch with feelings. As I write I think of a woman patient who is presently working on engaging such hermetic energy. The situation is this: she has a very strong feeling function, and a weak thinking function, and whenever she is disturbed by her husband's behavior or his response to her, she has great difficulty communicating with him. When she attempts to approach him, she becomes very emotional and shows him by her voice, gestures, and words that she is agitated. Sometimes she cries, or raises her voice, or babbles without a clear point of view. He becomes uncomfortable with this level of emotion and defends himself by diminishing her feelings and becoming even more entrenched in irrelevant points of logic than he normally is. Consequently, over time, they are able to resolve very few conflicts and they build up more and more resentment-producing encounters in which she blows him away and he pronounces her crazy from his "rational" position of remoteness.

My patient is learning to keep an image of a tricksterish woman in mind before she approaches her husband with a problem. The trickster-image gives her some distance from her emotions and supports her improvising creative ways of talking to her husband about her issues. She tries to shape-shift mentally to the propensities of a thinking type, and to approach the issues logically, instead of from her dominant function, feeling. She reports that such behavior is very difficult for her, like focusing on speaking a foreign language with which one is only barely familiar. Even when she is successful in engaging her husband in a good dialogue, she comes out of the experience exhausted. However, the results are beginning to validate her work, and the relationship is looking more possible than it did some time ago. While she has some resentment about being the one to "change" herself to accommodate the relationship, she is the partner who is able to do so at the moment, and perhaps, later, the husband will learn to reciprocate. At least she now sees some hope that she can eventually make that request by means of her new communication skills. She also sees that she need not deny the strength of her emotions just because for the time being she does not share them with her husband. She is learning to care for her emotions by guarding, rather than exposing them in a hostile milieu; not a portrait of ideal intimacy, but perhaps a step on the way.

Every woman does not have this struggle. To some women the capacity to think like a trickster comes naturally, and is not the ordeal that it is for my patient. One can see in dysfunctional families some boys or girls who have the wits and courage to forego feelings of loyalty and fidelity to the family, and so escape the family net. Such children have a strong hermetic animus with instinct for escape.

Others stay and patiently try to work things out and absorb the distress without breaking up the family, even if it costs a great sacrifice to their personal development. Not that there cannot be wisdom in that way, too. Let me digress from the subject of hermetic animus to say that I have seen a contemplative or yin approach to problem solving work miracles in some families or personalities. Psychology's bias would have us believe that the ego is a masculine complex, and individuation itself a masculine process. But women would say to that, "You don't know the half of it!"—the feminine half, that is.

Optimally, ego-development requires a yin-yang reciprocity in functions, and it is the overvaluing of the yang-functions which has led to psychology's penchant for pathologizing introversion. Yin functions are also quite important for good adaptation to the outer world, as well as the inner world. Jung's concept of individuation conjures up different images in different people, and my image concurs with that of Jungian analyst John Beebe who suggests that individuation is the development of integrity, not change in character structure.[16] Integrity implies an honest admission of the mutual existence and interplay of opposite aspects of the psyche. For instance, feminine and masculine values exist; yin may supersede in one situation, yang in another.

We tend to think of Tricksters in yang-terms, the yin being covert. Then a woman with hermetic-animus might be thought of as unfeeling. Common prejudice would have us believe that a survivor, calling upon some assertive energy, will forever be an aggressor, as if we can divide personalities into carnivores and herbivores. But if the feminine aspects of psyche are also supported, they bring sensitivity and balance to the tough, assertive, solar, or tricksterish aspects of the personality. Some cultures encourage men to be nurturant and sensitive to feeling as well as independent and survival oriented. Similarly, women who appear tough and indomitable can drop that protection and expose true vulnerability when they are feeling safe and cared about. We can speak of emotional and sexual vulnerability as related, but not identical. The opening of a woman's deep levels of sexual responsivity usually depends on abandoning herself emotionally as well as sexually. However, there is no simple formula for a woman's arrival at such a feeling of sexual safety. For one woman the security of a persistent, steady partner makes her feel safe; another needs a partner absolutely free of anxiety, even if unreliable; for another, an equally vulnerable and self-disclosing mate; for another, being content with herself regardless of her partner's qualities.

To consolidate these musings about the hermetic animus, we can say simply that male and female qualities can co-exist comfortably and consciously in one personality, and also within the Trickster Archetype as it moves through the personality. We do not have to sacrifice masculine for feminine, or vice-versa; in fact we are at a distinct advantage regarding survival if we can remain flexible. With respect to gender identity, a generation ago most analysts took a firm stand; it was considered very important that a clear identity of masculine and feminine be modeled and presented to the child. Today the subject is clouded. Formation of gender identity in the child is a subject only tangentially related to the themes of this chapter, and in addition, the subject deserves volumes of its own. To barely touch the perimeters of that subject, let me say that I find a healthy beauty, balance, and order to gender differentiation. Yet the boundaries defining that differentiation are in transition, as is every boundary at the moment, and what used to be "normal" is now not so clear. For the moment we can enjoy the dance without boundaries, with unknowing, with new boundaries, or we can struggle to protect the old gender boundaries, or all of the above.

WOMAN AND THE TRICKSTER ANIMUS

Observations of women who have arrived at powerful positions in society show that usually they have had fathers who did not treat them in a typically authoritarian way, nor expect stereotypical feminine behavior of them. One study reports that fathers of politically powerful women approved their being nurturant *and* aggressive.[17] We might see them as encouraged to accept healthy animus qualities in themselves, to enjoy their assertiveness and centrifugality. There is nothing to suggest that they cannot also enjoy the stereotypical feminine qualities as well; only ignorant unconsciousness could hold that we must choose one or the other.

Trickster exists in the psyche in both masculine and feminine form, each maintaining respective survival skills, though the archetype has been dominated by male images as most aspects of the divinity have been in Western cultures. Probably the Trickster seems male because of the pre-modern vision of women as primarily homebodies, child-bearers, and mothers; we have been given few examples of women enjoying and surviving the open roads and adventurous life. Even Amelia Earhart did not come back to tell us that we could survive as adventurous members of a community. But of more significance than women's being planted sociologically is the fact that women's trickiness has usually been well hidden, almost invisible.

In her study of Biblical women, Susan Niditch proposes that the Israelite women had to be tricksters, as they were forced to follow the typical pattern of marginal people. Their power was private, and behind-the-scenes, for their rights were unstable "in a culture in which powerful women are regarded with suspicion, as unnatural and evil."[18] Often woman tricksters manifest only through their husbands or children, especially their sons. This was true of most Israelite women.

Niditch calls our attention to the successful trickery of women in Genesis through the following examples, which I have condensed:

Sarai and Abram are co-tricksters as they travel through alien territory as brother and sister, considered safer than revealing their truth as a marital pair. Sarai goes along with her role, and is chosen as a wife by the Pharaoh. She manages to conceal her identity, and as a result, benefits accrue to her and Abram. Eventually, God sends a plague and the secret is brought out.

Niditch's second example is Rebekah, who, by secretly promoting her favorite son, Jacob, determines the course of the clan and thereby fulfills destiny according to God's will. God prefers Jacob to Esau too, and gives him all the advantage. When Jacob hesitates to fool his father on his deathbed, fearing to be cursed instead of blessed, Rebekah offers to take the curse upon herself. Mother and son succeed in winning Isaac's blessing, and Rebekah maneuvers Jacob out of the way of Esau's vengeance. Niditch says:

> Rebekah's wisdom is a wisdom of women that involves listening closely…and working behind the scenes to accomplish goals. It is a vicarious power that achieves success for oneself through success of male children, a power symbolically grounded in the preparation and serving of food. It involves as well a willingness to sacrifice oneself.… Such is woman's power in a man's world, and it is not the sort of empowerment to which most modern women aspire. It is the power of those not in authority…one who is part of a male-centered world and is not in open rebellion against it, but who nevertheless subverts its rules indirectly…a power of mockery, humor, and deception.[19]

Oppressed people of any group can identify with this description. Rachel and Leah participated in tricking Jacob into marrying the elder first. Later they co-conspire to leave their father's land with their husband, Jacob. Feeling exploited by their father, Rachel steals some sacred objects from his household (teraphim) to bring away with them. Her father, Laban, discovers the theft, chases after them, and searches through all the tents for his possessions. Finally he arrives at Rachel's tent. She has hidden the stolen goods under the camel saddle and sits on them. Rachel refuses to rise, using the excuse that she is menstruating. Undermining Laban's authority by exploiting her femininity in the dangerous power of the blood, she plays upon his fear of her uncleanliness that sets her apart from all that is deemed "normal," i.e., male.

Tamar is the trickster-heroine of a story of very complex social structures around marriage and widowhood. When her husband dies, her father-in-law,

Judah, orders his second son, Onan, to father a child by Tamar in order that she should have a place in society. Onan jealously cohabits with Tamar without impregnating her; he "spills his seed" (onanism) to avoid sharing their father's legacy with more offspring. God shows his displeasure at this selfishness by killing Onan. Judah should have next given Tamar to his third son, Shelah, but probably fearing that Tamar was a witch who kills her lovers, or the beloved of a demon who refused to share her, he sends her back to her father in the liminal state of neither virgin, wife, or mother. "Tamar, the person of uncertain status, is thus the perfect candidate to become a trickster. Through deception she is able to confront those with the power to improve her status and to gain what she desires."[20]

Hearing that Judah's wife died and he is coming to a nearby place, she disguises herself as a prostitute and waits for him at the edge of town, using the age-old trick of sexual allure to get what she wants—in colorful street language, "turning a trick." Not recognizing his own daughter-in-law, Judah, in the liminality of widowerhood, is seduced and unknowingly impregnates her. Before he leaves she manipulates him into giving her a few of his identifiable personal items. Now that she is pregnant she again becomes the charge of the house of in-laws, not her own father's. She returns to Judah, as is her right; but he rejects her as evil and orders her to be burned. Then she produces his possessions and tells him that the owner is the father of her child. Recognizing his own objects, Judah accepts his responsibility for the sexual liaison and for not giving her to Shelah as law prescribed. Tamar's power as a matriarch is established when she gives birth to twins, one of whom contributes to the genealogical line of David.[21]

More often than not, women in ancient trickster stories are victims or pawns of contests between male tricksters, or else they are depicted as depraved and judged vengeful, conniving, and sexually aggressive. An example of the latter is Potiphar, the Pharaoh's wife in the Biblical story of Joseph. She attempts to seduce Joseph, and when he refuses her, she employs another of the oldest of women's deceits and accuses him of attempted rape. In this case Potiphar attains no power by her trickery but becomes merely an episode in Joseph's heroic journey.

The Bible contains other stories of disempowered women who found devious or passive-aggressive means to fulfillment. Esther, a powerless woman of a powerless group, triumphed through a combination of courage, cunning, and loyalty. Not exactly powerless was Judith, who was a wealthy widow; but she prayed to the God of the lowly and oppressed to help save herself and her people by overcoming her adversary. Women have been known to use trickery to become independent, or to remain dependent. Women can escape from the possessiveness or protectiveness of mothers, fathers, and husbands, without overt rebellion. We can manipulate others, including the government, to take responsibility for us. A favorite contrivance is pregnancy. Pregnancy can be used as an animus advantage as well as feminine fulfillment. As an animus advantage, I mean that pregnancy can be a convenient device used to stay at home with mother, or to get away from mother, to get a husband, to keep a husband, or to get on welfare and remain a child of the state; it is often a means of acquiring status or getting love from someone who will be dependent on us for a long time—we can count on a baby to stick around.

Another animus device is holding others by exerting emotional power over them. I refer to an animus device in the sense that some contrived behavior springs from an intention to manipulate oneself into a position of advantage, and not from true feeling for another. The web of caring becomes entrapment when a women holds a man by appealing to his sentimentalism about the child's need to have biological parents together, or appealing to his rescue fantasies by seeming unable to cope emotionally without him, or by becoming physically ill, or otherwise inciting guilt. (Men resort to these devices, too.)

Such unconscious "arrangements" shape the first half of life. Like many adolescent girls who fall into the dark, Persephone's abduction is written into her destiny as a "mother's daughter"; her fulfillment or destiny required being drawn to the underworld as an escape from her mother's majestic power. By deciding to eat the fruit of Hades, Persephone moved out of the role of the passive child, and took a willful, though seemingly innocent, part in separating from her mother's world. She became a separate person without directly confronting her mother. A different configuration is presented in the relationship between Jesus and his mother. There the vignettes we are given about their interactions indicate that Mary was concerned, but allowed Jesus his own power and freedom to live beyond her limitations. Unlike Persephone, he was able to be straightforward and confronting of his mother. (Yet his celibacy raises questions. Was celibacy necessary for his individuation, for his mission to be fulfilled, or was he merely emotionally bound to his mother?)

More illustrations of the animus-dominated web of caring are found in Hera's myriad manipulations (including her retaining Argus as we have seen); they were her means of keeping Zeus attached and their marriage viable in spite of his disdain for intimacy. Hera represents the part of the psyche that preserves and perseveres in relationship in the face of fear of rejection and indifference. She refuses to deny her own instinct for mating, she insists on holding to commitment, she will not be deterred from her serious devotion to the Other. Her jealousy, like Persephone's inevitable rape, is predetermined. In Hera's case her inevitable jealousy is determined by the nature of a passionate woman's coupling with a narcissistic, patriarchal partner. So the psyche finds ways to trick us into having our desires fulfilled without direct confrontation of our basic conflicts.

In contrast to Persephone and Hera, who are both caught in behavior determined by their roles in relationship to another, Scheherazade is completely and competently her own person. She is an excellent representation of the successful and conscious woman trickster, who not only fools the homicidal king, but transforms his small-minded wickedness. So powerful is her vitality that he not only spares her life, but falls in love with her. In the manner of the creative Trickster, she is a transforming agent, not just a clever survivor. She combines all the positive qualities of the Trickster: she lives on the edge, keeps her cool, excels at communication, and combines being clever with being warm and kind, which all enable her to win out over the power complex represented by the king.

Melusina, Soul of Mercurius

Conspicuous by their absence in Jungian literature are references to the female counterpart of Mercurius, known to the alchemists as Melusina. Jung reports that she was frequently portrayed as a water-nymph with the tail of a fish or snake, a variant of the mercurial serpent.[22] She was said to dwell in the blood—what a metaphor for the universal spirit who imbues humans, body and soul! Legends about her allude to these events: her descent from the whale of Jonah (probably ultimately from Leviathan); her birth in the womb of Mystery; her seduction by Beelzebub into practicing witchcraft; her power to cure incurable diseases, to change shapes, to know the future, to cause storms. She lives in the philosophical tree and is, with Lilith, an aspect of Mercurius. Melusina/Lilith is his female serpent-daimon who seduced Adam and Eve. She is the Holy Spirit of which Mercurius not only partakes, but with whom he identifies. Why, then, do we never read about Melusina as the agent of individuation?

Jung writes of the events in Eden as, "the Creator's whimsical notion of enlivening his peaceful, innocent paradise with the presence of an obviously rather dangerous tree-snake 'accidentally' located in the very same tree as the forbidden apples."[23] The dangerous tree-snake was our queen of individuation.

Mercurius was known to the alchemists as containing the opposites. His feminine aspect, Melusina, was a temptress, responsible for the visions that appeared to one's mind. This is a recurrent archetypal image—woman embodies and/or evokes man's visions. Man carries the potential ideational seed, and woman extracts and brings it to fruition, enabling man to see it, to have it embodied. The visions were recognized by the alchemists to be both sensible and nonsensical, and the alchemists saw their task to be the extracting of the wisdom of Melusina by distilling it out or burning it off from the nonsense. One can only imagine what the nonsensical visions might contain.

The influence of such an anima force strikes terror in the hearts of the uninitiated male, and though the alchemists dared to hold her, little has come down to us about Melusina. By uninitiated male, I mean the man who has avoided rather than confronted the strong feminine—the bitch, the Medusa, the murderous mother, the manipulative mistress, the Amazon, the shrew. All of us are accessible to fearsome aspects of the feminine, and all of these feminine monsters are accessible to engagement. Few men learn to engage them; it is easier to withdraw, to avoid, and, when she shows up in a partner, to drop that partner for another who hides it better (for a while, at least).

The alchemists hoped to distill out what was troublesome and irrelevant from their essential elements. I believe that we are, in our ethical development, about where the alchemists were in their scientific development. If we succeed in surviving and producing descendants who are capable of ethical evolution, perhaps they will look upon our primitive morality with astonishment and, we hope, compassion. Our moral task seems to be to distill out the essence needed to provide the human community with a workable minimal agreement on what is "sensible," or at least minimally acceptable. How can we ever come to trust each other that much? Where is there ethical ground to stand on? And where is the feminine in this mercurial journey?

The image of female who is part fish and lacking genitals comes up frequently in women's imagery. A woman sculptor had an experience similar to Jung's when he was "told" the substance of his book, *Answer to Job*, by a figure who sat on the end of his bed during an illness. Annis McCabe was sitting at her kitchen table when a story began pouring itself into her mind. She grabbed whatever writing tools she could find, including the window shade which she used for paper, in order to not lose the offering. In the sculpture inspired by that fantasy, the writer/artist produced a woman crucified, who has the tail of a fish or serpent and is attended by a dolphin who swims at the foot of the cross.

This is a repetition of the alchemical image of Melusina, which came through the artist's unconscious though she had never heard of Melusina nor has she read in the area of alchemy. The fantasy contains the image of the female-spirit in the philosophical tree, she who is connected to all spheres, earth, heaven, and water, who dwells equally comfortably in the unconscious as in the conscious world. Now sacrificed and immobilized, she is a redemptress who awaits resurrection. The crucified woman is not a new image. Sylvia Perrara shows how the Sumerian Inanna prefigured the death and resurrection of Christ, as did the myth of Persephone.[24] And for those who have eyes to see, the feminine is crucified repeatedly.

As for the mermaid, I find her showing up in drawings by little girls of latency age who are emerging from the parent's world into the world of brothers and partners. Recently the fairy tale of "The Little Mermaid," who evolves through love and trials to become human, had a revival as a successful movie. Essentially the mermaid has to make the inner journey from the patriarchal animus to the world of the heroic partner. These recurring images touch profound chords in the deep psyche. Jung experienced these chords resonating in himself when he found alchemy's philosophical tree, and the serpentine tree-dwelling feminine spirit, and saw the significance of the alchemists' fantasy for our age. While the patriarchal spirit draws the soul away from matter and into abstract notions of power over nature, the feminine spirit draws the soul away from its civilized trappings and into union with nature, where dwells the maternal matrix. John Dourley discusses this image in terms of the recurrent shamanic motif:

> It symbolized the ascent of the soul upward to its higher truth, often depicted as the anima, sometimes in the form of a snake, who drew the shaman toward his eternal bride or celestial wife (*CW 9*, par. 115), the nyami, his familiar protective spirit and also nourishing mother (*CW 13*, par. 460). In his appreciation of this motif, Jung evidences the ambiguity and danger attached to entrance into the world of the heavenly bride or Great Mother. Not to do so is to remain divorced from the energies of the Spirit world, unable to feed or heal oneself or others. But to enter into a permanent bond with one's celestial wife is to lose one's consciousness to her in psychotic removal from the everyday world (*CW 13*, par. 457). Thus the shaman's successful incest with the Great Goddess must be one of entering in and return if the shaman is to mediate the life of the Spirit to the community.[25]

Shaman, alchemist, mystic, and artist all risk union with the divine, and return to share the benefits with their community. But to some extent we all experience this cyclical descent and return, at least unconsciously, as we descend through sleep into the maternal dream-world, and arise refreshed to create ourselves anew. We also experience the other world when we give in to the quiet, receptive state of mind that allows us to create a reverie, poem, drawing, song, dance. The continual efforts to maintain consciousness can be seen, not just as a dragon-slaying by a heroic ego, but as labor contractions. The union of the soul with the Goddess of Nature as she exists in the outer world and in one's inner world and body is the story of an ever-recurring incarnation. First in stillness we receive her in reverie or creation, then we bring the fruits of that union to consciousness; that is the coming of the Divine Child into the human psyche, midwifed by the hermetic androgynous principle in its capacity to transform.

Sophia, Soul of Yahweh

It is essential to recognize this process on a larger scale as the anima of the collective psyche draws our human souls toward awareness of the distance we have created for ourselves from our maternal matrix. As life-sustaining source, she informs us of the artificiality of our world, its growing separation from all that nourishes us spiritually. She appears crucified on the tree because there is no support for her dwelling in the living tree of our psyches as long as they are tuned to artificial materialism. Edinger's image is of the Holy Spirit, like the Gnostic Sophia, fallen into the darkness of matter. This fall, represented by the crucifixion, calls for a resurrection and dwelling in the living tree, the tree of life which includes all beings.[26]

> Why should I spend my life
> searching for Sophia? Even the search for Sophia,
> I said to myself, is vanity.
> The wise are remembered
> No longer than the fool.
> For as the passing days multiply,
> All are forgotten.
> At last, I observed,
> The wise and the fool
> Die the same death!
> What good is Sophia then?
> I found no answer;
> So I came to hate life.[27]

The Old Testament repeatedly tells of humankind's search for Wisdom, the feminine spirit who was with God from the beginning of creation. The word for "spirit" takes different genders in different languages. Hebrew *ruach* became the Greek *pneuma*, a feminine noun which was translated into Latin as the masculine *animus*, shaping and masculinizing the meaning of the Trinity and medieval Christianity. The roots of our Western religions were possibly based on a Mother-Father-Child trinity originally.

Wisdom, also known as Sophia, is described in the Old Testament as she who protects and inspires life into her children (Eccl 4; 12-14), the tree-of-life (Proverbs 3 : 17), holy, one, gentle, eloquent, active, steadfast, unspotted mirror of God's goodness, before the light, reaching from end to end mightily and ordering all things sweetly, and no evil can overcome her (Wisdom, Chapters 7 & 8). Gnostic texts indicate that Sophia was an essential component of early Christianity, so apparently her significance decreased as masculine interpretations influenced religious thought and came to be the norm.

Running counter to the present-day Christian dogma of Three-in-One masculinity, is the image of Sophia as Holy Spirit. It is not a far reach to see the similarities between Trickster, Holy Spirit, and Sophia in terms of their mediating from the beginning of time between God and earth, in terms of their wisdom and communicative focus. For those who find her, the magnificent Sophia holds great treasures:

> If life is an adventure of great experience
> Sophia knows the past.
> Sophia can predict the future.
> Sophia knows what has happened and
> what will be.
> Sophia can interpret oracles and
> solve riddles and mysteries.
> Sophia has foreknowledge of omens and signs.
> Sophia has foresight of miracles and wonders,
> of beginnings and conclusions,
> of this age and all ages.
> Thus, it was that I resolved;
> that I set my heart,
> on having Sophia come into my life;
> and live my life with me.
> Knowing she would counsel me

in prosperity and good times.
Knowing she would comfort me
in grief and troubled times.[28]

These texts proclaim the omniscience and mercurial cleverness of the Goddess, her Logos qualities, but notice that they do not give a complete picture of a Goddess with Eros qualities. The closest she comes to Eros is that she comforts. Because it is not said, we have to assume that, in giving comfort, she might be warm and physical, more grounded in nature. Or, we must look to other goddess images for reflection of the wholeness we seek in terms of more earthy, erotic, sexual, nature-oriented, and tricksterish qualities.

Lilith, Soul of Satan

The earthier aspects of Sophia seem to have been rejected, split off, and attributed to Lilith, whose image has been associated with nature and physicality for at least 4000 years. Her first known appearance on a Sumerian relief, around 1950 B.C., pictures her as a beautiful, sexual woman with talons for feet, a fourfold snake turban on her head, vulture wings on her shoulders, accompanied by lions and owls.[29] This portrayal is typical of that of nature goddesses, which often include inhuman qualities of the lower-body, such as fishtails, or bird or animal feet. Sometimes Lilith resides in a nest in a tree; in the story of Gilgamesh she became a wandering spirit when he cut down her tree. Later legends associate Lilith with the tree of Good and Evil in the Garden of Eden. Her image has undergone changes throughout the centuries; sometimes she is associated with the Birth Goddess, and sometimes with death and wickedness as the fallen, rejected feminine principle that destroys women in labor and sucks the blood of newborns.

Hebrew legends are the only remaining sources that tell us of the images attributed to this ancient goddess. The legends refer to Lilith as the primordial predecessor of Eve. While she is not referred to as a daughter, as Satan (Samael in the Hebrew Zohar) is called a "son" of God, she could be a fitting Anima to Satan. In contrast to Eve, who came second to Adam, Lilith seems to have been coequal with or preceding Adam, as Satan was, and she struggled with Adam for equality, symbolized in her refusal to always take the inferior position in sexual intercourse. Because of this act of pride she was cursed by God and banished. She hid herself in the sea, and visited Adam at night, ravaging him while he dreamed. With Adam's sperm she gave birth to demonic children unfit for human partnering. When forced back into exile by Adam with the help of angels, she changed into a nightmarish creature who haunted pregnant women and kidnapped infants because of her jealous rage against

Eve and her children. She was said to come between couples during intercourse causing the man to be impotent and the woman barren.[30] Like other dark and tricksterish women, she was considered evil and witchy and held responsible for inciting dangerous sexual feelings in men. Lilith is associated with the phenomenon of the lamia or succubus, who takes possession of men in their sleep and uses their energy for her own sexual fulfillment, leaving them drained and depressed.

In her aspects as the Good Mother she is Sophia, also known as the Shekinah of the Cabbala. (Jewish mystical teachings based on Hebrew scriptures and stemming in terms of publication to about 300 A.D). Ean Begg writes:

> Lilith's greatest triumph is recorded in a sixteenth-century Cabbalistic writing where, as a result of a piece of divine wife-swapping, following the destruction of the Temple, God relinquishes his consort, the Matronit (identical with the Shekinah) to Samael/Satan and takes his queen, Lilith, to be his bride.[31]

Legend claims that in her many incarnations, Lilith had a child by Elijah, married Moses, became Hagar, the first wife of Abraham, and also became the Queen of Sheba.

> The Queen of Sheba's visit to Solomon provides an important link in the continuum that runs from Lilith to the Black Virgins of Europe, through the refrain from the Song of Songs: "I am black but I am beautiful." For in the massive exchange of gifts between Solomon and the Queen, she departs with the two greatest gifts of all, Solomon's wisdom, and the child that she will bear, Menelik, ancestor of the royal line of Ethiopia, on whom Solomon bestows the ark of the covenant.[32]

This suggests that Lilith symbolizes the equality of the masculine and feminine in God. We might think of Lilith's counterpart to be the Virgin Mary, even if her image carries the pure and innocent, but none of the earthy aspects of the feminine. Nowadays we hear many reports of the Virgin Mary appearing to people to appeal for humans to relate more peaceably with each other, or to take better care of the earth. The many occurrences of visions of the Virgin Mary around the world today can be thought of as compensatory messages from the feminine principle in the collective unconscious. Like Lilith crying in the wilderness, and like the cry of Merlin, (which we will discuss later) she calls for repentance toward the goddesses of nature for the well-being of society.[33]

The story of Lilith also cries out through the symbolism in the novel *Beloved*, by Toni Morrison. Shirley Stave notes that Morrison, in giving voice to Lilith,

> …exposes the patriarchy's limited understanding of motherhood. Morrison's use of the Lilith material, then, sanctions female defiance of patriarchal authority at the same time that it allows an unsentimentalized view of motherhood and the complexities that accompany it. Only when the demon mother is deconstructed can mothers and children interact as full human beings, free of mythologies that would limit and damage them.[34]

Psychologist and writer Barbara Koltuv tracked Lilith through centuries of Hebrew literature and multi-cultural folklore, including the amulets that are still used in some cultures to protect marriages and infants from Lilith's rage. Lilith's rage is born of her failure to be recognized in her authenticity, and particularly in her earthiness, by the patriarchal godhead. She lives on in the psyche to protest, even to screech in her owl form, against oppression of the feminine nature. Koltuv says:

> Lilith is that part of the Great Goddess that has been rejected and cast out in post-Biblical times. She represents the qualities of the feminine Self that the Shekina alone does not carry. The first of these is lunar consciousness, which is a connection to the cycles of waxing and waning: life, death, and rebirth….The second rejected quality of the Goddess that Lilith represents is the body—instinctuality, and sexuality…. Third, both Lilith and the Shekina represent the rejected Goddess' quality of prophetic inner knowledge and experience over logic or law…. The fourth and final female quality carried by Lilith is that of God the mother and creatrix, in addition to God the father and creator. In this sense, Lilith is Adamah, the feminine red mother earth of woman's nature. She is the part of the feminine Self that modern woman needs to reconnect with in order to no longer be a spiritual outcast.[35]

Lunar consciousness, instinctuality, intuition, maternal creativity—these rejected feminine attributes call for inclusion in our images of the divine.

Binah, Soul of Chokmah

Looking again to the Cabbala, we find another ancient image of the Goddess accompanying the Trickster. The Cabbala describes a metaphysical system called the Tree of Life that defines experience in terms of divine influences (Sephiros) which vivify and sustain all things. All things have their origin in the Ain—

Nothing, Infinite Space. One hypothesis is that the Ain, this abstract negativity, concentrated itself into a central dimensionless point, which became The One, Keser, the first Sephirah. Keser became the source or Primal Cause; by reflection of itself, it forms an Eidolon, duplicate. Cabbalistic scholar Israel Regardie states: "Now, also, we have the commencement of a vibration established, for the number one vibrates alternately from changelessness to definition and back to changelessness."[36]

The current issuing from this One is the primeval mercurial intelligence, Chokmah, the second Sephirah; the two give rise to a third, Binah, the Great Mother; and from these three, all else issues.

Chokmah is Wisdom, male, vigorous, active. Binah is Understanding, female, receptive, the vital power that brings together all forms and carries out the plan of the Divine Logos, Chokmah. She is the Shekinah or Holy Spirit, or Upper Mother. (Her Eidolon or Daughter is the Shekinah of the tenth Sephirah, Malkus, the sphere of matter.) According to Regardie, Chokmah encompasses Thoth, Hermes, Athena, and Maat as emanations of Wisdom; Binah encompasses the universal power of illusion—Maya, and goddesses Kwan Yin, Isis, Kali, Shakti, and Taoist Yin. Binah is the cosmic root substance, objectivity in its purist abstraction, as Chokmah is the essence of consciousness. We could translate Binah as Soul, Chokmah as Spirit.[37] Here we have Wisdom (Chokmah) portrayed as masculine, and identified with the Goddess of Truth (Maat) and Gods of Communication (Trickster Gods Thoth and Hermes), and partnering Maya (Binah), the Goddess of Illusion. The linking of these archetypal figures throughout the ages, and the difficulty in pinning down gender qualities, is of the nature of the subject. Much of what legend and myth teach is passed down orally, and translations of both written and spoken stories differ. In view of what we have seen of the attributes of Trickster gods throughout different cultures, Chokmah and Binah united can be understood as an androgynous Trickster god/goddess who accompany the unifying principle, the Keser.

The axiom of Maria Prophetissa is actualized in the Cabbalistic creation story. Besides expressing itself in the process of the Tree of Life, according to Regardie, the axiom of Maria is referred to by Lao Tsu, who teaches that "Tao produced Unity, Unity produced Duality, Duality produced Trinity, and Trinity produced all existing things."[38] The Cabbala maintains that there is an abyss separating these first three Sephiros from the remaining seven; the tenth and last, Malkus, manifests as our external universe.[39] Again we have what seems to be a natural propensity to interpret creation in terms of a trinity, but, in contrast to the Christian trinity, the trinity of the Cabbala includes the feminine principle.

Goddesses of Transformation

Hecate, Aphrodite, Baba Yaga, and Isis are other goddesses resembling Trickster in their transformational and nature-enhancing aspect. Athena, though not a nature goddess, is also transformative in the individuation process, and is attributed to Chokmah (Thoth) as Wisdom. In the story of Odysseus, Athena transforms herself at times into a man, a boy, and a young girl in pigtails in order to facilitate the hero's individuation process.

A very different image from Athena is the Russian witch-goddess, Baba Yaga, who lures us deep into the primordial psyche, then presents herself as a beautiful young woman, a loving mother, or a devouring ogre to test our mettle. Trickster always puts us into a position of choosing between good and evil when they are often in disguise. Related to Baba Yaga is the Greek Hecate, who contains all the transformations reflected in the phases of the moon. And the love-goddess, Aphrodite, mother of Eros, is the temenos for relationship which transforms through love. We will discuss Hecate in more detail later.

Isis, venerated wife and mother, is probably the most comprehensive representative of the female Trickster goddess. For one thing, like Hecate in her triune nature, Isis's image allows women of all ages to identify with and emulate her. While her roles as a devoted wife and mother, and teacher of weaving, spinning, grinding grains, and cooking, endeared her to women, she also was an enchantress who provided the stability of an alchemical vessel for the transformation of Osiris. Her magic was allied to the wisdom of Thoth, the Trickster god, and manifested in her gift of healing. When Osiris was killed by Set and thrown into the Nile in a chest, Isis divined that the chest had washed up upon the coast of Byblos and been enfolded by a sapling. She "knew" that the sapling had become a tree which had been incorporated into a pillar at the palace.

Disguising herself, she secured a place at the palace as nurse for the royal child, where at night she transformed herself into a swallow and circled the pillar, mourning Osiris. Like Demeter, she tried to give the royal child immortality by placing him in the fire, but was interrupted by the frantic mother. Isis then was forced to reveal herself. Her astonished devotees gave her the pillar, and so she returned home with Osiris in it.

Some say Isis recognized the pillar by its fragrance, demonstrating a sensitivity to seemingly ordinary events and sensations, such as we saw in the story of Herakles who recovered his life through the odor of the quail (Chapter I). To those who are receptive, a smell, a tune, or some small object may mean the difference between death or despair, and life or hope.

Later the pillar was rediscovered by Set, who smashed it and cut the corpse into pieces. Isis then searched out the pieces of Osiris' corpse and reassembled him with the help of her sister Nephthys, Set's wife. Isis and Nephthys are both portrayed by the Egyptians as birds who fly about the dead, mourning. With long wings Isis enfolded the body of Osiris and attempted to transmit the breath of life to him. Though she was unable to bring him back from the other world where he remained king, so great were her generative powers and her receptive sensitivity, that she conceived his child, Horus. She invoked the protection of Thoth against Set for her son.

In her role as nourishing mother Isis is also represented by the cow. The story of Isis at her most cunning, championing for her son's place as heir to Osiris's throne, tells how she bested Set in his attempt to dishonor Horus. Under pretense of peace-making, Set attempted to rape young Horus and discredit him in the eyes of the other gods. Isis knew Set's tastes, and prepared an irresistible salad for him, into which she secretly added Horus's semen. Set ate, conceived, and became the laughing stock of the other gods.

Isis as the intrepid lover and clever mother who not only protects her child, but outwits his enemy, is an inspiration to all women, not only mothers. She is the ideal model for anyone who grieves the loss of a loved one, for her actions illustrate the psychological processes experienced by anyone who is bereft: that is, when we suffer such a loss, we want to go back over our life with the loved one and pick up every memory, every fantasy, every psychological piece of them that is possible to gather and hold on to. Isis does that, and also shows us that, once the re-membering of the loved one has been done, it is possible to go on and involve oneself in life.

Isis embodies the nurturant and mercurial functions in wonderful balance. Like all transformative cooks, she prepares alchemical food which works magic. Recently two movies have played on this theme: *Babette's Feast* and *Like Water for Chocolate*. In each film the alchemical feminine is represented in a woman who, by nurturing those she cares for while remaining alert and attentive to the forces around her, creates a new reality. In each movie the hermetic woman is surrounded by dark forces capable of swallowing her psychologically. But so strong is her life-force, emotional power, and desire to generate sensual pleasure, that each of the women not only overcomes the threat of annihilation, she creates a memorable miracle of love that is close to immortal.

While Isis is to me the most complete, there are other goddesses and sorceresses, such as the goddess Metis, who are known for their intuitive wisdom. Most of these feminine figures carry some part of Trickster's qualities, but have less relationship with humans than does the typical Trickster god. The myth of Metis is of interest here in that she was the victim of a trick. It was prophesied that, as Zeus' first wife, she would bear a son who would be as wise as she. Zeus, threatened by the possibility, swallowed her while she was pregnant; but the child was a girl, Athena, whom Zeus could only birth from his head with the aid of Hermes. Ginette Paris explains that Metis became the name Greeks gave to a kind of intelligence shared by Hermes and Metis, a prudent and reflective wisdom, intuitive, perceptive, intimate with the ways of nature, cunning.[40]

Jean Shinoda Bolen suggests that this myth is still unfolding. Metis, by trusting Zeus, allowed herself to be tricked into oblivion, and her feminine wisdom was swallowed up in patriarchy. But perhaps she will find her way out and the prophecy will be fulfilled. Perhaps her son, a new male deity who is wise, trustworthy, and able to relate intimately with woman and nature, is evolving in the collective unconscious. Bolen refers to this as the missing god who will replace the old patriarch and rule with an all-loving heart in intimate relationship to the feminine.[41]

Bolen's vision of the missing god is similar to that of the trickster/feminine nature god/goddess whose rise we are focusing on here. We have no model for such a male divinity in western theology, though there are individual men who embody this degree of psychological development. This psychological evolution has not been communicated through the collective unconscious to the god-image. Neither do we yet have on a collective level a model for a female divinity who is both wise, sensual, and warmly intimate with her man. It is not feasible to regress and pick up an Isis or an Ishtar or a Metis from another century. Each society has to find its own solution to the missing deities through its own dialogue with the spiritual world.

CREATIVE CRONE HECATE

George Sand, Babe Zaharias, Mae West, Minnie Marx (mother of the Marx Brothers), Sarah Bernhardt, Gertrude Stein, Isadora Duncan, are just a few famous women who expressed trickster features, such as capacity to improvise and create, express androgyny, span worlds. When I ask audiences for examples of contemporary hermetic women, they invariably name entertainers who push pass the limits of conventional morality. These entertainers carry so much weight of collective projections that they sometimes collapse under their personas of archetypal proportions. Less subject to the hoopla of fame are women poets, who serve as exemplars of the hermetic, free-spirited energy of this era—Denise Levertov, Adrienne Rich, Diane Wakoski, Marge Piercy, Sharon Olds, and many more. (And though she is not of this era, let us not forget the liberated Wife of Bath.) Women novelists—Margaret Atwood, Doris Lessing, May Sarton, Anne Rice, numerous others—manifest trickster qualities of "seeing-through," combining irony and compassion, cosmic vision, and sensuality, as do Georgia O'Keefe, Judy Chicago, Annie Liebowitz, Mercedes Ruehl, Candice Bergen, and many women artists and filmmakers. And, whereas in the past women in positions of political public service usually exemplified the more serious Athena or Artemis, I expect from the examples of females in the US Congress, that we will see more political women transmitting the trickster-current into the collective consciousness through public-service.

Woman's capacity to touch her witchiness seems essential if her creativity is to have vibrance.[42] And to speak of either witchiness or creativity, invokes the Trickster in woman. Of course, Hecate, chthonic witch, is the Greek goddess who most resembles Hermes, and is close to the souls of creative women. She is the guide of souls, and three-cornered pillars were built to her at the crossroads of Ancient Greece. Our prejudices may keep us from appreciating her glory. In her primary place as crone, we may find her wisdom with us even as young girls, but it is difficult for a young woman to expose her Hecate-wisdom without being scapegoated in this youth-possessed society. Even our prepubescent girls are conditioned to begin hiding their wisdom in order to be liked.

Hecate's three-phased trinity was composed of a moon goddess, sometimes known as Selene; an earth goddess, sometimes known as Artemis; and an underworld goddess, Hecate, in her crone and androgynous form. Another schema refers to the three goddesses in one as the new moon, Persephone; the full moon, Demeter; and the dark of the moon, Hecate. In this representation Hecate resembles Hermes, whose threeness is not named, but is visually depicted in images from antiquity as three-headed, and with a three-pronged staff. This threeness continues later in the representations of Mercurius as a three-headed serpent or dragon and a three-spouting fountain of the *aquae vitae*.[43]

The aspect of completion also evokes the number four when thinking of Hermes and Hecate. As guardians of the crossroads, guides to the underworld, and companions on the way to death and paradise, they acquaint us with completion. Hermes' birth made a full house of twelve divinities on Mt. Olympus. He was born on the fourth day of the fourth month, which the Greeks held sacred to Hermes. In his primitive form of a stone structure (the herm) at the convergence of roads in ancient Greece, he is always situated at the intersection of four directions. In threeness we encounter instability, energy, dynamism; we are led into labyrinths of mystery and the uncertainty of good and evil. Three is the escape from duality. For humans to be ruled by three suggests a sense of headlong momentum, a careening from advantage to disadvantage to advantage. Like the spirit of this dying twentieth century, three keeps moving with little sense of resolution or repose. No purpose can root, no rule can take hold. In our restless era we seem to have come to the end of rulers and rootedness. How do we find meaning in our seemingly purposeless momentum? We are provoked to ask, "In what realm of the divine are we dwelling, and what does that divine spirit, be it triune God or Goddess, expect of us?" In this time of rapid transit and instant communication, we must recognize that we have put our trust in the hands of, not rationality, not logic, but Trickster, god and goddess of chance, of communication, merchants, thieves, gamblers, rescuers, adolescents, borderlines, clowns, storytellers, sociopaths, inventors, musicians, healers, journeyers, gypsies, and freaks. But apparently we are responding only to the frenetic aspect of the Trickster and not ready to rest in the security of four.

When Aeneas in his search for his father sought out the wisdom of the prophetic sorceress, Sibyl of Cumae, she brought stability to his journey through the underworld by sacrificing four black bulls to Hecate, the goddess of the underworld. Sibyl acted on the principle that four brings resolution to the instability of three. Jung emphasized the significance of the doctrine of the Assumption of Mary into heaven, as an acknowledgment by Christianity of the need for completion in the male Trinity. Buddha had his four-fold path. It is too soon or too late to know how our epistemological ground would feel if our divine trinities were completed by a member of the opposite sex. Would she be quite such a shadowy figure? A fully empowered Mary along with the Father, Son, and Holy Spirit? Hermes in his female role? A masculine member to Hecate?

Hecate's mysteries also flourished in Rome, where she was honored as the personification of nightmares, and patron of riders. Today, in our prejudice against age and powerful women, she is more often an apparition of terror, who with her dog guards the gates of Hades. She appears with Priapus, establishing herself as sexually permissive; she rules snakes and dogs, those ambiguously diabolic benefactors; she is Goddess of Marriage and Birth and she sends madness (a combination which some find not incongruent).[44] Kerényi writes:

> At every new moon she there received cakes and smoked offerings as did Hermes. With Hermes she guards the gates, and with him, too brings wealth and good fortune to barns. She has hardly less to do with fruitfulness than has Hermes. Associations with a kind of eroticism that one might find crass and vulgar and a connection to souls and spirits are

> characteristic for her. The same is the case (and the problem) for Hermes, and with him it is even more problematical since we can now compare father and son also from this angle. On the lofty level of the idealistic, ingenuous Eros, with his passion for self-sacrifice and for reaching out beyond his own life, the union of phallus, soul, and spirit seems conceivable, but on this low, Hecatean level…? We must recall that the Hermetic essence, seen in its most ancient representations, may only to us appear so low and vulgar, whereas there, where Hecate ruled the world of northern Greece and Thrace in the form of "Aphrodite Zerynthia," it is precisely the crassest that is the holiest and most spiritual.[45]

Kerényi has hit the essential nerve that our society is struggling to take in: Crass is holy. We dash and falter between these two—crass and holy—as if they were separated by an abyss. But an examination of other cultures tells us (in case our own feminine instincts have been muted) that this is delusion. Erotic love and spirituality co-exist.[46]

SACRED EROTICISM

The ability to enjoy eroticism, sensual and emotional, is an attribute of the ancient goddesses. Recognizing its power, societies must find ways to access and enjoy the erotic without being overwhelmed by indulgence or made impotent by repression. Hindu art exalts sacred eroticism. However, because it is indomitable and sacred, even in Hinduism the power of lust has demanded limitation. For example, at one time in India, Kama, God of Desire, was worshipped as the first god, the creator and god of phallic love. He was depicted in lovely form. Perfumes, mango blossoms, and sandalwood paste were lain before him. With the rise of more ascetic Buddhism and Jainism, Kama became identified with the magician-tempter of Buddha, and became synonymous with dark forces. Legends tell of the meeting of Kama and Shiva. The power of the yogic fire from Shiva's third eye destroyed the god of lust. Pupul Jayaka writes of this legend, that it symbolizes the physical disappearance of the face and limbs of the presiding deity of erotic love from temple and household shrine.

> Kama became Ananga, the bodiless one, only remembered in the secret vrata rituals of women and in the saturnalian spring festival.…The image and presence of Kama…could not be annihilated: his fragrant face, his lotus eyes, his sensuous limbs, and the inextinguishable fires fused with the new emergent deities. The numerous vratas that centered around the worship of Surya, Siva,

and Krsna reveal the subtlety with which the transformation was accomplished.[47]

This God of Desire still survives in somewhat subdued form in other deities, and the power of erotic love is recognized in tantra and bhakti yoga.[48] The Hindu gods are related to Eros, but appear much more physically grounded, and in that sense, Dionysian. The relationship of the Hindu gods of love to Trickster is hinted at in the description of Indian vratyas (wandering magicians). They combine Hermetic and Dionysian aspects. These black-clad yogi traveled in the company of a bard and a prostitute. During solstice festivals after harvesting, they arrived to waken the earth, and drew mandalas on the cart which served as an altar. As they performed secret rites and chants, the bard and prostitute performed ritual intercourse to ensure fertility.[49] Throughout cultures, the Trickster appears with similar qualities; though not a love-god, he is always friendly toward the feminine and all that is fructifying and natural, and often appears when sexuality is evoked.

Lust is sometimes denigrated as being dangerous to society by upsetting domestic harmony and abetting overpopulation. But the dark onus of lust seems to have fallen like a heavy cloak of chastity upon the feminine while the masculine escaped. Women are still given principle responsibility for the management of lust. Therefore, lusty women are often scorned, or killed, while lusty men are adulated. The feminine aspect of lusty Trickster was hidden, its receptive qualities exaggerated to be devouring and attributed to the witch, while the phallic aspect remained open and appreciated. The feminine with any Trickster characteristics, not only lustiness, tends to be perceived as dark and foreboding, witchy, and not friendly to humans as Hermes and the other male tricksters are. The familiar male-female split renders the hermetic feminine evil and witchy, while the hermetic masculine is acceptable, or even good; this is so not only in western culture. Instinctuality is associated with witchiness in the feminine in many cultures. Ulanov says:

> Unmoved by human values, a witch's mind bears the cold-blooded quality of instinctual life far beneath the warm-blooded values of human feelings. She is not to be educated or reformed or touched by human culture. The closest she comes to human affect is her irritability, fretfulness, bad-temper, and malevolence.[50]

We are reminded of Lilith, who was cast into evil ways by God because she wanted to be an equal sexual partner to Adam. The witch has to carry her instinctuality alone and with spite, instead of in harmony with her loving nature, which has been rejected. (Hell hath no fury like a woman scorned.) Frustrated by the separation of sexual and loving feelings, and with no possibility of harmonious gratification of both, women do tend to become irritable!

An important function of women's gatherings has always been to provide an outlet for a kind of lusty, assertive humor, so little tolerated in mixed company. Less technological cultures allow many opportunities for women's gathering, usually while engaged in domestic tasks. But our lifestyle for many years in Europe, America, Japan, etc., has discouraged meeting at the well or quilting party or coffee klatch, and women complain to me that they have a hard time finding or creating such healthy camaraderie. Trickster is very present in my woman's therapy group, and usually she comes in the form of Baubo. With no overt direction on my part—I am non-intervening in this long-term group and function chiefly as a sustainer in the background—the group has evolved into a safe place for the women to express their "uncivilized" feelings. Violence, grief, unadulterated sex, bitchiness, affection, and all manner of "inappropriate" thoughts come to surface, accompanied by tears, anguish, and a lot of laughing. The women have invented a private pantheon: Tawanda, Goddess of Domestic Violence; Latrina, Goddess of Dirty Work; Rantia and Ravia, Goddesses of Premenstrual Syndrome; Iwanna, Goddess of Conspicuous Consumption, etc.

Native American cultures accepted sexuality as part of nature and were relatively unburdened by guilt or by projections of dark lust onto the feminine. Perhaps that explains why autobiographies of hermetic women are more common in the Native American literature than in the European or Asian…women like Grandmother Twylah Nitsch, part Seneca and part Oneida. She learned through a divine revelation, a vision, that there have been a series of worlds, and in the fourth world the greatest division took place when humans created a god and placed him as a male deity somewhere out in the clouds. This created the greatest separation between humankind and the Great Mystery; but this needed to happen in the history of the earth, says Grandmother Twylah.[51] There were important lessons to be learned through this experience.

The inclusion of the erotic as a valid and sacred aspect of our Goddess-given nature must occur in order for the creative witch to be incorporated into modern life where her vitality can help to reconstruct our weak-spirited society. We desperately need the infusion of the full-bodied, intimate feminine instincts.

Women of Spiritual Power

Even though the patriarchal attitude pervades Buddhism, the feminine principle appears to me to be more developed there than in Christianity, especially in Tibetan Buddhism and American Zen centers. The Dalai Lama, steadfast in spite of being ousted from his homeland by the Chinese communists, publicly compassionate and good-humored instead of hateful and bitter, manifests an aura which marks him as an example of a man in excellent relationship to the Trickster. By this I mean that he incorporates Trickster and yet is not dominated by it. Through his enforced exile and the sorrowful ordeal of the displaced Tibetans, his religion is being more widely disseminated, his cause more respected. He outclasses his enemies, he outshines evil, and he reveres the feminine. Jack Kornfeld described an audience of Buddhist monks and nuns with the Dalai Lama, who, hearing the nuns recount tales about the discriminations made against them in their own monasteries, held his head in his hands and wept.[52]

Pope John Paul II also reveres the feminine in that he has dedicated his life to Mary. However, both John Paul II and the Dalai Lama head patriarchal religious systems, where, as in government, the sacred are separated from their sheep by their special charge of holiness from on high. The halos and coronas of sainthood stretch, like the royal crown, toward the sky-gods to illustrate the connection between the head and the upper spirits. Hierarchical values prevail, and women are not equal to men in status. In contrast, some religions, like those of Native Americans, respect the lower planes of nature and animal life and the lower half of the body, while keeping their spiritual energies embodied and making the ground sacred.

Despite the diminishment of the feminine in the patriarchal religions, the trickster woman makes her power felt, one way or another. For example, anecdotes about synchronistic happenings continue to build around the figure of Mother Meera, a holy woman residing in Germany who has attracted many devotees.[53] There are great yoginis whose reputations as powerful, free, and independent spirits are known in spite of the fact that they live most of their lives in seclusion.

The Tibetan religion has many holy women. This story is from Khetsun Sangpo Rinbochay's exposition of Tantric practice:

> It is said in Atisha's biography that everyday he saw a woman who was at times crying and at others laughing. Finally he asked her, "Why is it that for no apparent reason you sometimes cry and sometimes laugh? Are you in any way mentally distressed?" "No, I am not. You people are, and so I cry." "Why?"

> "The Tathagata essence, one's own mind, has been a Buddha from beginningless time. By not knowing this, small complications follow from such a small base of error for hundreds of thousands of sentient beings. Although their own minds are Buddhas, they are in such great confusion. Not being able to bear the sufferings of so many beings, I cry. And then, I laugh because when this small basis of error is known—when one knows one's own mind—one is freed. Enjoying the fact that sentient beings can so easily released from suffering, I laugh, knowing that they are ready to be liberated."[54]

In that story we see the Trickster woman in a wide gamut of possible relationships to the human: warm and compassionate, realistic and not sentimental, distant enough to get the broad picture, and intimate enough to hold it with intense emotion, able to contain it all without a need to control or force things to a conclusion.

A contemporary Tibetan lama, Namkhai Norbu, described his memories of a great dakini, A-Yu Khadro, who lived in a small, windowless hut with an old man and an old nun as assistants at the foot of a cliff. Over a period of time Namkhai Norbu received valuable teachings from this woman who was 113 years of age when they met. We can glean a flavor of her from his first impressions after a three day journey to her hut:

> When we entered the Khadro's room for the first time only one butter lamp was lit.... She did not look particularly ancient. She had very long hair that reached her knees. It was black at the tips and white at the roots, Her hands looked like the hands of a young woman. She wore a dark-red dress and a meditation belt over her left shoulder. During our visit we requested teachings, but she kept saying that she was no one special and had no qualifications to teach.... The more compliments we offered her, the more deferential she became toward us. I was discouraged and feared she might not give us any teachings.[55]

He camped overnight at a river nearby. The next morning the nun and her niece came to bring him back to A-Yu Khadro.

> Many more butter lamps were lit and she touched her forehead to mine, a great courtesy. She gave me a nice breakfast of yogurt and milk and told me that she had had an auspicious dream that night of her teacher.... He had advised her to give me the teachings.[56]

The Self provides such a variety of lessons; we get them through wisewomen, tricksters, difficult partners, dreams. In the past two weeks I have heard of two dreams by two women I know, miles apart from each other, containing the same image: blood is pouring from a deep wound in the earth. These both being strong, creative, healthy women, I take these dreams as archetypal messages to the collective consciousness from the depths of the unconscious.

VIVIENNE, SOUL OF MERLIN

Finding another attitude toward nature, other than conquering it, suggests another period of history and another Trickster figure. Throughout history leaders and heroes have depended on their trickster sidekicks, such as jesters, informers, and seers, for help in governing, outsmarting enemies, and providing comic relief. Even in our democratic form of government, vice-presidents and relatives of the president have frequently been put in this role. One such figure was Merlin of Uther's and Arthur's courts. There is significant evidence that the legends about the great seer, trickster, and advisor to kings was based on the life of a historical person, a Merlin who existed in the Lowlands of Scotland at the end of the sixth century.

Whether or not the historical Merlin existed, an archetypal Merlin was thought to be one of the Celtic poet-seers whose prophesies provided an essential function of connecting the society with the word of God. His story, historical and mythical, is relevant for our times, as Nikolai Tolstoy argues:

> Like ours, his was a time of upheaval, destruction and rebirth. Civilization was collapsing in the face of barbarian invasions from the East. In 542-43 bubonic plague swept through all Europe as far as the British Isles, causing mortality in all likelihood proportionate to that resulting from a nuclear war. Cities were abandoned to dogs and crows, robbers infested the countryside, and ordered life everywhere appeared collapsing to its close. Educated men prognosticated and even welcomed the coming end of the world, and apocalyptic images and visions abounded.... Thus Merlin's inspired prophesies of the ordered succession of coming kings possessed a deeply cosmic significance.[57]

After a glorious period of service to his community, legend has it that Merlin undertook the journey to the Otherworld by ascending the Tree of Life in a ritual self-sacrifice, paralleling the deaths of the Celtic God Lug, the Norse Odin, and Christ, and thereby entering the realm of Melusina, the tree-dwelling serpentine nature goddess.

Another version of the ending of Merlin's story tells that he fell in love with an enchantress, Vivienne, who tricked him into teaching her his magic, then used the power against him, trapped and immobilized him as her captive. In both cases, whether by choice or fate, Merlin was absorbed by the forces of nature and his female counterpart.

Jung was intrigued by the story of Merlin, whom he referred to as "son of the devil and a pure virgin" and the dark brother of the Christian hero, Parsifal. In Jung's understanding, Merlin was a parallel figure to Parsifal, rising in the collective unconscious of the twelfth century to complete the one-sided Christian image of the hero. Jung associated the fate of Merlin with the withdrawal of the great nature spirits in the wake of excessive emphasis on the "progress" of Christian civilization.[58] In fact, Jung seems to have had a "Merlinish" journey to the Otherworld in mind when he built for himself his retreat at Bollingen where, he stated, "I am in the midst of my true life, I am most deeply myself."[59] At Bollingen Jung honored that part of his personality who, in his own words,

> has always been and always will be. *He exists outside time and is the son of the maternal unconscious....* At times I feel as if I am spread out over the landscape and inside things, and am myself living in every tree, in the plashing of the waves, in the clouds and the animals that come and go, in the procession of the seasons.[60] (italics-DM)

I have observed this retreat-dream in many men, and I think it is a fundamental way that men, particularly those who have led very active and assertive lives, find fulfillment in union with the anima, that is, an anima of pure nature. Sometimes this becomes a thorn in the side of their women partners, who dream of a lively social life. Many couples come to face this issue at the point of retirement. "At last," says she, "he now has time for relaxing with friends, going dancing, having dinner parties, traveling to Paris." "Alas," says he, "wouldn't you rather work a farm, build a log cabin deep in the woods, camp out on this desolate beach with me alone?"

We might think of the retreat fantasy as man's descent to his Merlin personality; or we can say he is expressing what Robert Bly termed the wildman, his chthonic nature which he may have had to suppress or split off from consciousness for years.

Jung had his own way and found his spot. By mistake the cornerstone sent by the quarry to Bollingen was a square stone of wrong proportions. Jung realized that the incident had meaning for him and instead of returning the mistaken stone, he kept it and inscribed it with carvings to express what the tower at Bollingen meant to him. On three sides he carved alchemical figures and quotations in a spirit of gratitude. On the back face of the stone he wanted to chisel *"le cri de Merlin"* for the rejected stone reminded him of Merlin, vanished from the world and the forest, whose cries are still heard. Jung says:

> In the twelfth century when the legend arose, there were as yet no premises by which his intrinsic meaning could be understood. Hence he ended in exile, and hence *"le cri de Merlin"* which still sounded from the forest after his death. This cry that no one could understand implies that he lives on in unredeemed form. His story is not yet finished and he still walks abroad. It might be said that the secret of Merlin was carried on by alchemy, primarily in the figure of Mercurius. Then Merlin was taken up again in my psychology of the unconscious and remains uncomprehended to this day![61]

Jung always felt that his message about the need for completion (inclusion of opposites) rather than perfection (exclusion of inferiority) was largely misunderstood.

As for Merlin, according to legend, having abandoned the world of time and space to unite with the world of nature, Merlin fell in love with Viviane. Studying the archetypal meaning of the relationship of Merlin and Viviane, Verena Kast asks:

> If Merlin is so united with forest, nature and spring, why must he still fall in love with Viviane…? Is the issue here that women must win back the magical power "the female magical power" that Merlin has? (Prophecy, of course, has been the province of prophetesses since ancient times.)[62]

Kast speculates about how we can understand why Merlin the enchanter becomes the "enchanted" and finds himself bound in union with a woman. One possibility is that "Merlin's tower would be a symbol of a womb, a place of transformation from no commitment, from the joy in the sudden fancy, from roaming, to binding relatedness in a love relationship."[63]

It is the nature of tricksters to evade committed unions. Are we supposing that Merlin, then, transforms, or allows himself to be transformed to a committed lover? Is not the term "committed trickster" an oxymoron? But isn't it also the nature of tricksters to keep us off sure ground, so that just when you have him pegged as a footloose journeyer, he transforms into a committed partner? But can one expect any partnership with Trickster to have any duration? Perhaps it is not that Merlin must fall in love when he unites with nature, but rather that he can, at last, give himself over to love, his heavy-duty extroversion being now subdued. Or that he can be still and quiet long enough to listen to his need for Viviane, his feminine soul. What do both have to tell us that could be useful to our society?

My idea is that Merlin will return when he can return with Viviane as an equal, in a way in which he can serve a world which truly respects the natural world, much as Native Americans once tried to teach the white invaders to do. The cry of Merlin, I believe, is a cry of anguish: it arose when, through his capacity for prophecy and his intimacy with the feminine, he foresaw the consequences of his civilization's progress. Foreseeing the soul of the world being buried in cement, plastic, and gas fumes, and the damage that that would do to the tempers of human beings, perhaps he saw as well how the feminine principle was being suppressed. Perhaps he saw that the magical power of women, as seen in Isis and Hecate, and as he gave back to Viviane, would be rendered useless for generations. Perhaps he saw that the feminine instincts would become too impotent in men and women to prevent the slaughter of innocence and hope.

Earth Woman, Soul of Coyote

We turn now from old world to new for mythic examples of Trickster and his feminine counterpart. Although the world was new to Europeans, its stories are ancient. In the Coyote stories of some of the Native American nations of North America, Great Spirit gives Coyote the task of creating the earth and the human beings. The creation of earth is accomplished by having the ducks dive underwater until they succeed in bringing up some mud in their webbed feet, one variant of the widespread earthdiver creation motif. Beginning in the east, Coyote traveled around spreading the mud to create the earth, whom he refers to as "Female Comrade, the earth."[64] The mud of which the female earth is formed is coexistent with the Gods, Great Spirit, and Coyote; nevertheless it is underwater, submerged in the unconscious until retrieved at Coyote's insistence. Coyote's work creates the history of life on earth, and then is finished. What happens when his work is done? The Native American story bears a significant similarity to Merlin's story which I think is worth noting:

> From the very beginning, Coyote was traveling around all over the earth. He did many wonderful things when he went along. He killed the monsters and the evil spirits that preyed on the people. He made the Indians, and put them out in tribes all over the world because Old Man Above wanted the earth to be inhabited all over, not just in one or two places.
>
> He gave all the people different names and taught them different languages. This is why Indians live all over the country now and speak in different ways.

He taught the people how to eat and how to hunt the buffalo and catch eagles. He taught them what roots to eat and how to make a good lodge and what to wear. He taught them how to dance. Sometimes he made mistakes, and even though he was wise and powerful, he did many foolish things. But that was his way.

Coyote liked to play tricks. He thought about himself all the time, and told everyone he was a great warrior, but he was not. Sometimes he would go too far with some trick and get someone killed. Other times he would have a trick played on himself by someone else. He got killed this way so many times that Fox and the birds got tired of bringing him back to life. Another way he got in trouble was trying to do what someone else did. This is how he came to be called Imitator. Coyote was ugly, too. The girls did not like him. But he was smart. He could change himself around and trick the women. Coyote got the girls when he wanted.

One time Coyote had done everything he could think of and was traveling from one place to another place, looking for other things that needed to be done. Old man saw him going along and said to himself, "Coyote has now done almost everything he is capable of doing. His work is almost done. It is time to bring him back to the place where he started."

So Great Spirit came down and traveled in the shape of an old man. He met Coyote. Coyote said, "I am Coyote. Who are you?"

Old Man said, "I am Chief of the earth. It was I who sent you to set the world right." "No," Coyote said, "you never sent me. I don't know you. If you are Chief, take that lake over there and move it to the side of that mountain." "No. If you are Coyote, let me see you do it." Coyote did it. "Now move it back." Coyote tried, but he could not do it. He thought this was strange. He tried again, but he could not do it. Chief moved the lake back. Coyote said, "Now I know you are the Chief." Old Man said, "Your work is finished, Coyote. You have traveled far and done much good. Now you will go to where I have prepared a home for you."

Then Coyote disappeared. Now no one knows where he is anymore. Old Man got ready to leave, too. He said to the Indians, "I will send messages to the earth by the spirits of the people who reach me but whose time to die has not yet come. They will carry messages to you from time to time. When their spirits come back into their bodies, they will revive and tell you their experiences.

"Coyote and myself, we will not be seen again until earth woman is very old. Then we shall return to earth, for it will require a change by that time. Coyote will come along first, and when you see him you will know I am coming. When I come along, all the spirits of the dead will be with me. There will be no more Other Side Camp. All the people will live together. Earthmother will go back to her first shape and live as a mother among her children. Then things will be made right."

Now they are waiting for Coyote.[65]

In this way, many Native Americans expressed their belief in an ordered universe that was moving toward completion. The essence of these messages of both Coyote and Merlin seems to be that our salvation is hidden within nature and in an anticipated feminine approach to nature.

The myths we have been hearing suggest that the Trickster gets things moving, reflects on his work, retreats into the world of nature while other powers have their moment in time, and reemerges in some new form bearing a feminine aspect in order to bring the work to completion. We might wonder if Coyote has returned with a vengeance, inundating us with more communicative devices than we ever wanted to know about, moving us around faster than ever with less perceivable boundaries. Earthmother is aging quickly under our fascination with excess and its experiment in overpopulation. When and how can the damage done to her be reversed?

Merlin and Coyote: have they reappeared as a final act? Have they brought their feminine aspects to the fore as yet? I think not, though they draw close. The anima aspect of these figures seems to me to be slowly materializing out of a shadowy background, like a photographic image gradually appearing in the developing process of the darkroom. This anima who has the perspicacity and wisdom of a trickster, and all the life-giving qualities of relatedness and caring that the feminine implies, is drawing close to all of us. We can feel her, almost see her, coming into focus. She is in our dreams, in our stories, in the experiences of visionaries, a bit of her in this woman, a bit in this man, as we all prepare on some level to recognize her when she comes into full view.

Rather than lay responsibility for the destruction of nature totally at the feet of the masculine, it must be said that some of the motivation for conquering nature came unquestionably from men who were trying to please women, trying to make life easier and more comfortable for their women and to lower the mortality rate in their children. What now can the feminine want? I think women want not only to feel free to contact their emotional and generative power, but also to have the value of their experiences validated and incorporated into society's fundamental structure. Perhaps the feminine and the Tnbrickster combined can bring creative solutions that enable us to have the best of both worlds, the world of technology and the world of the nature gods and goddesses.

CHAPTER V

ETUDES IN PARANOIA

Milan Kundera's heroine, Agnes, in the novel, *Immortality*, feels besieged by noise, greasy fast food, tasteless clothing, mannerless people, and a general lack of aesthetic sensibility. She abhors the ugliness around her:

> Suddenly frightened by her hatred, she said to herself: the world is at some sort of border; if it is crossed, everything will turn to madness: people will walk the streets holding forget-me-nots or kill one another on sight. And it will take very little for the glass to overflow, perhaps just one drop: perhaps just one car too many, or one person, or one decibel.[1]

At the dark heart of the paranoid complex we come to such a border; at first it appears a nebulous possibility, then there is a shift in levels or shades—is it a shadow, a rim, an unmarked crevice in the dark? Like Othello, we scan and scrutinize, wanting, yet not wanting, to find the limit we dread and need. Then there is that last step across the border, and the dear Desdemona in our soul is as good as dead.[2] Once the border is crossed and our suspicions justified, only a wise trickster can scramble the boundary again and get us back to hope.

Most of us are familiar with this paranoid complex. We come to this border from time to time: Am I imagining things, or am I being stalked? Is this coincidence, or am I the victim of a plot? Was this an accident, is this a streak of bad luck or am I jinxed? In a relationship the complex marks the line between trust and loneliness. For the person with a paranoid personality disorder, the tent is pitched here, on the borderline between hope and hopelessness. And here few can stand to camp with us—but Trickster can. She sees in the dark and has no fear of crossings. So here let us consider some of the murky borders that thrust themselves in front of us regularly in our society, borders that make us question our reality: the borders of truth, of goodness, of aggression.

LIES

> I want to unfold. I don't want to stay folded anywhere, because where I am folded, there I am a lie.
>
> R. M. Rilke[3]

Earlier in this book I have described our era as one of unfolding the shadow, or in Rilke's terms, exposing the truth. In the process of exposure, a shadowy mist envelops truth. Where is the line between promoting an image and distorting truth? Falsehoods pervade everything from campaign promises to fake breasts, from radiation experiments to hair coloring, from savings and loan scandals to a president's infidelities, from polite omissions to false personalities. A prototypical African story related by Robert Pelton shows how the Trickster god, Eshu, plays with notions of truth and falsehood:

> Once two friends owned adjoining farms. They dressed alike and were in all ways a model of friendship. Eshu decided to make them differ. He used to walk each morning on the path between the two farms, and one day set out wearing a multicolored cap, variously described as red and white; red, white and blue; or red, white, green and black. He also put his pipe at the nape of his neck instead of in his mouth, and let his staff hang over his back instead of his chest. He greeted the friends, already working in their fields, and passed on. Later they began to argue about the color of his cap and which way he was going.... Soon they came to blows. When they were brought before the king, Eshu confessed to igniting the quarrel because, "Sowing dissension is my great delight."[4]

To appreciate the story we need to know Eshu as an exuberant, erotic, playful mediator between gods and men, like Legba, but with his characteristic vengeance and anger more prominent. Eshu is essential to daily life among the Yoruba who give him the first sacrifice of the new year; build shrines to him at the entrances of compounds, markets, and crossroads; and anoint his pillar each day with palm oil. He stirs up human troubles so that men will offend the gods and have to offer sacrifice. The gods are hungry for sacrifice, and Eshu, the wicked dancer, provides for the greedy gods! In the story we have recounted the two friends are inseparable and unobservant of boundaries. Eshu fools them by causing each to miss what the other sees. Their quarrel establishes them as separate from one another and reveals their suppressed animosity.

Pelton, extracting from a story told by Thomas Merton, tells us that:

> One of the sayings of the desert fathers tells how two old brothers tried, for the sake of humility, to start a quarrel, but failed because they were detached even from their own opinions. Here, (in the Eshu story) on the contrary, there was surface harmony, but underneath lay suspicion, anger, and violence.[5]

Eshu shatters the false peace between the two friends by confusing the limits of truth. This may throw some light on the value of the discord in our society being stirred up from deep within its institutions and structures. Perhaps the peace of post-World War II USA was a surface peace—not a true peace, but an undifferentiated habit of polite calcification which began to be shattered in the tumultuous '60s, as previously unquestioned truths were questioned.

Clearly the USA is not the only country to have had its peace shattered. Other countries are going through cataclysmic losses of old traditions. Since the fall of the USSR, the fragmented Soviet states have seen a drastic increase in overt crime, one of the effects of the shattering of false peace. The peace of totalitarianism is an example of the calcification that tricksters attack. One of the most obvious bits of double deception between the old communist government and the New Soviet Man was the supposed love of labor without capital gain. A favorite Russian joke was, "The communists pretend to pay us; and we pretend to work!" Another deception was revealed at the lifting of the bans on churches in Russia after the demise of the communist government; then the survival of religious spirit which had existed covertly for seven decades became obvious. For years the Russians pretended to be atheists, but the desire for worship of something beyond the state could not be extinguished.

Like the need for excitement through a good fight, and the need for tenderness through a gentle touch, the need for a spiritual experience that holds all the pieces to a central point is fundamentally human. The need for completion and meaning, which Jung considered to be the unique contribution of human beings to the universe, has never been suppressed. A need for meaning motivates us humans to keep trying for some kind of reconciliation of our disturbing experiences of divine cruelty and mercy. Our genetic makeup seems to evince a spiritual appetite.

What is diminished, if not shattered worldwide, is not only the peace which results from a belief in the truth of our governments, but also a peace which results from the acceptance of the authority of churches. The structures, not the spirit, of religion seem to be under attack, some from outer antagonistic forces, others from self-destructive forces. The human drive for spirituality continually seeks channels and rituals for expression, but many people feel betrayed and lied to by representatives of existing religious institutions. An appetite for the spiritual tries to nourish itself on sports, or art, or self-growth, or the political State, or extraterrestrial pursuits, all of which are constructive but ultimately disappointing without a transpersonal dimension. Shattered is the peace that former generations experienced through the security of belonging to a "true" church.

Perhaps the Trickster has been provoked to play mischief with religious institutions because they have excluded exactly those contents that are needed to infuse life into their dry bones: femininity, instinctuality, and inclusiveness. Today those contents, absent from most institutionalized religions, are being exposed repeatedly through dreams, collective imagery, and collective patterns of behavior, and if we listen to those expositions we will find ways to dialogue with an inner source of divine wisdom. But how do we transpose that dialogue—between conscious mind and the inner wisdom which honors diversification, and the instinctual, and the feminine—into a visible religious context? The peace of most cultural institutions has been maintained by excluding femininity, instinctuality, and tolerance of differences, and therefore is a false peace, like that of the neighbors who did not expose their differences until stirred up by Eshu.

Edinger describes our present state as an emergence of spirit, rather than an end: "God has fallen out of containment in religion and into the unconscious of man, i.e., he is incarnating."[6] Incarnating, I would add, inclusive of darker, more feminine, and more humorous aspects. The dark, comely, sensuous, and clever Shulamite is pushing her way up through the cracks in the marble floors of the Western monolithic cathedral. This is happening in each of us; each must make a personal effort to contact the inner wisdom. Additionally, we are required to make a collective effort to contact our personal revelations and communicate them through dialogue as a community if our culture is to prosper spiritually.

Connection with inner wisdom (also known as Sophia, or the Shulamite, or the Shekinah, to mention some of Wisdom's names) as we do through the revitalizing potential of the unconscious, and the challenge of response to each other, we may discover new skins for our spiritual wine. A woman told me that she had dreamed of being given a chalice; instead of dark, full-bodied wine the chalice contained candy…sticky sweet and lacking substance, spirit, or nutritive value. In her next dream or active imagination, she might throw the insipid contents to the floor, take the empty chalice to the altar and demand the blood of life, perhaps consecrating the wine herself.

Again, here is how Edinger amplifies the passion that is implied in that dream:

> For us an adequate knowledge of the psyche is probably a matter of life and death. If the emergent God that wants to be born in man is not humanized and transformed by a sufficient number of conscious individuals, its dark aspect can destroy us.
>
> As it gradually dawns on people, one by one, that the transformation of God is not just an interesting idea but is a living reality, it may begin to function as a new myth. Whoever recognizes this myth as his own personal reality will put his life in the service of this process. Such an individual offers himself as a vessel for the incarnation of deity and thereby promotes the on-going transformation of God by giving Him human manifestation.[7]

I expect "the emergent God" of whom Edinger speaks to include many more feminine values, as a result of Trickster's shaking loose the inflexible structures of our culture, and challenging their truths.

A legend recounted by Israel Regardie about the origin of the Egyptian Tarot cards suggests that there were Cabbalists who predicted the deconstruction of religions and who felt the need to protect and maintain spiritual awareness, and particularly knowledge about the tree-of-life and the Sephiros, in some form accessible to the individual outside of the organized church. It is a legend that reflects the influence and cleverness of the Egyptian trickster god, Thoth, as he acted through the persons concerned with preserving truth:

> The adepts of antiquity, seeing that a period of spiritual degradation and intellectual stagnation was about to descend upon Europe with the advent of the Christian Era, considered how to preserve their accumulated knowledge. They wanted to reserve it for a later time when people would be spiritually advanced enough to receive the truth, yet make it accessible to those who were already able to devote themselves to the study. Several plans were suggested and discarded, until one adept proposed reducing all knowledge of the universe to symbols suitable for use as a game. Thereby the wisdom of the ages could pass unnoticed by the herd, while presenting clues to those in search of truth. An adept-artist painted seventy-eight hieroglyphs representing

symbolically some particular aspect of life and the cosmos. So the Tarot deck has come down to us as hidden truths, and it is said that should a person be incarcerated without instructions of any kind, it would still be possible to obtain from the cards an encyclopedic knowledge of the essence of all religions, sciences, and philosophies.[8]

Today we seem to be encoding spiritual values in a number of unorthodox ways, not as well planned and thought through as in this legendary example of the Cabbalists, but nevertheless, holding on as best we can to truth, and hiding it from destructive forces when necessary. Some ways that come to mind are the interest in studying archetypal themes; individual and small group spiritual studies or rituals; the passing along of spiritual knowledge through songs, dance, movies and stories; and, in the spirit of Trickster, exploring lying to the brink of nihilism. Ironically, the more we become wise to the lies we are asked to believe in order to comply with collective positions and attitudes, the closer we come to an appreciation of truth as a spiritual value. And, through the proliferation of electronic networks, it is hard to imagine that any one lie could be hidden from the public for very long.

A woman had the following dreams on two successive nights. In this extraordinary period of 48 hours, the dreamer was approached by forces suppressing religion, truth-telling, and the humble feminine ordering principle. Without delving into her personal shadow in her dream protocols, as we read her dreams we are reminded that these three subjects are under attack in the larger objective psyche:

> DREAM 1: Pope John Paul II is beaten to death as he waits to get on a plane at an airport. I ask people who saw it to describe the scene. They make downward striking motions with their hands. Then I am in a church where a dead man lies. It is not the Pope, but a minister. As we leave the church others are chastised, perhaps shot.
>
> DREAM 2: I am trying to convince someone to tell the truth. It is the press versus individual expression. I say, "No matter what happens, one should tell the truth…no matter who gets in trouble."
>
> DREAM 3: Annie, the housekeeper, is dead. A hymn comes from a church, "O let all who suffer, let them come to the water."

I was struck by the repetition of a process in the dreams, like the progression we have seen in the myths of Coyote and Merlin. There is first death of the spiritual authority, then a struggle for truth, then a sense of work completed; finally, a hymn (Let them come to the water) leads to *solutio*, the symbol of reflection, purification, and renewal. Water purifies through inclusion; we are absorbed and united with the whole through immersion, and upon re-emerging, are born anew. Again we are brought to these images: completion, reflection, purification through immersion, and the opportunity for the emergence of a new development, as I superimpose imagery from the Trickster myths upon this client's dream material.

The myths suggest this process also: Trickster's completion of his work, withdrawing into a state of reflection and purification through immersion in nature, and a (promised) return in completion with a feminine principle. Now, this cycle may be ancient and repetitive, so is there any new truth to be gained by observing it? What seems new to me for our times in this schema is the notion that there could be a period of withdrawal and reflection, instead of a relentless effort to slay the dragons that threaten progress. We have been given images of progress that move swiftly to defeat enemies of progress, but few images of allowing ourselves to reflect on what is happening and what the consequences of action will be. We kill an unwanted plant with a chemical which subsequently poisons the ground water; hence, we treat the ground water with chemicals which in turn cause disturbances in the bodies of the drinkers. Then we medicate the drinkers, creating reactive side-effects. In the end, we find, too late, that the cure for the side-effects was in the plant which was killed originally. To this kind of scenario, Trickster and his Woman, who slows him down, say, "Wait! Don't rush into heroic solutions. What seemed true may not be the whole truth. Let's get another perspective and reflect on the big picture." Jung spoke of a "reflective instinct" which transformed a natural stimulus-response process into a conscious content.[9]

There is a certain resistance toward facing the truth when one is in a hurry to come to a solution or conclusion. At such times we may be so invested in the endpoint or goal that we gloss over the accuracy or relevance of the process taken to achieve the goal. An old Irish saying reflecting the human tendency to compromise the truth when in haste is, "The devil is very quick!"

Another situation in which we tend to compromise the truth or ignore real facts is when we are particularly fond of a belief, and want to maintain its value in spite of evidence that contradicts the belief. The struggle for truth has preoccupied religions for at least two thousand years as each religion claims to have "the Truth," whereas to a Trickster-eyed view, each one has a partial truth. The relationship in Christian theology between the God of Truth and Satan, Father of Lies, resembles the relationship between the high gods and tricksters in other theologies. Satan's presence at the dawn of creation is true of such tricksters, as are Satan's tricky interventions that harass both God and humankind and create discord in relationships between all three, God, human, and Devil or Trickster. But unlike the typical Trickster god, Satan's actions serve only himself and lead to terminal pain, not eventual benefit. Satan's prideful antagonism toward God is uppermost, and humans are his pawns. Trickster, though, remains the benefactor of humankind.[10] But when and why, then, would he affirm lying? How are we to understand that the God of Liars guides us to the moment of truth? We are asked to suspend ordinary operating standards in order to permit access to the God of Truth/Lie that might otherwise remain submerged and hidden in banality.

Moved by the God of Liars, we lie, to different degrees and in different ways. Small children usually experiment with lying. It is a sign of intelligence and ego-strength, as they learn to separate from authority and explore their own reality; it is a sign of emerging awareness of the psyche, a way of showing that the inner world has its power, too. Through deliberate lying the child demonstrates that he has achieved an important distinction between literal and imaginal realities. With a growing sense of community, children tend to respect the group vision and norms and give up lying during the middle years. However, adolescents often find it necessary to protect themselves with false leads. If relationships are primarily positive, adolescents eventually discern that lying erodes trust, and trust is an important comfort, especially with respect to those closest to us. Adults sometimes lie by withholding truth, afraid to pay the consequences of being messengers of bad news or controversy. To the extent that we withhold truth, even when controversial, we miss out on fully participating in life; to hearken back to Rilke's words, we remain "folded." Yet folds can be exciting; the unexplored dimension invites intrigue and exploration. Lying is not merely nihilistic, but sometimes expansive and creative.

Lying—regardless of the length of its consequences—is momentary in nature, not long-ranged. We lie by closing our eyes—the "evil eyeblink," or refusal to see the truth. We lie to extend possibility and thereby have a sense of participating in creation. For instance, a patient who feels ashamed of her poor education leads people to believe she is a college graduate; others fabricate exciting life-histories or exaggerate their accomplishments. It is fascinating to watch people in group therapy mislead the group by withholding information. When our psychic stamina is weak, we lie to maintain inflation, to protect our narcissism, to avoid expending energy, to vent our envy. With luck and good will we grow toward a degree of complexity that makes truth more risky and exciting than being folded;

risking more and more of truth we become larger than fear and falsehood. The greatest evil persists in its lie, until the bond between the liar and her lie is greater than any other bond.

In this area of truth-telling, any change in the collective handling of truth will have to be built from the bottom up—from the individual of integrity to the honest group, as Kohlberg demonstrated could be done. Truth-telling clearly cannot be dictated from on high, but must be gradually established through small acts of trust, multiplied exponentially. When one cannot risk trust, one chooses the lie as one's partner and lives well within the secure boundaries of paranoia. Nevertheless, Trickster is there as well.

EVIL

> Whatsoever I've feared has come to life
> Whatsoever I've fought off became my life
> Now I'm doing time cause I fell on black days.
> *Soundgarden* (alternative rock band)

In this description by Soundgarden of what Jung would describe as "living out the shadow," we get a glimpse of the double-edged quality of what we call evil—on one hand, it is what we fear; on the other, it is what we desire. The question of whether a *principle* of evil exists is reborn continually in our psyches. Each time we ponder a moral choice, a dialogue between inner forces weighs the consequences and makes us wonder about the author of each possibility: do we answer to a god or a devil? Phenomenologically, when we risk a moral choice, we dip down into the depths of our private moral foundations. We wonder which is the path of Good, which the way of Evil? Even the most sophisticated of us eventually comes to this dim basement of the spirit at some time. What shall we do? We must cast our faith into one choice or the other. But is there such a thing as evil beyond our experience of wrongdoing that we have been conditioned to feel, an evil force that exists outside of every particular culture's notions of right and wrong, an evil force that exists beyond our projections of our personal shadows?

On a cosmic scale, it seems to me that the question of absolute evil can never be answered; every instance of destruction can be interpreted as having some ultimately positive purpose, and what appears as evil can only be judged relativistically from the human point of view. But from that human, historical experience, it seems there is no question that evil exists, and that we may choose it.

Ethicist Nell Noddings identifies three forms of evil: natural (disease, death, disasters); cultural (poverty, war); moral (deliberate infliction of unnecessary pain).[11] I would like to look at these forms of evil in terms of the idea of *privatio boni*, considering evil as a privation or absence of good. Theologians have long debated whether evil exists as an entity in itself. The debate was kept alive by Jung and theologian Victor White, and it continues today.[12]

Kerényi says: "We should not hesitate to search for the primal cause of evil. Once we see it clearly, we may be less evil than we are now."[13] Kerényi's words reassure me. Nevertheless, in the nineties I have to admit that trying to talk about evil strikes me as naive, perhaps absurd, and at the very least, an opening to ridicule. Therefore, in the name of Lilith, I proceed.

The debate focuses upon the question, "Is there an evil force in nature, or is natural evil simply an absence of perfection?" We might see the "faults" of nature as evils, yet a perfect natural world is inconceivable, in so far as there would be no movement or change. Darkness, pain, and death are necessary for regeneration, but only from the point of view of the individual ego can darkness, pain, and death be considered evil. Reason alone cannot encompass any conclusions regarding the nature of evil in the natural world. As a positive force, each disease represents some organism's right to life, and even death can be seen as an absence of those factors which support life. Also, death is a necessary part of the cyclical life process. While we might ask why the universe should be cyclical instead of permanently sustained in a pleasant state (paradise), we have no guarantees that such stability would be more to our liking (more "good") than the present state of affairs. Certainly experience would be less intense. Even with its suffering, this may be the best natural world, because it exists and sustains life, exactly due to the features we think of as imperfections. Still, we wonder, does it have to be quite so painful? "To gods all things are beautiful, good and just; to man one thing is unjust, another just," said Heraclitus.[14] But did the gods think it through?!

What of Nodding's second form, cultural evil? Is it absolute? Like natural evil, cultural evil can be seen as an absence of factors necessary to maintain pleasant conditions, and not necessarily a result of an evil principle at work. Cultural "ism's" are misguided dreams, and become destructive through ignorance of their future consequences and of their effects on the broader world screen. War, genocide, and group hatred certainly feel bad and lead to destruction on both sides, but neither side can be identified as pure evil, for each side is thinking of its own good or the survival of its own values. Even a suicidal group sacrifices for the sake of some ideal.

Noddings third category, moral evil, is complicated by individual decisions and determinants. Evil by deliberate choice, especially when the choice is to take pleasure in hurting another, lends strength to the argument that evil is not just an absence of good, but a viable force to contend with on the psychological level. In examining my phenomenological experience of an evil principle, I find that I can only experience evil when I am fully emotionally engaged, and unable to distance myself philosophically. Staying in the intellect is always less messy than factoring in emotional data, and intellectually I can be as clear as Victor White about a god who is all good (for example, by defining good as that which exists, and evil as the absence of existence). But examining my own capacity to choose evil deliberately, and projecting that capacity onto others who are similar to myself, the phenomenological experience is one of having a choice of being deliberately destructive or not. I can easily imagine identifying with a nasty streak of meanness which negates any positive force. Certainly, sad to say, I have wished harm to others.

Envy of God has traditionally been given as the origin of human evil. Derivatives of this envy of God translate into the envy of parents by the child, or therapist by the narcissistic patient, as a response to feeling deprived and estranged. Feelings such as envy can foster great suffering both in oneself, and when imposed on others. Ought we then to define envy as an absence of good feeling and therefore not a cause of evil in itself? But what of envy which provokes the wish to destroy its object? What if the envious one kills her rival because she feels less adequate? Can we say she acts because of an absence of good, or because of the presence of a willingness to kill?

In another case, the desire to have a perfect world fosters great suffering. Is the desire for perfection an evil in itself, or an absence of good? To envision a world free of inferior beings who cause trouble and use up resources does not seem such a terrible idea in the abstract; but when the Nazis carried out their concept of perfection by murdering the retarded, mentally ill, homeless, homosexuals, gypsies, and Jews, someone had to actualize the idea, had to look into the eyes of another and will them to die. Such cruelty, even for a "reasonable" cause, seems unarguably evil. Yet murder with similar justification by means of "just" wars, euthanasia, capital punishment, and abortion is acceptable to many of us who can justify the killing.

Still another case of evil most of us can relate to: disciplining children to teach them right from wrong seems reasonable; but who can justify the damage to body and soul in a child actually beaten or broken-spirited? Many of us can remember a particular teacher who seemed to enjoy breaking spirits in the name of building character. Was she evil, or just dimwitted? The willingness to carry through ideas and feelings that impose pain and suffering on others when we know there are alternatives may be evidence of an evil principle. While we may not author the ideas and feelings that come to us, we have a part in judging them as doable.

One definition of evil is that which is not able to be transformed. Then there is no repentance, no wish to change, and no regret.[15] Another definition considers evil to be betrayal.[16] Still another definition is the refusal of life, the denial of being. Kerényi, after finding no evil principle among the gods in Greek mythology, concluded that murder as an act of "utter evil" and not a purposive separation, belongs only to man, not to god nor beast. Not that joy in cruelty does not exist among the gods and beasts, but Kerényi defines evil as "desiring to kill." He believes that it is impossible to not cause suffering, but that "we must strive for a kind of education that will teach man not to kill, and to cause as little suffering as possible."[17] Karen Armstrong describes the evolution of Satan from a loving angel to a figure of "ungovernable evil."[18]

Once, in the inwardly focused state that I am often in at the end of an analytic session, I did something that a patient took as dismissive, when actually, I was preoccupied by concern for her. The patient returned for her next appointment in a rage, having perceived me as uncaring. She reported that during the days between our meetings she had found herself with violent feelings toward me. She thought with pleasure about eviscerating me with her bare hands, tearing me apart. The patient had recognized this as a familiar state; she had been there before. She knew that allowing herself to remain in this state of hateful fantasy would prevent her from focusing on other things. "I would lose myself," is how she put it. The more she imagined my violent death at her hands, the more she wanted to imagine it. Finally, during the separation between sessions, anticipating that she would "lose herself" this way and feel very depressed, exhausted, and out of touch with reality, she began to try to suppress the thoughts. Over and over she put the thoughts out of her mind, until gradually she could look at them objectively.

What veil separated her from acting on this murderous feeling, rather than deciding to suppress it?. What experience of loss is contained by this murderous fantasy? How much should I encourage it to be spoken of so that the loss can be lived out, and when do I advise someone to put it away? What may be lost in the act of suppressing the fantasy? Before I had to make these decisions she made a conscious choice to not entertain the fantasies, and was able to refocus her attention and not become depleted by the hatred. She remembered the state of her rage and brought the experience to her next session, so we were able to talk about what we each had experienced. Of course I want to explore the full extent of her fantasy and her hatred. But I am not advocating suppression of feelings when I suggest that sometimes it appears that we know all we need to know about our hatred, and have only to choose how we will use ourselves. Psychologist Carl Goldberg, in a study of malevolent behavior, concluded that evil deeds are learned by doing. "Each decision to rationalize a contemptuous act makes it easier to perform subsequent contemptuous act. Inevitably the result is an addiction to rationalizing cruel, insensitive behavior."[19] He points out that opportunities to choose between good and bad occur continually in daily life, and how we respond influences future choices. Will I be an instrument of death, or of pain, or will I put my hatred behind me and become an instrument of peace, communication, perhaps art?

Clarissa Pinkola Estes suggests that when we refuse to entertain evil, we drive it down into the deepest layers of the psyche "where all creation is as yet unformed, and let it bubble in that etheric soup til we can find a better form for it to fill."[20]

Popular questions about evil usually turn on degrees of freedom of choice. In the example above, my patient was able to reflect on her choices, and was not driven totally by passion. Through several notorious cases in the courts in recent years involving homicidal parents, homicidal children, homicidal spouses, homicidal arsonists and assassins, homicidal competitors in the sports world, celebrities who have killed or molested children or have sold deadly drugs to children, it has become obvious that the public in general is not able to define a murderer as a "bad" person. We are so moved by the psychological dimensions of murderers, so understanding of motives, and so rich in identification with the shadow, that we are reluctant to bring a verdict of guilty onto anyone. We seem to only blame the circumstances or society. This is discouraging to those whose job it is to protect others. It may be a sign that there is evil at large and it has the upper hand; yet, it could be a sign of movement toward greater objectivity and differentiation of evil, that we are more able to see and empathize with the total person, and not just with two-dimensional illusions. For victims, this means great frustration and sadness; for perpetrators, compassion; for all, the awesome reality of the complexity that is human.

In addition to considering forms of evil as Noddings does, I find it useful to differentiate attitudes toward evil. We can examine evil philosophically, psychologically, and phenomenologically. To look at evil philosophically, as a cosmic force or universal principle, for example, one can rationalize and accept evil as a necessary balance of positive-negative charges. Psychologically, evil can be rationalized as a response to some stimulus, or a complex expressing itself through an individual who perceives it to be justified. Both these approaches demand a detachment from the subjective feelings of an embodied human spirit. To achieve either of these two approaches we assume an inflated position, an archetypal mindset which places us outside of the human condition.

Jung must ignore the omniscience of God to question God's goodness; that in doing so Jung makes himself a blasphemer and judge of God, the Unknowable Mystery beyond all good and evil. Yet psychologically we recognize that Jung touched that place in each human being who feels some part of his or her fate to be unjust. This, it seems to me, was Jung's impassioned answer to those who posit the concept of *privatio boni*.

If evil is substantive, as Jung maintained, from where does it originate? "All evil comes from man" is a belief attributed to Basil the Great of the fourth century. But Jung asserts that if we credit humanity with being the source of evil, we create a tremendous inflation; has man or woman the power to spoil God's creation? Jung cautions that if we reduce evil to an "absence" or "nothingness," who will take his shadow seriously? Whose responsibility is the serpent in paradise? Who is the author of Lucifer's arrogance? If God is the author, must we split God into light and dark?

Victor White's position is held today by those who interpret Jung's insistence on substantive evil to be a form of Manichaeism. But Jung persisted in identifying his God-image as containing both good and evil in a mystery beyond comprehension; furthermore, Jung's image of the Tremendum wants humans to relate in a human mode, with curiosity and emotional availability. White told Jung that if evil was not an "absence of good," he could see no meaning or motive for integrating his shadow. For him, the shadow was a "good deprived of good."[21]

The image of an all-good God is relatively new in human history. Images of divine figures who incorporate evil principles are ancient and are frequently feminine in mythology. Mesopotamian mythology had a sea-monster, Ti'amat, as the feminine enemy of the creator. Paradoxically she inhabited the sea, the womb of all conscious beings, which suggests that she was both life-giving and death-giving. She represented absolute matter, and was split by spirit in the form of her son, Marduk. Also in earliest Judaism, evil was portrayed as a cosmic principle, usually a sea monster, who would periodically emerge and suffer defeat by other cosmic forces. Jews also posited the Golem, an evil colossus who came to life when a magic word was placed under its tongue.

In the Cabbalistic Tree of Life (see Chapter IV), the root of evil is found in the fifth Sephirah, Din (God's Stern Judgment), which is balanced by being paired with Hesed (Mercy). Sometime in early Judaism the figure of Satan appeared, a son of Yahweh who could only act with Yahweh's approval, which meant that Satan's evil originated in Yahweh. But later, probably influenced by Zoroastrianism, Satan gradually acquired the reputation as the source of evil.[22] Instead of a god or gods who contained potential for both good and evil, Satan became known as God's adversary, the shadow of an impossibly good and frightening God; but unlike Trickster, Satan within Christianity came to be considered a symbol absolutely evil; as such he is the antithesis of the sacred.

Karen Armstrong states that the Zohar constantly defines evil as something that has become separated, or which has entered into a relationship for which it is unsuited. Therefore, Din (Stern Judgment) is beneficial, unless it is separated by Hesed (Mercy), in which case it becomes destructive.:

> One of the problems of ethical monotheism is that it isolates evil. Because we cannot accept the idea that there is evil in our God, there is a danger that we will not be able to endure it within ourselves. It can then be pushed away and made monstrous and inhuman. The terrifying image of Satan in Western Christendom was such a distorted projection."[23]

But even though the monotheistic religions separated good and evil, there have been hermetic figures within the ranks who were illumined by the spirit Mercurius, as shown by their appreciation for paradox, their inclusiveness, and their capacity to relate to all factions, including the most humble. For instance, a sixth century Greek Christian using the pseudonym of "Denys the Areopagite" saw God as having two natures, one which turned toward us and was immersed in creation, and one far side which stays in eternal mystery and is ineffable. Denys believed that every Christian could achieve ecstatic union with God through paradoxical prayer that takes us out of our intellects and our senses, and into a place of silence. Also, he believed that ecstasy was found in the humblest of things and smallest of gestures.[24]

Another hermetic figure was the twelfth century Iranian Sufi, Yahya Suhrawardi, who made a life's work of unifying Islam with Greek and Oriental philosophies. He claimed all sages preached a single doctrine, and he identified Hermes with Idris in the Koran and Enoch in the Bible. He integrated seemingly unrelated studies of physical science, metaphysics, pagan philosophy, monotheism, and mysticism, and was known as Master of Illumination. He was also a creative artist who helped Muslims find symbols of meaning for their lives.[25]

The Rabbis of the first century also used paradox to glimpse the mystery of God and liked images of "glory" and "Holy Spirit" to remind themselves of the inadequacy of words to describe God. Armstrong tells us that one of the favorite synonyms for God was the Shekinah, derived from the Hebrew word meaning to "dwell with" or "pitch one's tent with." This was an image of a God who accompanies us in our wanderings and is always an accessible presence on earth.[26] The Rabbis stressed community as "one body, one soul," which was the "New Temple",[27] just as Christians saw themselves as the "body of Christ."

On the cosmic plane of mythology Trickster is never simply evil, as Satan has become in the normative Christian tradition. Trickster, for one thing, is not motivated by pure pride, as is Satan, and his evil mischief relieves some of the tension between gods and humans, promoting good feeling in the long run. Not only does Trickster make fools of humans, but also of himself and other divinities. He exalts the lowly, and thereby becomes closer to Christ than to Satan. As we saw in the story of the trial of Hermes for the death of Argus, Hermes accepts responsibility for his evil deeds in the same spirit as Christ, whereas Satan creates tension by setting himself up in total rebellion without any guilt or effort to redeem himself. In contrast to Trickster, Satan represents a singular one-sidedness, and would never distance himself from his evil to admit regrets, whereas Trickster would never be caught in so unilateral a position.

A trickster figure avoids serious evil by his complexity; we might say, his excesses are performed in moderation. We find in myths and folk tales that he is guilty of each of the seven deadly sins at one time or another, but never lingers long enough in any sin to become entrapped in it. Perhaps this is the best model he can give us for the fix the world is in: Don't dally with inflation. Don't linger in madness. And especially, resist being trapped in pride and arrogance. Trickster also escapes being evil by his natural good-will toward men. Male and female tricksters model for us the possibility of self-love without hubris. Without a great investment in pride, competition becomes just another way of relating playfully to our fellow players, and not a cause for fighting to the death.

Trickster, unlike an absolute evil principle, brings relativity into being and has made itself felt in the Christian Church (unofficially, not through dogma) through certain rituals, usually carryovers from pagan celebrations. One of these was the Fool's Mass, a popular spoof of the Mass during medieval times. Held in the church, it included satirical ceremonies and sacrilegious figures, such as braying asses substituting for choirboys.

The Trickster, like Christ, spans and mediates the lower and higher worlds. From the bestial to the mystical, from the base, contemptible *prima materia*, to the pearl of great price, divine life moves with the swiftness of death. Judaism's and Christianity's relationship to matter has been extremely ambivalent, at times holding physical matter sacred, at times repudiating it. The importance of the material world, especially the body, has been verified by Christianity's basic belief: that God assumed a human body, underwent death, and was resurrected. That soul and body will be restored to unity at the second coming Christians believe was modeled for humankind by Christ, and confirmed by the doctrine of the bodily assumption of Mary into heaven. Nevertheless, the body and its instinctual desires was considered a danger to an attitude of unselfishness required of Christians. The image of a pleasure-seeking body, dwelling place of the Trickster Archetype, came to be more associated with Satan's realm than with Christ's (see Chapter IV).

Currently most clergy who accept psychological attitudes believe that a good relationship to the body is essential to self-control and the capacity to act altruistically, and that repressive methods of discipline are not conducive to a healthy degree of self-esteem, self-control, empathy. Psychologists would agree that fear and punishment do not deter antisocial behavior, any more than repressive governments can eliminate spirituality. But early in the history of Christianity, stoic influences led to Satan appropriating all the chthonic power. Being concerned with bodily pleasure and well-being came to be associated with the devil. This trend left Christ the man and his virtuous mother looking limp and pale, and gave Christians no model for healthy instinctual vitality.

The Christian church's intention to interpret the laws of nature has, in today's antiauthoritarian world, led to discord. Christians, lay people and clergy, are not easily convinced of the divine inspiration of the church's leaders, nor of what doctrines can be considered free from historical and humanly personal influence and representative of purely natural law. On questions of morality, particularly where they involve sexuality and death, not all Christians are willing to grant their church infallibility. An example of discord within the Catholic Church is the issue of gender of priests. While providing the patriarchal leadership demanded by the Catholic Church, Pope John Paul II intends to respect the feminine principle and sees the church's refusal to admit women to the priesthood as compatible with the will of Mary. Catholic feminists cannot accept this as truth.

Jung maintained that the split in Western culture between the gods of nature, which came to be personified in Satan as absolute evil, and the god of spirit or Logos, incarnated as the Christ, would always be the source of great suffering. He pointed to the Gnostics and alchemists as healers of the split by their attempt to reconcile these opposites. The alchemists did not see Mercurius as the antithesis of God, although they assumed there was some linkage to Satan on the dark side. They saw that every substance and event had its dark possibilities. Jung wrote:

> In the Christian mentality the dark antagonist is always the devil. As I have shown, Mercurius escapes this prejudice by only a hair's breadth. But he escapes it, thanks to the fact that he scorns to carry on opposition at all costs. The magic of his name enables him, in spite of his ambiguity and duplicity, to keep outside the split, for as an ancient pagan god he possesses a natural undividedness which is impervious to logical and moral contradictions. This gives him invulnerability and incorruptibility. the very qualities we urgently need to heal the split in ourselves.[28]

To trust the hidden truth in each of us and to try to remain undivided, open to our pathologies and evil possibilities, seems to be our key to healing from the evil we suffer.

> I turn your face around! It is my face. That frozen rage is what I must explore—Oh secret, self-enclosed, and ravaged place! This is the gift I thank Medusa for.
>
> *May Sarton*[29]

Violence

> Writing saved me from the sin and inconvenience of violence.
>
> *Alice Walker*[30]

One morning I watched a TV news-show hostess interviewing the author of a popular cartoon show noted for its amusing portrayal of children engaged in violent, self-destructive, and pornographic behavior. The author is defending his artistic right to satirize and to focus on the obscenities of youth. His characters are meant to illustrate the mentality of "latch-key" kids growing up without the influence of a reflective attitude modeled by thoughtful adults. He admits the humor is aimed at adults, not children. He appears cool, cerebral, impeccably casual. Also interviewed by phone is a woman representing a parents' group that is concerned about the influence of TV violence and obscenity on the psyches of children. She appears concerned, articulate, impeccably conservative. To the author the answer is simple: If you don't like it, don't let your kids watch it. The woman-representing-parents argues that parents cannot have perfect control over what their children watch at friends' homes, nor over the influence on them of a society which bombards its members with obscene and violent messages. Behind the very sophisticated facades of these two people the passionate forces that fuel their well-tempered argument strain for expression. We hear the growing edge, we feel the heat rising. Finally the author's hostility breaks through the glass of political debate and slashes at the mother with a caustic remark about the probable stupidity of her children.

The hostess cheerily evades the depth of the struggle and wraps up the piece with a chirpy gush of pleasantry toward the angry man in her studio. We get only a glimpse of the woman-representing-parents somewhere out in the world beyond the studio as she unflinchingly takes this cut without retaliating. The surface image of the well-appointed, poised young woman holds still in front of my eyes for a split second, and then I see the bear mother within her as it leaps out of her body and across the airwaves, crashing through the studio. With one swipe of her massive paw she wipes the supercilious hostess out of her way and goes for the author with claws bared. Off fly his little granny glasses; his impeccable collarless shirt is becoming stained. The studio empties. A quick thinking cameraman calls the animal control unit who rush over with a tranquilizer gun.

Meanwhile, a bag lady, curious about the pandemonium as people dash out of the studio, wanders in. Seeing the frenzied animal, she sits down and opens up a stale pastrami on rye which she places between herself and the raging bear. When the animal control team arrives the bag lady is amusing the bear-mother with some street stories. The bleeding author cowers in fear. Perhaps he, too, is an innocent, unaware of the damage he perpetrates. As the needle pierces the thick fur of the beast, the author whimpers with relief and is carried to an ambulance. The meddling bag-lady is sanctimoniously shooed out and off the premises. She heads for a nearby garbage can to replenish her food supply…

I turn off the TV which has gone to commercial, and ponder the rage inside me that fed this fantasy. I'm familiar with this violent bear-mother that comes over me when I know that children are being mistreated, and when adults refuse to look at their responsibility in the corruption of innocence, even the innocent in themselves. The smug perpetrator of violent television art reminds me of the violated child in me, and the violence I have done to the innocence of others, but he does not appear able to take in the pain of this. His arrogance renders him non-reflective and non-negotiating. The violence I refer to is not just overt sexual and physical abuse of the sort that social services investigate constantly these days. I am thinking about the thoughtless, deceitful, withholding, manipulative, neglectful kinds of things done to children, even in the name of good parenting, or good entertainment, or good, clean fun. Like enjoying shaming them. Like avoiding relating to them. Like this cartoonist who draws children hurting old people for a few laughs, and caustically insults a parent when she tries to tell him why this bothers her. Like me, when I come at my children with emotional guns blazing in the frenzy of needing to control nature—their nature, my nature, our milieu. In these ways we teach children that anything that grows is worth cutting down, when we should be teaching them to plant and water small growing things.

But parents are in a position today that may have never existed before in the history of mankind; they have no group mores to pass on which can be supported by the community. Even children of small sects and closely knit families cannot be totally isolated from the larger society with its mixed messages because of mass communications. No matter what their parents or extended family believe, children today learn many of their values from the media. With violent crime such a virulent blight on our society, a vital question arises about the role of art and entertainment in reflecting and fostering violence. Whether we see art as imitating life or shaping it, we cannot deny art's power to articulate morality.

A trickster attitude would be in favor of artistic expression. But Steven Spielberg, for one, expresses some restraint in exercising his license as an artist. The Oscar-winning director of the movie *Schindler's List*, points out that while he does not advocate government censorship, there is a "fine line between censorship and good taste and moral responsibility." Speaking of a recording company's decision to distribute a rap song about cop-killing, Spielberg says,

> Had I been head of Warner's, I wouldn't have. I would have said my conscience won't let me scream, "Fire!" in a crowded theater.... I've always been full of hope...but we can't just sit back and be inactive and simply hope things are going to turn out all right for our children and their grandchildren.... We have a duty to voice our opinion and to work to fix the world.[31]

In discussing issues of evil and morality in the cinema, Jungian writer Martin Schlappner notes that film noire looks at the criminal from within with an attempt to understand him; such films present an ambivalent, non-judgmental view of criminality, and are not interested in morality or immorality. They are certainly in the realm of Trickster. But Schlappner describes the great Alfred Hitchcock, Eric von Stroheim, and Federico Fellini as film producers who sent clear and deliberate moral messages. Schlappner says:

> Evil is not always evident; it may also be concealed in good, but also in the most inconspicuous, the most trifling of our actions which, because we do not hale them before the judgment seat of our ethical principles, do not seem to involve our responsibility. The criminal, who is shown us in the tempting light that evil often emits, makes us aware of our own inclination to do evil in one way or another.[32]

Schlappner shows that Hitchcock approaches life with a lens open to human guilt—guilt in the context of suspense and distanced by the "irony of wisdom."[33] This style is of the essence of the Trickster: it allows wisdom to emerge through irony which distances us from our suffering.

On the other hand, von Stronheim, Schlappner says, "does not take refuge in ironic aloofness, he reacts passionately to the ways of men…"[34] The ways of men are to seek totality, "open to consuming evil, to the hurtful and menacing, who harbors the will to evil as an integral part of a full life, for a full life demands something more than smug virtue."[35] Von Stronheim's creations portray the multidimensionality of human nature, including love and the cruelty that follows love's desperation.

Finally, Schlappner presents Fellini as an artist who is not only interested in human suffering and guilt, but passionately interested in man's salvation in this world and the next:

> To him the mystery of man is the confluence of the mighty irrational currents of spiritual existence, of love and salvation, humility and incarnation—and in the center of the concentric layers of reality is God, the key to all mysteries.[36]

Fellini cannot be accused of being incognizant of Trickster's wisdom; the characters in Fellini's movies reflect his grasp of trickster insightfulness. In fact, Lopez-Pedraza shows that Fellini presented images of Priapus that were brilliant in capturing the freakish and hermaphroditic nature of this archetype, particularly in the movie, *Satyricon*. Yet Fellini steps into another archetypal realm when he enters the passionate and heroic struggle for salvation, as Schlappner explains happens in Fellini's *Il bidone*.

Great artists liberate the interplay of multiple archetypal forces within a life, or a work of art. Like the wandering waif in a Fellini film, the soul moves through all shades of joy and suffering and hopes for more. The Trickster accompanies the soul in this movement and bids us not to identify with the feelings of the moment. We might say that Trickster, with his long-range vision, informs us of what Fellini knows. "Human existence on its way to divine grace: that is Fellini's answer to the question of the meaning of evil."[37]

But on this earth we cannot honor the Trickster alone; in the name of Hestia I must confess my fear that the irony that pervades today's world would have us see it all as a gigantic amusement park where children can be bounced about from one house of horror to another with no serious consequences. I do not want to distance myself from that fear. Lest we think all entertainers are oblivious to this horror, I like to recall that it was a comedian who stopped in the middle of his hilarious performance and spoke out against child abuse with a passion and conviction that may have been out of character for a trickster type in itself, but could reflect a combination trickster and nurturant parent.

In promoting violence we lean toward a sado-masochistic orientation where one tries to overpower another. In the adult-child relationship, the power-inequity, and with it the possibility of violence, is in the nature of the relationship. Every parent must admit, albeit reluctantly, that feelings and images of violence are constellated by the helplessness of children. When this fact is obscured by sentimentality and idealization of the child, the danger of literally, but unconsciously, treating the child violently is more likely. Therefore, great mindfulness is necessary if we are to learn to bring up children with a livable exposure to violence and images of violence.

Psychologists know that imagining the forbidden is homeopathically therapeutic against impulsive destruction, but we do not know much about the optimal age-levels for exposure to the forbidden. I have a strong bias against presenting children with images of taboo subjects which are not natural to their level of maturity; we will return to this theme in the discussion of "Innocence" following.

I think of the evolved feminine as not denying the presence of violence and sadism in the psyche, but, being close to her maternal core, she is attracted to the Trickster, not because he distances us from suffering, but because he removes walls and hierarchies that isolate persons in their suffering. Those barriers which close off the suffering from both the sadistic and the compassionate can be dissolved by the humor and imaginal play of Trickster. Another way of saying this is that the Trickster helps us to see that the sadist and the victim are a pair, and can each benefit by finding the other in themselves. By his refusal to take sides, the Trickster allows us to find a centering principle.

The inability to bring our suffering into balance around a central core or witness, is the human factor in the perpetuation of personality disorders, those hubless webs of unfinished reaching.

All of these associations arise as I ponder my fantasy of the raging bear-mother. And I wonder, too, if this imagined scenario reflects anything about models of psychotherapy. I do know therapists who operate on the model of the evasive television hostess, not only indifferent to passion, but avoidant of it. I am not describing a containing attitude, with which a therapist receives the patient's material reflectively, sincerely, and non-reactively; by evasive I mean that the therapist cushions emotion with distancing techniques that render the emotional tone powerless. I have been like this at times, when the pain of what was presented before me was more than I could take in, and where I forgot it, even before the session ended. Or when I impulsively tried to insert a note of hope without hearing out the patient's sorrow.

As therapists we can also function as the animal control team, eager to prevent any learning experience that would bring pain, even if it means growth. I have been like this, too, controlling out of fear and lack of faith in the Self. For instance, I can cut-off a patient's violent thought with a violent dismissal, instead of taking it further and deeper. And some therapists function as the curious bag- lady, who probably most represents the spirit Mercurius. Then I remember a therapy session of the day before:

A man of forty sobbed about a former stage of his life. He remembered how he used to drive home from work exhausted, dreading the moment he would have to enter the home; the ordeal of having to relate to wife and small children; the burden of responsibility of those who depended on him staring him in the face; himself, struggling with his fatigue and resentment; the effort of pretending to love it. He admitted this with enormous shame. Worse yet, he admitted, he used to have a fantasy that some act of God would destroy them all and take him out of his miserable emotional indebtedness to his family. As we talked more about this, I learned that he didn't feel any guilt or shame when he used to drive home with this destructive fantasy. It had remained in the realm of wish-fulfillment in a way that resolved him of any responsibility for his own cruelty. Cruelty could be projected onto the Divine, leaving his energy free to feel sorry for himself. I wondered if my patient could imagine that he, himself, would perform the perfidious act that would relieve him of his responsibilities. He said that at the time he could not have considered that thought; and in fact, at the moment he still could not imagine that he could do anything directly to get rid of his past or current loved ones. The closest he can come to his cruelty is to realize that some terrible part of him would at times welcome their death.

But his psychic space is larger now, and can hold both these contents at once—he can feel his cruel desire to have his loved ones eliminated, and he can also feel how bereft he would be to have them gone. In object-relations theory we could say that he has negotiated the stage of the paranoid-schizoid position and has arrived at the capacity for depression, a genuine accomplishment. He is able to contain love and hatred of the "good breast" at once, not to have to separate his loving self and his cruel self. But he could not imagine doing the cruel deed that would result in the death of his loved ones. Therefore, it is still possible for his cruel self to be more differentiated. Evil is still blurry in the area of his taking responsibility for the killer in himself. As of now, only nature can be accused of wanting to kill. But he wants death to others. He will have to meet the killer in himself in some way, at some time, and, we hope, before it expresses itself too dangerously. Every person has the killer within. Few want to come to know it. In analyzing the development of evil self-image, Grotstein explains that the murderer establishes contact with his own agony from which he distanced and projected onto his victim.[38]

This man holds in his awareness the childhood memory of being told often by his mother that she wished he were dead. He also remembers sadistically being teased, and teasing his younger brother. With terrible regret for the pain he has caused, he accepts the fact that there is no way to amend what was lost, except to use it in being a more compassionate human being now. He is large enough now in his perspective about his own cruelty to try to see it objectively and use it creatively in his avocation as artist.

Here is a contradiction: I expressed a passionate wish not to cause suffering to others, yet I would have my patient welcome his inner murderer, and I also am about to speak in praise of violence. What is our responsibility toward violence? Is the enjoyment of violent games, movies, thoughts, likely to lead to criminal violence? How do we come to know the killer inside ourselves without creating a more and more dangerous environment? Can we enjoy symbolic violence without increasing the urge to inflict violence? What does an ethical parent teach children about violence? Should we try to stop violent games? A teacher says that one of the most popular videos for young children is about road construction; as much or more than watching sappy singing dinosaurs, children love seeing explosions, bulldozing, and machines dumping tons of concrete into cavities in the earth. Do we want to encourage this, or discourage this, or just enjoy it as sublimated anality?

The great appeal that killing has always had for us in story and art is evidence of our need to know about and deal with the feelings that accompany termination. A friend who teaches sociology tells me that when asked to anonymously reveal a secret wish, three-quarters of his class of college students admitted to wanting to kill someone. As we watch Lady Macbeth or Terminator or Pagliacci or Road Runner we come a little closer to the hateful parts of ourselves, and of the violent Self. Some of us seem to need to vicariously experience the violence repeatedly; perhaps we are those for whom the archetypal energy of the predator has been more strongly evoked in us while an avenue for expression has been less available. There is evidence to indicate that those who are not in touch with their own violence, or who have had little experience with having been provoked to violence, are less interested in seeing violence portrayed symbolically; there is some evidence as well that if one is allowed to react to some provocation of violence by expressing it symbolically, even at a later time, that there is relief of tension. But I do not know of any evidence to suggest that repeated experiences of violence, either real or symbolic, ever extinguish violent behavior. Instead, there is more evidence to suggest that using violent means to accomplish things becomes addictive and contagious, and requires at some point a decision to cease.

In body therapy the physiological manifestations of violence are encouraged and enacted with the therapist. Why is this catharsis not addictive, but instead actually lessens the possibility of acting-out violent impulses through homicide or suicide? Because each expression of violence is subjected to the fire of consciousness and the cooling water of reflection. The therapeutic vessel is the container for a refining alchemical process, decreasing the possibility that the angry feelings will burst forth at some moment of unpreparedness. The feelings become known and their cues are anticipated so they can be met with foresight. Most games and movies of violence differ from therapy in that they allow no time for cool down and reflection. In these violent games action builds upon action and no alternative is offered but action. The feminine principle of reflection and contemplation is often missing. Nor is there an opportunity to physically ventilate and exhaust one's energy through the large muscles as in violent sports.

Violence is wonderfully exhilarating; it is enhanced by testosterone, it excites the flow of adrenaline, it reaches beneath the layers of cliché and phony politeness to the visceral self and moves us, moves us out of pain, out of deadness, out of apathy, out of indifference, and raises us to feeling strong and large. It is the harbinger of spring to the depressive. We need it, because it is. It is foolish sentimentalism to believe that we can become so refined spiritually as to eliminate violence from our repertoire of human experience. We must figure out how to enjoy violence without causing others to suffer. We must learn to play with our love of violence through sports, music, drama, engineering, and art, to limit it to those enclosures, and then to reflect on it in the shield of Athena so that it does not bleed into our relationships with innocents. We can only do this by making these activities available to everyone, but particularly to children and adolescents, on more than a spectator's role or through video games. The body has to be engaged, not just the mind and one or two fingers, which may eventually become trigger fingers.

Unfortunately our society does not recognize the power of drama and art as much as it does sports. Thanks to sports we can offer up a day to the worship of the gods of the Super Bowl: Herakles, Wotan, Yahweh, Set, Mithra, and the like. But why not also play with violence through art? If it were available before suffering hardened into hate, wouldn't most teen gang members prefer to spend eight hours a day rehearsing for *West Side Story* or practicing martial arts than literally killing each other over drugs? Yet we pay choreographers and dramatists and poets almost nothing; we cast them aside like dregs when they could provide the creative redemption of our miserable adolescents' enslavement to materialism. If we rewarded artists who worked with children with anything near the money spent on arty ads for cars and cola, we might make a dent in the suffering of the young.

It will take energy and creative planning to resolve the problems of violence in our so-called civilization. Some forward-thinking educators have taken up the challenge and have involved students in extra-curricular artistic productions and non-competitive games. At the same time, politicians cut funds for such "frills." It will take more of us from all professions to slow the movement toward that last step across the border of paranoia.

SEX

A story from the Winnebago Trickster Cycle tells that Trickster took an elk's liver and made a vulva from it. Then he took elk's kidneys and made breasts, put on a dress, and transformed himself into a beautiful woman. She let various animals have intercourse with her. Then she went to the village and courted the chief's son. The chief's family prepared a feast for her—that was her real motivation for the courtship. The chief's son was pleased with her, and they married and had children.[39]

Trickster's liminality is wreaking confusion in the whole realm of sexuality, today as always. In the battle of the sexes it makes a difference as to whether we want to battle to the death, or just to put up enough of a fight to make the union in the little death more pleasurable. In the former camps are those who go for the jugular—the violent rapists, exploiters, prick teasers, and ball-breakers. In the latter camps are provocateurs, challengers, and pleasure-seeking-thrill-enhancing-mottle-breasted-risk takers. The demarcation between the camps has probably always been bleary, but under the scrutiny of current sexual politics…well, we are certainly clear about our confusion. A female challenger thinks she is inciting a possible partner to show his strength by engaging with him in verbal or emotional fireworks; if he is a member of the hostile camp he will interpret her assertiveness as an attack on his manhood. Then he may withdraw, leaving her disappointed, or attack, leaving her bruised instead of fulfilled. Or, a male provocateur hopes his risqué jokes are evoking exciting fantasies which may make him a more desirable partner; to the woman who associates foreplay with pain or humiliation, he appears to be an exploiter or would-be rapist, rather than the potential friend and lover he saw himself to be. One looks at the solidarity in the women of Lysistrata with nostalgia for a time when sexual politics were so clear-cut, and the battle lines drawn with such good-will.

Kerényi consulted Greek mythology for an answer to the question, "What is evil?" In examining the ambivalence the Greeks felt about ritual sacrifice, Kerényi gives an example of the ritual of the bull killing in Buphonia which was always followed by a ritual trial. "All who had participated in the sacrifice were haled before the court; each attributed the murder to someone else; in the end the knife was pronounced guilty and thrown into the sea."[40]

This evokes comparisons with the notorious case of the man who was castrated by his wife ("little woman," "old lady," "better half"). The jury could not find him guilty of wife-abuse, nor could another jury find her guilty of willful mutilation. We can conclude that the decision was about the same as in Buphonia: the knife did it, and should be punished severely.

Castration and other forms of mutilation are ancient expressions of hatred toward another or oneself. Rape and castration have been standard war crimes, self-mutilation a reaction to grief, castration and disfigurement favorite means of revenge, or signs of oppressive power. David paid a bridal price in Philistine foreskins long before Freud declared fear of castration the linchpin of culture. Clitorectomy, a bloodier form of foot binding, is still performed on women in some parts of the world.

Still, it is the consensus of people I've discussed this with that male castration images are prevalent in contemporary culture. Unlike the movies and cartoons in my earlier memories, today's contain plentiful examples of men being wounded in the groin, often by a woman or a child, or the family dog. If my observation is true, this reflects and contributes to a growing awareness of a theme Trickster stories emphasize: the vulnerability of males. The once-emblem of invincibility, the penis, is admitted to be a delicate, immensely sensitive, essential, exposed, and accessible body part. Perhaps the occurrence of this theme is a sign of the diminishing power-differential between the sexes. We can all be hurt. Furthermore, we can wipe out our entire species without too much effort by bombs, bacteria, genetic meddling, and indifference to natural resources.

Children today are bombarded with sexual data. Unfortunately, it does not make them sexually smarter, because it is not presented in the context of relatedness. Those of us who are privileged as therapists to intimate conversations with children and adolescents know how often their sexual data is full of error. Worse, adults and adolescents themselves do not realize how ignorant the young people are, and we adults trust them much more than we should on the basis of what we think they know. They know many physiological facts that are incomplete and unconnected to meaning and affect. What is most disturbing about the sexual information deluge is that it leaves no room for innocent exploration. Adolescents have been given very specific and graphic pictures of how sex is supposed to be before they ever have a chance to develop their own pace and tastes.

Children are robbed of important self-discovery by too much information too soon. The information is foisted upon them before they are naturally ready for it or curious about it and before it is situated in a loving relationship. This loss of opportunity for imagination and for sexual meaning is sad, for without that, sex is perfunctory and intimacy does not occur. I cannot foresee a way to protect children from big screen sex. We can only try to keep them alive to the possibility of intimacy by fostering imagination; for example, through story—especially the stories of the family and our own relationships in the real world of human connections—we convey a sense of continuity and durable care.

We are getting better at acknowledging the need for sexual freedom, touch, and affection, but not true intimacy, which requires honesty and self-disclosure. Wilhelm Reich's description of the "orgasm reflex" includes much more than genital climax. It includes a full-body response and an emotional response that involves deep awareness of the partner. Problems in our culture with intimacy are evident in that breast-feeding is still discouraged, naturalness of bodily functions is still discouraged, expressions of passion are discouraged, aging is discouraged, we are over-sanitized and deodorized, and death is hidden.

In a creative society a different set of expectations around sex, marriage, and family could allow new ways of preserving the sanctity of all three. Imagine, for example, a society where sacred male and female prostitutes provided sexual experience in ceremonies of affection for anyone who so desired, where marriage was free from sexual obligation, and families bonded by natural affection and not by law or the demands of sexuality. We could entertain such possibilities, at least to discuss them, in order to survive. The international congresses on population issues are a good beginning of an opening process.

Innocence

The sacrifice of innocents is an archetypal theme which exposes a basic human fear of annihilation. This theme is recapitulated in the individual, whose pursuit of life necessitates a sacrifice of innocent symbiosis or unconsciousness.[41] As a society we need to look at our unconscious participation in this primal pattern. The task is to keep the possibility of a place of innocence viable in the inner world as well as in the world of our outer children, and not to allow that place to be overrun by cynics and pessimists. A concern of sociologists is that the increasing excessive individualism and self-orientation in our culture are leading to a breakdown in community life and in the mental health of individuals. An absence of strong group cohesiveness and mores is especially hard on our children who are exposed to lots of cynicism and little support. James Hillman offers insight into the ambivalence we demonstrate towards children, as it reflects the abandonment of the archetypal child. In the way we treat our childlike dependencies and creativity, we indicate that we cannot bear the child.

> Either we repress or we coddle this face of our subjectivity. In both cases the child is unbearable: first we cannot support it at all, then we give way to it altogether. We follow a pattern contained in the word "abandon" itself, alternating between the opposite meanings of "losing" and "releasing". On the one hand we free ourselves of a condition by letting it go from us, and on the other hand, we free ourselves by letting go to it.[42]

If we were alive to the Divine Child, there would not be such an exclusive division about what experience is appropriate for adults, and what is relegated to the child as inferior. Damage of innocence and innocents, the slaughter of hope, is where some instinctual parental presence in us would draw the line on irony, where we would cry out against a combination trickster/sadist that would fool us into believing that indifference to a child's pain is beautiful, clever, and sophisticated. Sadism toward children is not typical of Trickster, who befriends humans, especially children, but it involves a dark Eros that plays on the forbidden, something that has been excluded from the adult imagination. In his commentary on the psychological relevance of the writings of the Marquis de Sade for penetrating the shadow, Thomas Moore points out that the shocking humor around the abuse of children that de Sade presents, liberates a dark truth that we would prefer to ignore.

> If we were to take an unbiased look at the place of the child in modern Western society, we would see a split attitude: on one hand parents try to give their children everything possible, with fantastic Walt Disney images of childhood, while on the other hand parents also dominate, bind, torture, and sexually abuse those sentimentalized children.... Rather than look for something malfunctioning in odd and destructive loves of children, Sade searches out a positive attraction to the evil that is the genuine seed of abuse.... Recognizing that we find the archetypal child in actual children, we could explore this hatred and love of the child.[43]

Innocence constellates sadism, and vice-versa, but many cultures acknowledge this and build in safeguards to give young children the right to grow up protected from excessive sadism. A notorious exception, in my opinion, is the British type of educational system which seems to accentuate sadistic treatment of young children. At an early age children are sent away to boarding schools, where discipline is often severe. Some parents do find any excuse to be away from their children. Nevertheless, there is a constructive parental component in the human race that attends more to the positive side of ambivalence, the wish to be close to and to care for its young. And although Mother Nature imposes suffering on every age group, it is hard to imagine a mother destroying children out of sheer sadistic glee. In myth and story, mothers who kill their children almost always do so in anguish to save them from prolonged suffering, or to sacrifice them in rage as a protest to the behavior of their fathers.[44]

The instinctual mother we usually picture as wanting to stand by that nugget of humanity that refuses to increase the suffering of children, that wishes hope and a chance to experience joy for all sentient beings, especially the young. Some cultures honor this protective attitude toward their young, and ritualize the exit from innocence by some initiation into adolescence. The initiation ceremonies may include some wounding, or at least the acting-out of a sado-masochistic dynamic in the fact of submission to the initiation. Such wounding signifies the end of a right to narcissistic purity, and an expectation that the adolescent will move out of the mother- world, become cognizant of evil, and accept responsibility.

Unfortunately, adolescents in most Western societies have to establish their own rights of passage, as the culture does not provide them. And the child's situation is not helped by the cultural male-female split that colors attitudes in every segment of society, from the way we treat our bodies to the way we express our souls. The polarized maternal complex infantilizes, while the paternal complex abandons. Sociologists hope that the merging of male and female roles will alleviate some of the ambivalence that penalizes the child in our culture. Sociologist Charles Derber notes that in patriarchal society men have monopolized attention and economic and social power, but that more active responsibility in child-care roles are giving men some insight into the rights and needs of others. He writes:

> The prolonged dependency of children, as well as the needs of infants for continuing special attention, necessitates on the part of the caretaker a transcendence of the egoistic mode; the needs of children are one of the major species considerations which powerfully counteract narcissistic tendencies and create in every society the need for some other-orientation.... In advanced industrial societies it is the narcissism of the male that has been acutely heightened and most urgently requires the counteracting restraint implicit in child-care roles. The intensive self-orientation of the male can change only if he is socialized to new roles that explicitly demand attentiveness to others. Since male worth is now contingent upon success in economic roles which require extraordinary self-orientation, male egoism is likely to be mitigated only by new expectations for men that involve a decline in pressures for self-directed achievement and a new emphasis on the ability to respond to people. A radical restructuring of the primary attention-giving (i.e., child-care) roles, where men, like women, are expected to develop a capacity to give attention to children, may be the most important element in such a change.[45]

A woman found herself having recurrent images of suicide. For no apparent reason, the picture of herself holding a gun to her throat and preparing to pull the trigger, came into her mind over and over for several days. After some resistance she was able to admit this to me. We traced the fantasy to her guilt at having gone to a lawyer to try to obtain child support after years of caring for two children with no financial help from their father. The assertiveness required in going to court brought up old injunctions: "You're not supposed to ask men for anything." "You're not supposed to fight over money." "Who do you think you are?" So deeply imbedded in her psyche was the division between her world of caring for children, and the "male world" of law courts and finances, that she felt she deserved to die for daring to cross the line. In destroying herself through her throat she could reflect the contempt she had introjected for speaking up, for having a voice in the matter. By demanding justice, she unleashed demons of anti-feminine introjects which we all absorb to some extent from the collective consciousness. It was almost enough to have her destroy the innocent in herself, as well as her children.

Fortunately we can see through some of the time-honored assumptions that have placed destructive constrictions on our human feelings as well as social behaviors for centuries. Still, moving them is not comfortable, or easy. We can have hope, or we can have paranoia; if we dare to hope, we can count on the accompaniment of the Trickster. The fundamental and survival oriented archetype we call Trickster is present in both sexes, present in decisions that determine the flexibility of the personality, that touch on authority and autonomy, and a sense of freedom. Though some may be born with stronger aspects of its influence than others, the important thing is whether we stand in good relationship to it, in which case we will enjoy curiosity, a sense of humor, a healthy balance of self-esteem and humility, an appreciation for the ironic, expressiveness, and an independent spirit; or not in touch with it, in which case we will be cynical, gullible, or overly idealizing of others, compulsively authoritarian or defiant, chaotic and fragmented or rigidly bound to systems, inauthentic, noncommunicative and devious. The kind of destruction based on competition and envy which we see now in politics and in the "bad-sports" world is not hermetic. It is heroism gone sour. What matters is how welcoming and respectful we are of the joyful Trickster Archetype, how willing to receive its epiphanies when they come to us in the form of man, woman, animal, or spiritual force.

Epiphany and Doubt

Magi only journey at night
like the guarded secrets of dreams
and, at morning, always arrive from the East,
the rising sun at their backs, haloing them in light.
You will have to shade your eyes
to watch them,
step by step,
approach you
with their request. They are not wise in usual ways

They cannot make a chair,
their soups are regrettable.
It is conjunctions,
    symmetries,
      balances
that interest them.

Heaven shakes, earth quakes.
As above, so below.
A star moves across the sky
and they are in the saddle
convinced an earth child
has yanked a string.
They come from a country of kites.
They also puzzle prophesies,
living in perpetual pregnancy,
awaiting the births of the predicted.
They unroll ancient parchments
to find new babies,
then read the wrinkles of the newborn
as testimonies of the past promises.
They are not your average observers.
That is why they have come to you
—why they come to us all.
Your replacement has been born.
They need your help
to tell them
where
they can find the child.
Lost in higher logic,
they will not see you blanch
or notice you are troubled.
They want to teach you the lost art of homage,
how freeing it is to be prostrate before promise,
They are the strangers
who have come to tell you
the truth
you have forgotten.
Do not try to trick them,
coaxing from their enthusiasm
murderous information.
It will not work.
Wise Men always go home
by another route.
You will end
by slaughtering hope
and you will not see
the fleeing child, your child,
reach for their gifts.[46]

CHAPTER VI

THE ANIMATED TRICKSTER

Will the human race survive much longer? Each day I listen to despairing tales, not from neurotic or self-serving egotists, but from conscientious, evolved persons who not only have no vision of Utopia, but have given up hope to create even a somewhat saner world. I see teachers who are so unappreciated, indeed, abused, that they abandon their profession in order to heal themselves; people with a will to work who are unemployable; ethical mental health professionals whose practices are failing in the face of competition by the fix-it-quick profiteers; people whose livelihoods depend on destruction of the environment; nurses who cannot stop to give loving attention to their patients lest they forfeit their jobs for being "inefficient" according to the pirates who control health care; people who make more money than they know what to do with but can't make love; parents who cannot let their children out of their sight without compromising the child's safety; adults who dare not walk outside at night. We are thriving with material goods, but barely surviving in soulfulness, and at great cost to hope.

To those who despair I say that I believe we may survive to make a better life, but we must advance in our ethical development as a species—and quickly—to survive. In wanting to survive, wanting to make a better world, I recognize a heroic mode, perhaps a childlike optimism, but not in contradiction to Trickster, who, as we have seen, is sent to earth to help humans and deliver us from our enemies.

Since today humankind's worst enemy is within each human being, my hope comes from observations of Trickster myths: myths which suggest that we could balance our current values which call so heavily on materialistic-heroic images of wealth and self-importance, with more feminine values of nurturance and compassion and more tricksterish values of playfulness and inclusiveness. Such myths and stories suggest that, with concentrated attention to the Trickster Archetype as a divine emanation, particularly as expressed in its feminine aspects, competition could be balanced with playful humor, arrogance with inclusivity, greed with openness, exploitation with nurturance. They suggest we, like Hermes, could "parent the Divine Child," in other words, put care of the natural world and of the innocent above all else.

We have seen that in many cultures a Trickster god is associated with a feminine counterpart. Several cultures have dreamed myths that connect an image of human fulfillment on earth with the reappearance of the Trickster and the Feminine Principle (Anima), as prominent presences.[1] I have suggested here that the Trickster and the Anima have been subdued and hidden in a devil image while the gods of scientific technology and warfare predominated worldwide. As the principle of evil becomes more differentiated, certain aspects of the positive Trickster and the creative woman are being retrieved from the dark shadow, a retrieval which could lead to an advance in our level of ethical development.

The question of significance of the pattern seen in the myths cannot be answered from a logical approach, but must be allowed to unfold with some degree of input and guidance from humans, the only finite beings who, as far as we know, are able to influence the pattern. Therapists understand this, because it is as a person unfolds in analysis, in ways that cannot be predicted or led, but can be allowed and shaped by dialogue with the non-controlling therapist. We have no control over the fact that the Trickster Archetype is surfacing so frequently now, but we can notice that a feminine aspect is nebulous and forming out of the shadow of the Trickster; and it is likely that a feminine aspect would shift the balance of archetypal qualities toward more relatedness, emotional connection, and tolerance for the beauty and darkness of the natural world.

The Dark Trickster and Anima

If we are to deepen ethically, we need divine help so as not to regress, not to fall back into a pre-patriarchal, undifferentiated state of domination by irrationality and by a fear of natural discomforts and disasters. We must be able to take what is best for us from all that we have learned about the caring matriarchal and careful patriarchal principles, and fashion that knowledge with wisdom into a creative society. No one of us need pretend to have any answers to how this should be accomplished, but each one of us deserves to hypothesize about what will help. Many possibilities are inspired by what we know of the positive aspects of the Trickster and the comprehensive, differentiated Anima.

In the worst possible scenario the dark aspects of Anima and Trickster could prevail. The dark Trickster brings the excitement of creative motion without emotional depth or compassion. The dark Anima lures us into irrational webs where we become enervated and spineless. Combined, they produce anarchy and disorganization, rash expenditures of energy toward no constructive purpose, a squandering of all that is valuable without regard for the future or respect for the treasures of the past, a preoccupation with pleasure without a balance of sacrifice, self-indulgence at the expense of future generations, the decay of memory, and the death of hope. We see much of this scenario before us now, for the Trickster and Anima have both been suppressed and vilified. Both need to be acknowledged and differentiated from the collective shadow so that the positive values of trickster and Anima can flourish. Jungian analyst Janet Dallett also writes about the confusion of evil, the feminine, and nature in the contemporary psyche. "Now we have to become conscious of the reality and locus of evil. Identifying with the good, light, true, and beautiful, or denying what lives in the unsavory dark have ceased to be viable options."[2] With growing awareness and differentiation of our experience of evil, we might stimulate a constructive integration of trickster and Anima into our world. Eigen notes: "In the mature personality irony and faith balance each other. Mystical vision and the requirements of situations meet."[3]

The world of a Trickster/Anima will manifest differently from a predominantly Trickster or predominantly Feminine world. Together the Trickster/Anima combination brings an attitude of opening: opening of boundaries, opening of physiological paths of energy, opening of communication channels between all groups, even between the patriarchal and matriarchal duality, and between the animal, human, and spirit worlds. With Trickster participating, however, there can be no simple pacifistic or spiritually airy Anima prevailing, because where there is Trickster there is down-to-earth physicality, sensuality, instinctuality. Neither can there be a return to a matriarchal, live-and-let-live-in-the-lap-of-mother attitude, because that would not allow for dialogue and the excitement of communication between different factors. While Trickster dismisses hierarchy, it does demand differentiation so there can be the richness of disagreement. If we survive to meet a new era, communication must span every possible duality. This would mean two-way communication between age-groups, races, religions, governments, animal species. This means that children's needs could be heard and responded to by adults, animals' needs could be heard and responded to by humans, adults could explain themselves to children, and humans to animals. Men and women could learn each other's languages, gender lines could be more relaxed and flexible, politicians could put communication with and welfare of their constituents above their personal ambitions and rich special interest groups.

And without a strong feminine presence, the world of trickster would run the risk of being short on empathy and reliability. The most consequential quality that the Anima brings to this unfolding is the orientation towards communicating feelings and maintaining relationships, especially with the young, the weak, and the silent, such as places of nature and non-verbal creatures. "Silence is the mother-tongue," says Norman O. Brown.[4] Trickster/Anima teaches the language of silence and the need to put feeling-relationships before merely cognitive and verbal contracts.

PARENTING THE DIVINE CHILD

Jung said:

> Everything now depends on man: immense power of destruction is given into his hand, and the question is whether he can resist the will to use it, and can temper his will with the spirit of love and wisdom. He will hardly be capable of doing so with his own unaided resources. He needs the help of an "advocate" in heaven, that is, of the child who was caught up to God and who brings the "healing" and making whole of the hitherto fragmentary man.[5]

Instead of relating to the parental projection of a mother-god as if we were children contained in the arms of mother (as matriarchal societies do), contemporary human societies have been acting more like children striving to please a powerful and ambitious father-god, or like heroic atheistic orphans pitting themselves against the power of nature. Today our culture struggles to find images to portray new stages of relationship to the Anima and Animus. We are beyond the parental stage of worship in many portions of human society, and the question is, as it is pressing in all gender-oriented relationships, how will these principles best be balanced in some equal and generative partnership?

One help would be for us adult humans to stop being the child, and to learn to relate to the Divine Child. We have conditioned ourselves with parental god-images to identify as children, rather than as responsible persons. Rather than relating to the Anima only as a child to a mother, or a dominator to a harlot, we could withdraw those projections and see the Anima in all her feminine aspects. To see the fullness of the feminine in the divine means we can accept her in ourselves. Then we adults could stop whining, demanding, and preening for attention, in favor of accepting the importance of good parenting within ourselves. To incorporate the motherly aspect of the feminine in our behavior toward the youngest members of our species, our hope, would be phenomenally constructive. We could outgrow seeking approval from others on whom we project power, and then focus on giving to those who come after us; we could choose generativity over narcissism, and nurture our future possibilities. To incorporate the aesthetic sensibility of the feminine would guarantee that the Trickster's love of disharmony and conflict would not be given reign to run rampant over the well-being of the young, but would be mediated to preserve child-life and enhance the creativity which children represent.[6] To incorporate the feminine appreciation for relatedness would enhance the values of cooperation and communal awareness over strife and competition. A true connection with the transcendent makes tribal loyalties and prejudices obsolete.

As an example of learning to identify ourselves as adults and parents instead of as children, let us return to the man with a strong trickster component in his personality whom I mentioned in previous chapters. He who was abused and hated by his mother, and who struggled for years with his violent feelings, had a profound breakthrough one day during a meditation. In analysis we had worked for many months on his feelings of self-contempt because of what he thought of as his "weakness" in the face of his violent resentments.

On this occasion he had come to a familiar memory: himself as a boy watching his mother rant in a typical tirade. Instead of running away to care for his inner wounded child (we had attended to that fearful part of himself often enough), this time he went toward her (imaginatively, of course). Seeing her childlike helplessness for the first time, he held her in his arms, and rocked her gently. She softened, cried, and he knew that she had always needed this. This moment of opening to her pain brought about the beginning of his forgiveness, and the end of his depression.

Who can explain why such a simple act happened at that time? Perhaps the same mother-child scenario could have been staged by the therapist, but would it have had lasting results? I trust more that it came about from within the patient, after long periods of focusing, holding, and going over his own feelings of helplessness until something transformed.

A few weeks later he dreamed:

> I am in a rural area at night. It is pitch black, and I am isolated and anxious. I come to a house in the woods, my house. I enter through a living room and

go to my room. A little later I come back into the living room and am amazed to see that someone has placed a huge candle burning in the doorway, which they have left open. I am terrified, because I am seen by something out there, which I do not know about.

His associations to the dream led to the realization that Something from the dark unconscious wants to make contact with him. It sheds light—awareness—at the threshold of two worlds; one the safe, secure hearth within, and the other the dark unknown without. The candle bridges both worlds, and may enlighten him if he dares to accept it. He felt the energy of the Something to be feminine, and connected it with his mother. Already she had contacted his compassion in his meditation. The dream presents a mercurial aspect which I have found is usually an excellent sign of a deepening process in therapy. Signs of Mercurius—threshold, open door, mysterious, secret observer—herald significant psychic movement.

INCLUSIVENESS AND COMPASSION

As in the dream above, Trickster loves to create and uncover secrets, and so do women. I picture these secrets as pockets, not folds. The self-disclosures of women writers, for example, Adrienne Rich, Anne Sexton, Sylvia Plath, and others, were criticized as too "confessional" by those who were made uncomfortable by the personal nature of their work. Yet these artists emptied their pockets to create a new level of honesty and intimacy between the sexes. The disclosure to the American people insisted upon by Hazel O'Leary, when she became the new Secretary of Department of Energy in 1993, of the true facts about nuclear testing and radiation experiments on unsuspecting humans is a perfect example of the integrated Trickster/Anima at work. After years of deception by authorities, barriers were removed and true information about life-threatening research was made available to the public; the Trickster gods of communication and the goddesses of life and compassion for living beings both moved through the courage of Hazel O'Leary.

Congresswomen have led in the movement to have pesticide companies made more responsible in reporting levels of safety; for example, the women have stressed the "child factor" to point out that levels of safety of pesticides in fruits need to be different for children than adults. The levels of toxins in dirt and grass where children play endangers them more than adults, and so on. Chemical companies tend to distort facts by downplaying the dangers of their products. Some women who value disclosure and safety more than profitable business, pushed to force drug companies to reveal that many drugs prescribed for women have never been tested on women, only on samples of male population. When women become aware of the Trickster within themselves, they can catch deception in others and avoid being victimized by demanding openness. And they avoid victimizing themselves by not obeying old punitive inner critics that invariably attack sensitive new possibilities in the psyche. They know that no sooner is the child granted some playroom in the psyche, than the sadist begins to sneak around. Opening possibilities have to be guarded.

Opening means inclusion: the ecumenical movement across Christian churches has emphasized their shared purposes rather than their differences. Native Americans share their advanced philosophy of life on earth and allow their sacred stories and ceremonies to be witnessed by other races (as we have gratefully done here). Male schools and clubs open themselves to women. Caucasian organizations open themselves to other races. Plant and animal species are included in the right to exist. Opportunities open to the handicapped. We have already seen the removal of the Berlin Wall; the beginning of the reunification of Ireland; the abolishing of apartheid; disclosures by governments of facts previously hidden from the people; inclusion of homosexuality as a valid choice; opportunities for all races to hold high public office; legal demand placed on mental health professionals to disclose side-effects of medications to mental patients; legal demand placed on all professionals to disclose evidence of child abuse immediately; opening of the home by women to share domestic chores and child-care with men; opening of the political and economic world by men to share wage-earning and top-dog status with women...all are moves toward inclusion which have great impact on humanity's self-image. If these openings don't please all of the people all of the time, they at least speak out to their inevitable purpose of community.[7]

Trickster/Anima dismantles the traditional limits by which women define themselves. New boundaries emerge. Old structures, and especially old social stratifications and calcifications dissolve. Creativity is the rule, rote role-playing is out. What matters is what comes from the heart. Creativity in child-care is a priority. As Rhea hid her child, Zeus, from devouring Chronos, woman hides the innocent—internal tendril and external offspring—from the giants of mass materialism. As Hermes rescued the baby Dionysus, Trickster/Anima rescues, values, and nurtures innocence. He/She fights the giants as all hermetic ones do: with every bit of wisdom, magic, and device to make a large safe space for the children of the world. The presence of the child in the psyche is an indicator of hope, just as the child in flesh and blood throws an anchor into the future of the species. Trickster/

Anima, retrieving the polymorphous child who contains all possibilities, is an image that can unite all of our frayed and fragmented shards. I like to believe that this unitive image is infiltrating the philosophical ground of contemporary cultures. Philosophers today question the ontological and epistemological roots of traditional ethics and ask whether our ethical criteria "demoralize" by supporting patterns of dominance and submission. They suggest that a focus on connection rather than on individualistic rights may lead to a more sensible ethic in our increasingly chaotic world.[8] As a result of feminine ethicists finding a voice, we are beginning to see attention given to "care" and "relatedness" in ethical theory, as well as the traditional concern with "justice" and "contracts." As one example of many, in addition to Gilligan (see Chapter I), I would call attention to Nell Noddings' "Relational Ethics."

Noddings is one of many contemporary philosophers who propose a morality which depends on the universal experience of natural caring first, and secondarily on our remembrance of that caring. "This strong desire to be moral is derived, reflectively, from the more fundamental and natural desire to be and to remain related."[9] When the sentiment of caring is not felt, the memory of that sentiment and value attributed to it, sustains the ethical ideal.

> The genuine moral sentiment arises from an evaluation of the caring relation as good, as better than, superior to, other forms of relatedness. I feel the moral "I must" when I recognize that my response will either enhance or diminish my ethical ideal. It will serve to increase or decrease the likelihood of genuine caring.[10]

Nodding explains that this experience of ethics is not merely "situation ethics," is not focused on consequences, and is not founded on the notion of universal love. Neither is it indicative of low self-esteem on the part of the carer; in fact, it demands solid self-acceptance and confidence to persist in dialogue without becoming a dictator or doormat. It is founded on receptive empathy which allows us to perceive what another is experiencing. Noddings frequently refers to Martin Buber's philosophy in her writing.

For example, in educating children, the relationship between teacher and student is valued above the subject matter. The teacher seeks "I-Thou" dialogue, not just response, from the student; he or she receives and includes the student's experience of the subject matter in the process. The teacher's first duty is to the ethical relationship between them.

> What matters is the student, the cared-for, and how he will approach ethical problems as a result of his relation to her. Will he refer his ethical decisions to an ethic of caring or to rules and the likelihood of apprehension and punishment? Will he ask what his act means in terms of the feelings, needs, and projects of others, or will he be content with a catalog of rules-of-the-game?... She meets him as he is and finds something admirable and, as a result, he may find the strength to become even more admirable. He is confirmed.[11]

I mention Noddings' work as only one of many attempts to humanize philosophical thought, and to underline the fact that it is the Feminine Principle moving through men and women philosophers that makes this humanizing influence palpable. And it is the Trickster archetype acting in conjunction with the Feminine Principle which creates the structural flexibility that makes change possible. Karen Armstrong writes: "The prophets insisted that cult and worship were useless unless society on a whole adopted a more just and compassionate ethos." She traces the essential feature of all major religions: compassion "a particularly difficult virtue. It demands we go beyond the limitations of our egotism, insecurity, and inherited prejudice."[12]

DEVOURING GIANTS: EXPLOITATIVE GREED

"Relational Ethics," based on a motive of natural caring, is harmonious with the Trickster/Anima values. But can such an ethical approach have any pragmatic value in twenty-first century society? If we look at the self-oriented-profit motive and the caring motive as two attitudes toward relationships, we can find many large groups, corporations and institutions who exemplify the former and show little caring for others. In American life the trend toward impersonal, large businesses which threaten to swallow up more human-scaled organizations, grows ominous. This is true even of universities and hospitals which have been taken over by the business mind-set. A college professor writes in protest of the business mentality that has invaded institutions of learning:

> The faculty are not primarily job development specialists or a bargaining unit. The faculty are a group of professional teachers whose work is to guide students in developing knowledge, skill, and wisdom, to lead them out into an ever new world. Education is not primarily a business venture whose purpose is to make money or to develop the economy. Education is not a military operation whose purpose is to defeat foreign competition. We do not need CEOs at the helms of our institutions. We are educators, and we

are in serious need of the leadership of some good deans and provosts, the discourse of some respected philosophers, the comprehensive paradigms of some visionary scientists, the aesthetic expression of some gifted artists, the example and the challenge of some good teachers.[13]

As long as they are beyond the power of the giants' influence, the youth of a society see these issues clearly (the Emperor's Clothes effect).

> Corporations cold turn ya to stone…
> No escape from the mass mind rape
> Play it again jack, and rewind the tape
> Play it again till your mind is locked in
> Believing all the lies that they're telling ya
> Buying all the products that they're selling ya
> They load the clip in omnicolor
> They pack the nine and fire it at prime time
> Sleeping gas, every home's like Alcatraz…
>
> *Rage Against the Machine*

The young see through the arrogance and manipulativeness of bureaucracies—the over serious drive to profit, the absence of communality, the self-aggrandizement. Youth, because they are not solidified into a position, are more tuned in to influences of both Anima and Trickster. Anima manifesting as an equal partner to Trickster requires authenticity in relatedness. One aspect of woman's attraction to authenticity is the capacity to negotiate. Noddings holds that women, accustomed to mediating between those who exploit them and those who depend on them, can take the lead in showing how to mediate between the oppressed poor and the oppressive rich, and other politically disparate groups.[14] In spite of trickster's reputation for lying, the mediating Trickster/Anima limits lying to deliberate game-playing. Anima demands that people in authority not disguise themselves or lie to their subordinates out of ambition or intrigue, but that dissembling be reserved for the realms of trickster only, for example, in art, entertainment, and play between equals, not with younger, smaller, or subordinate persons, and not when life is at stake.

These issues of authenticity and relatedness have little to do with economic systems. Capitalism and communism share a single problem, which is that they are usually separated from a spiritual principle. Capitalism doesn't have to be dirty to survive; it has proven its worth and can survive with ethical standards, for successful business does not demand exploitation of the innocent. But giants are power-hungry; if they are hermetic in their wiles, it is in the service of the power-drive, and not generativity. Many developers think not one bit about the next generation as they destroy acre after acre and small business after small business for a quick profit. Developers are some of the richest but most morally moronic of our species. We have a plethora of seminars and business schools teaching "management skills" which claim to emphasize the ability to respond to people, but which actually teach only manipulation and power strategies, as if people are chess-pieces in the corporate game. For example, most fast-food chains earn fortunes for their executives, but provide no health care or job security for their employees, many of whom work inhumane schedules. Some schools and businesses today are no more humane than nineteenth century sweatshops.

Unfortunately, health care givers, such as hospitals and health insurers also fall into the corporate giants' game. Even some mental health professionals have been mesmerized by business management techniques. Being principally devoted to profit will eat the soul out of the work of psychotherapy and medicine. An attitude of compassion, especially towards the younger and weaker members of society, by health professions would change the face of medicine as it has become under the aegis of big business. The presence of trickster/Anima, our original healing divinities, must be cultivated again by the health professions.

An example of a contemporary businessman with heart was the person who had the creative thought of exchanging guns for toys. By arranging deals with toy businesses he managed to remove hundreds of guns off the street, gave some positive attention to the young, and presented them with a role model as a male who cares about his fellow- human and does not need to support violence to prove his manhood. Another creative business idea is the Time Dollar, a currency based on time where one hour of service earns one credit, a service credit. The idea of time-service credits is "a whole new approach to self-reliance and community building."[15] Celebrities and large corporations could put money back into ecology, educational and cultural centers, instead of only personal acquisitions. We can hear the CEOs laughing at such frivolous propositions; still, creative approaches to business give one hope that a cooperative system of managing supply and demand can evolve which will make our present competition for money look barbaric and clumsy, especially as that competition makes us more and more the enemies of nature.

PARENTING NATURE

Women are considered by some to be more appreciative of nature than men. If so, one explanation is women's early identification with mother.

(Women are) outside the nature-assaulting parts of history...less avid than men as hunters and killers, as penetrators of Mother Nature's secrets, plunderers of her treasure, outwitters of her constraints.... If men had felt all along more closely identified with the first parent...we would not now be so close to the irrevocable murder of nature.[16]

Whether Dinnerstein is right about the origin of woman's association with nature, her observations that an association exists seem accurate. It would seem that women's cyclical physiological and emotional makeup, so affected by the regular monthly hormonal rhythms, also significantly contributes to identification with nature. Very early in life a woman learns that she does not consciously control many of her natural processes. Menses, breast development, attracting an appropriate mate, childbirth, all involve waiting periods, whereas men are accustomed to quick results, in sexual matters particularly.

Archetypally, nature has always been a mother. I suspect that will not change with different social roles for men and women. The identification of Anima with natural processes makes the feminine principle the likely mediator between humans and nature. Trickster and Anima blend in their reverence for the natural world. We need them to teach us to regain our lost affinity for nature and our capacity to survive ordinary conditions of the real world without artificial devices. For many this would mean a great sacrifice—to stop running from nature and accommodate to her, to conserve resources and energy, to learn again to play outdoors. As adults, to be outdoors to supervise play and keep play areas safe and to enjoy interacting with children. To value the plants and animals, to learn to communicate with them and to have a sense of stewardship and responsibility for these less adaptive creatures. The Bible gives man dominion over nature, but we can choose whether to exercise dominion as enslavers, or dominion as nurturant stewards. Modern barbaric hordes attack life with concrete, plastic, and a terrible appetite for wealth.

Visualizing a nurturant stewardship inspires us to put the welfare and the health of the young above the advantages of accumulating material goods or attaining status in a class-conscious atmosphere. To see the fallacy behind so-called "labor-saving machines" which rob us of simple pleasures, simple jobs, and the pleasures of depending on each other. To learn to enjoy the company of plants, animals, children, and each other so as not to need to frantically grasp for entertainment by machines. To enjoy our own bodies, their natural looks and smells and miraculous processes of life, their capacity to adjust to climactic change, their sensuousness and capacity for pleasure that is not based on artifice or false appearances or prowess, but on the exquisite senses of touch and kinesthesis combined with the excitement of sensitivity to another's feelings.

The world of trickster/Anima is colored by Trickster's capacity for transforming and the feminine capacity for grounded caretaking. Together they enjoy the seriousness of play and the sacredness of the hum-drum. Together they foster a spirit of cooperation above competition, an appreciation for the transcendental within the obvious, more the spirit than tenets of religion, more the spirit of the marriage than the rights of the partners, more the spirit of the family than the ambitions of its members, more the spirit of the work than the status it brings, more the spirit of the game than the prize and pride, more the pleasure of the innocents than their exploitation, more the suffering of the neighbor than the inconvenience he causes, more the spirit of the tree or bird than its usefulness. Someday, perhaps, we will rest in the faceless, nameless wonder of the Great Mystery. In the meantime, while we need literal images, we can sing to these embodied spirits, Hestia and Hermes, as Homer did:

> Come, both of you inhabit this beautiful house with mutual feelings of friendship.... Hello, daughter of Chronos, you too, Hermes, with your gold wand. As for me, I will remember you in another song.[17]

And so, I hope, will we.

CHAPTER I. SUPERMAN IN HELL

1. See Robert Jay Lifton, *The Protean Self: Human Resilience in an Age of Fragmentation* (New York: Basic Books, a division of HarperCollins Publishers, Inc., 1993), published while this book was in process, for elaboration on the history of fragmentation in our culture. Lifton's rich profusion of examples from life and the arts amplifies the cultural unsettledness and underlines the message about which he and I, unbeknownst to each other, were moved to write. Lifton refers to the archetype of Proteus, the shape-shifter, to illustrate the fact that cultural fragmentation results in either opening/embracing attitudes or closing/protecting attitudes on the part of persons attempting to survive. I am using the Trickster Archetype (Hermes, instead of Proteus) to illustrate similar ideas. My approach is more archetypal and introverted, in that I am exploring more closely the intrapsychic experience of evil and the relationship to the archetype, while Lifton concentrates more on the interpsychic and sociopolitical factors. We are both concerned with how people survive.
2. Gossip columnist Liz Smith (of *New York Newsday*), in an interview with Lawrence Linderman: "I'm like all gossip columnists: a moralist at heart. To be a preacher or a gossip columnist you have to be like Savonarola, a little nuts.... Bad gossip drives out good gossip. Gossip has been totally vitiated today by this explosion of interest in it, especially by television which has made it worse than ever...when shows pay for stories, people will do anything for money, such as releasing hospital records, which is despicable.... No one ever went broke underestimating the taste of the American public. Howard Stern and Rush Limbaugh have been number one in nonfiction. *The Bridges of Madison County*, which is an idiotic book, was the best-selling novel in the country...look what's happening to our colleges. We have all the learning of Western civilization being debased by pressure groups who want...to act like what happened in history didn't happen." *Modern Maturity*, Sept. 1994, 62-69.
3. William Doty notes that the elevation of the Trickster Archetype in his role of mediator is illustrated also in medieval manuscripts where the figure of Mercurius is placed on the title page at center of the whole range of disciplines of learning and science. (Personal communication).
4. Amitai Etzioni, *The Spirit of Community: Rights, Responsibilities, and the Communitarian Agenda* (New York: Crown Publishing, 1993), 3.
5. It is disconcerting to realize that a similar situation existed in Germany before Hitler seized power. The Holocaust Museum in Washington, DC, summarizes that time succinctly in its exhibit on pre-Nazi Germany.
6. Billy Graham at the presidential inauguration of George Bush.
7. Rafael Lopez-Pedraza, *Hermes and His Children*, (Switzerland: Daimon Verlag, 1977), 51.
8. Ibid., 51.
9. Dorothy Dinnerstein, *The Mermaid and the Minotaur* (New York: Harper & Row, 1976), "What has kept (men's view) so short-sighted has been...the strength of their vindictive, grabby feelings. To maintain a longer, more enlightened view, these feelings...would at this point have to be pulled back in, and kept under control, by a more powerful effort of will than they (men) seem to be able to muster."
10. Edward Edinger, *Encounter with the Self* (Toronto: Inner City Books, 1986), 55.
11. Norman O. Brown, *Life Against Death* (Wesleyan University Press, 1970), 302. Brown's thesis is the progressive triumph of the death instinct manifested in the exalting of undesirable, as avarice by our civilization.

12 Henri Desroche, in *The Sociology of Hope*, quotes from M. Weber: "Only he who is capable of being amazed by the sequence of events can question himself on the meaning of the universe," 4. (Translated from the French by Carol Martin-Sperry, Routledge and Kegan Paul, London, 1979.)
13 *CW18*, par. 1398 (New York: Princeton University Press, Bollingen Foundation, 1963).
14 See Edward Edinger, *Transformation of the God Image* (Toronto: Inner City Books, 1992), 80, on science fiction as a voice for the collective unconscious.
15 *CW*, "Answer to Job," par. 658. (see ch. 5, n. 17).
16 Erik Erikson, *Ghandi's Truth: on the Origins of Militant Nonviolence* (Norton, 1969). See also Carol Gilligan, *In a Different Voice* (Cambridge, MA: Harvard University Press, 1982), 103-105. Gilligan discusses the relationship between Erikson and Ghandi in greater detail.
17 Murray Stein, *Solar Conscience, Lunar Conscience* (Wilmette: Chiron Publications, 1993), 108, for more on Promethean consciousness, hubris, and the denial of conscience in modern psychotherapy.
18 Adolf Guggenbühl-Craig, *The Old Fool and the Corruption of Myth* (Woodstock, CT: Spring Publications, 1991).
19 John Cornwall, *The Hiding Places of God* (New York: Warner Books, 1991).
20 Banesh Hoffman and Helen Dukas, *Albert Einstein, Creator and Rebel* (New York: New American Library, 1972), 193.
21 Karen Armstrong, *A History of God* (New York: Ballentine Books, 1993), 148.
22 Told to me by Tim Sanderson and Ron Kledzik. I like Estes's image of sending the Evil One to a comfortable asylum (see ch. 5, n. 14).
23 Marie-Louise von Franz, interviewed in "The Geography of the Soul," published by "In Touch," Summer 1993, by Centerpoint.
24 *C. G. Jung Letters*, vol. 2, ed. Gerhard Adler, in collaboration with Aniela Jaffe, tr. R. F. C. Hull (Princeton: Princeton University Press, 1973), 434.
25 See Edward Edinger, *The Creation of Consciousness* (Toronto: Inner City Books, 1984), 59, for this quote from Jung's letters, and also for his inspiring elucidation of Jung's myth and its implications for the future of civilization.
26 Ibid., 90.
27 Eugene Ionesco, *Rhinoceros*, tr. Derek Prouse (London: John Calder Publishers, 1958).
28 Lawrence Kohlberg, *The Psychology of Moral Development* (San Francisco: Harper & Row, 1984); Lawrence Kohlberg, *Consensus and Controversy*, ed. Sohan Modgil and Celia Modgil (Philidelphia: The Falmer Press, 1985).
29 Carol Gilligan, *In a Different Voice* (Cambridge: Harvard University Press, 1982), 62.
30 This is not to say that every man thinks in a predominantly masculine style, nor every woman in a predominantly feminine style, any more than we can say that every man values independence more than attachment. It does imply that there are gender differences in principle, reflected in generalized differences between males and females.
31 Rosemarie Tong, *Feminine and Feminist Ethics* (Belmont, CA: Wadsworth Publishing Co., 1993).
32 Charles Derber, *The Pursuit of Attention: Power and Individualism in Everyday Life* (Oxford: Oxford University Press, 1979).

33 Erikson, *Ghandi's Truth: On the Origins of Militant Nonviolence,* 251. Other definitions: "Morality: How one behaves according to a sense of right and wrong; ethics: how such a sense is explained and advocated; moralism: refusing the ethical proofing of morality" (Wm. G. Doty, personal communication). And, morality: "the process of entering into one's destiny and nature with responsibility;" moralism: a "fixed notion about what one's nature requires,. . . a defense against morality. (Thomas Moore, *Dark Eros: The Imagination of Sadism* [Woodstock, CT: Spring Publications, 1995], 108-109.)

34 M. K. Ghandi, *Satyagraha* (Non-violent Resistance) (Ahmedabad: Navajivan Publishing House, 1951). "A Satyagraha will always try to overcome evil by good, anger by love, untruth by truth. There is no other way of purging the world of evil."

35 See Thomas Moore, *Dark Eros: The Imagination of Sadism*; see also Chapter III.

36 Lopez-Pedraza, *Hermes and His Children,* 56.

37 See Emory Sekaquaptewa, "One More Smile for a Hopi Clown," in *Parabola,* vol. IV, no. 1, Feb. 1979.

38 Ann Ulanov and Barry Ulanov, *The Witch and the Clown* (Wilmette, IL: Chiron Publications, 1987), 192.

39 Clifton Snider, "Victorian Trickster," in "Psychological Perspectives," no. 24, Spring/Summer, 1991, 90-110.

40 Ibid., 98.

41 William Willeford, *The Fool and His Scepter: A Study of Clowns and Jesters and Their Audience* (Northwestern University Press, 1969), 4.

42 Though shape-shifting is an important ability in all tricksters, other mythological persons are noted for shape-shifting too. Lifton cites Proteus as shape-shifter model for the "Protean self."

43 Linda Leonard, *Witness to the Fire* (Boston: Shambala Publications, 1989).

44 Temple Grandin, 120, quoted in Oliver Sachs, "An Anthropologist on Mars," *The New Yorker,* Dec. 27, 1993, 106-125.

45 Ibid.

46 Michael Fordham, *Jungian Psychotherapy,* (Wiley, 1978).

47 Thomas Moore, *Dark Eros,* 18.

48 Stuart A. Kirk (Columbia University) and Herb Kutchins (California State University) in *The National Psychologist,* vol. 3 no. 5, Sept./Oct. 1994, 12-13.

49 Barry Holsteen Lopez, *Giving Birth to Thunder, Sleeping with His Daughter* (Kansas City: Sheed Andrews and McMeel, Inc., a subsidiary of Universal Press Syndicate, 1977), 66.

50 Ulanov, *The Witch and the Clown,* 192.

51 For more on male arrogance and female servility see Rosemary Tong, *Feminine and Feminist Ethics* (Belmont, CA: Wadsworth Publishing Co., 1993), 36.

52 See Allan Chinen, *Beyond the Hero: Classic Stories of Men in Search of Soul* (J. P. Tarcher, 1993), for stories relating to the Hero/Trickster relationship in masculine psychology

53 This episode of "Politically Incorrect with Bill Maher" aired April 4, 1995, on Comedy Central.

54 Gerald Adler, speech to American Academy of Psychotherapists, Oct., 1994, New Orleans, LA.

55 Phillip J. Brantley and Patricia B. Sutker, "Antisocial Behavior Disorders," in *Com-*

Notes to Pages 48-61

prehensive Handbook of Psychopathology, ed. Henry E. Adams and Patricia B. Sutker (New York: Plenum Press, 1984), 439-471.
56 Adrian Raine, Ph.D., "American Psychological Association Monitor," vol. 25, no. 8, Aug., 1994.
57 Jan Volavka, *Neurobiology of Violence* (Washington, DC: American Psychiatric Press, 1995).
58 Roger Sperry, *American Psychological Association Monitor,* August, 1993.
59 *American Psychological Association Monitor,* January, 1994, vol. 25, no. 1.
60 Brantley and Sutker, "Antisocial Behavior Disorders," 471.
61 Desroche, *The Sociology of Hope*, 3.
62 Erikson, *Ghandi's Truth.*
63 Michael Eigen, *The Psychotic Core* (Northvale, NJ: Jason Aronson, Inc., 1986), 120-124.
64 Lifton, in *The Protean Self,* 82, approaches a similar concept in noting that survivors have two options: to open up or to shut down. Opening characterizes what he calls the "Protean self"; shutting down, the "fundamentalist self." Survivors often use a combination of the two, including protections such as numbing, guilt, suspicion of counterfeit nurturance, and struggle for meaning.
65 Karl Kerényi, *Hermes: Guide of Souls* (Woodstock, CT: Spring Publications, Inc., 1986), 62-63.
66 *The Homeric Hymns,* tr. Charles Boer (Woodstock, CT: Spring Publications, Inc., 1970), 140.
67 Gilligan, *In a Different Voice.*
68 Marie-Louise von Franz, "The Problem of Evil in Fairy Tales," in *Evil,* ed. The Curatorium of the C. G. Jung Institute, Zürich, (Evanston, IL: Northwestern University Press, 1967), 114. See also James Hillman on smell and image-sensing, *A Blue Fire* (New York: Harper & Row, 1989), 60-64.
69 Edith Hamilton, *Mythology* (Boston: Little, Brown and Co., 1940), 19.
70 *The Homeric Hymns,* tr. Charles Boer, 62.

CHAPTER II. THROUGH LENS AND LOOKING GLASS

1 Heather Valencia and Rolly Kent, *Queen of Dreams: The Story of a Yaqui Dreaming Woman* (New York: Simon and Schuster, 1991), 176.
2 Deldon A. McNeely, *Touching: Body Therapy and Depth Psychology* (Toronto: Inner City Books, 1987); Malcolm Brown, *The Healing Touch* (Mendocino: Life Rhythm, 1990; and Michael Eigen, *The Psychotic Core*, 351-357, on the importance of infantile gazing for the development of self-feeling.
3 Erich Neumann, *The Origins and History of Consciousness,* tr. R. F. C. Hull (Princeton, NJ: Princeton University Press, 1970).
4 Meister Eckhart, *A Modern Translation,* tr. Raymond B. Blakney (New York: Harper & Row, 1941).
5 See Lopez-Pedraza, *Hermes and His Children,* esp. 105-121.
6 See Clarissa Pinkola Estes, *Women Who Run with the Wolves* (New York: Ballentine Books, 1992); see also the poetry of Sharon Olds.
7 Edward Edinger, *The Creation of Consciousness* (Toronto: Inner City Books, 1984), 38-45.

8 C. G. Jung, *Mysterium Coniunctionis* (Princeton: Princeton UP , 1963), *CW 14*, §215.
9 For more on Justice and Nemesis see Mary Daly, *Pure Lust: Elemental Feminist Philosophy* (Boston: Beacon Press), 275-279, for discussion of appropriate rage in the face of a justice that blindly punishes the oppressed.
10 Valencia, *Queen of Dreams*, 270.
11 Mariann Burke, *Advent and Psychic Birth* (Mahwah, NJ: Paulist Press, 1993), 136.
12 Willeford, *The Fool and His Scepter*, 35.
13 C. G. Jung, *Memories, Dreams, Reflections* (New York: Vintage Books, 1989), 39-43.
14 Gary Astrachan, "Hermes, der Argustöter" in Gorgo, Zeitschrift fur archetypische Psychologie und bildeschaftes Denken, 1991, Heft 20, 20-46.
15 Sir James George Frazer, *The New Golden Bough*, ed. Theodore H. Gaster (New York: S. G. Philllips, Inc. 1972), 512. See also N. O. Brown, *Life Against Death*. Brown interprets the herm reductively in terms of the anal stage of psychological development.
16 Robert Pelton, *The Trickster in West Africa* (Berkeley: University of California Press, 1980).
17 The theme of licking the eyes to remove mucus and unleash supernatural power recurs in African tales. See T. O. Beidelman, "The Moral Imagination of the Kaguru: Some Thoughts on Tricksters, Translation and Comparative Analysis," in Hynes and Doty, 112.
18 Pelton, *The Trickster in West Africa*, 120-122.
19 Ibid., 123.
20 Ibid., 124.
21 Milan Kundera, *Immortality*, tr. Peter Kussi (New York: Harper Perrenial, 1992), 29.
22 Martin Schlappner, "Evil in the Cinema," in *Evil*.
23 Kundera, *Immortality*, 127.
24 Patricia Berry, *Echo's Subtle Body* (Woodstock, CT: Spring Publications, 1982).
25 James Hillman and Michael Ventura, *We've Had a Hundred Years of Psychotherapy and the World's Getting Worse* (San Francisco: HarperCollins, 1992).
26 Kundera, *Immortality*, 30-34.
27 Hillman and Ventura, *We've Had a Hundered Years of Psychotherapy*, 63.
28 Nathan Schwartz-Salant, *Narcissism and Character Transformation* (Totonto: Inner City Books, 1982), 61.
29 Pelton, *The Trickster in West Africa*, 4.
30 Schwartz-Salant, *Narcissism*, 36.
31 Pelton, *The Trickster in West Africa*, 64.
32 Ibid., 65.
33 Ibid., 76-77.
34 Derek Walcott, *Collected Poems 1948-1984* (New York: Farrar, Straus and Giroux, 1986), 328.

CHAPTER III. SCRUPLES AND SOUL DOCTORS

1 Pelton, *The Trickster in West Africa*, 67.
2 Ibid., 68. Also note societal integration of Gilligan's differentiating "hierarchy" and

"web," as described in Chapter I.
3   Ibid., 45.
4   Mircea Eliade, *Shamanism* (Princeton: Princeton UP, 1964), 392.
5   Ginette Paris, *Pagan Grace* (Woodstock, CT: Spring Publications, Inc., 1990), 99.
6   Lopez-Pedraza, *Hermes and His Children*, 9.
7   Kerényi, *Hermes*, iv.
8   Jung's term for the capacity to allow a solution in the form of a symbol to resolve the tension of a strongly binding conflict.
9   Hynes and Doty, 209.
10 Armstrong, *A History of God*, 220.
11 Chloe Madanes, *Strategic Family Therapy* (San Francisco: Jossey-Bass Publishing, 1981).
12 Ibid., xvii.
13 Albert Ellis, "Ethics and the Therapist's Honesty," in *Voices*, vol. 28, no. 3, Fall 1992, 31-33.
14 Darrell Dawson, "Constraint, Ethics, and Compassion," in *Voices*, vol. 28, no. 3, Fall 1992.
15 Thomas Moore, *Dark Eros*, 41.
16 Peter Mudd, tape of lecture given to analytic candidates.
17 Lopez-Pedraza, *Hermes and His Children*.
18 For a beautiful illustration of this principle, see Janet Dallett, *When the Spirits Come Back* (Toronto: Inner City Books, 1988).
19 Nathan Schwartz-Salant, *The Borderline Personality: Vision and Healing* (Wilmette, IL: Chiron Publications, 1989).
20 Alfred Plaut, "A Case of Tricksterism," in *The Journal of Analytical Psychology*, vol. 4, no. 1, 1959, 35.
21 Paris, *Pagan Grace*, 98-99.
22 See Lopez-Pedraza on pornography, 113 f.
23 Pelton, *The Trickster in West Africa*, 281.

CHAPTER IV. TRICKSTER WOMAN

1   Stein, *Solar Conscience, Lunar Conscience*, 89-92.
2   Kerényi, *Hermes: Guide of Souls*, 59.
3   Ibid.
4   Jung, *MDR*, 354.
5   Kerényi, 64.
6   Jean Bolen, *Gods in Every Man, Goddesses in Every Woman* (New York: Harper & Row, 1989).
7   Armstrong, *A History of God*, 124.
8   This is true for very old men as well, as if sex without youth is dangerous and undignified, regardless of one's gender and sexual preference. Which leads to another example of gender inequality, that is, the gap in society's perception of what constitutes "old" in men as compared with women.
9   T. O. Beidelman, "The Moral Imagination of the Kaguru: Some Thoughts on Tricksters, Translation and Comparative Analysis," in Hynes and Doty, 181.
10 Dinnerstein, *The Mermaid and the Minotaur*, 147. Also see page 89 in Dinnerstein

for a compilation of references on anti-female attitudes. Also see Marilyn French, *The War Against Women* (New York: Summit Books, 1992).
11 Thomas Moore, *Dark Eros*, 137.
12 James Hillman, in a lecture to the National Congress of Jungian Analysts, Boston, MA, Oct., 1993.
13 Lopez-Pedraza, *Hermes and His Children*, 105-115.
14 Ulanov, *The Witch and the Clown*, 207.
15 Ibid., 13.
16 John Beebe, in a lecture to the National Congress of Jungian Analysts, Boston, MA, 1993.
17 Dorothy Cantor and Toni Bernay, *Women in Power* (Boston: Houghton Mifflin Co., 1992), 111.
18 Susan Niditch, "Genesis," in *The Women's Bible Commentary*, ed. Carol A. Newsom and Sharon H. Ringe (Louisville, KY: Westminster/John Knox Press, 1992), 25.
19 Ibid., 20.
20 Ibid., 22.
21 Ibid., 23.
22 *CW13:* §172 (Princeton: Princeton UP, 1963).
23 Ibid., §288.
24 Sylvia Perera, *Descent to the Goddess: A Way of Initiation for Women* (Toronto: Inner City, 1981).
25 John Dourley, *A Strategy for a Loss of Faith* (Toronto: Inner City, 1992.), 106.
26 Edinger, *Encounter with the Self.*
27 Aurora Terrenus, *Sophia of the Bible* (Santa Cruz: Celestial Communications, 1988), 12.
28 Ibid., 68-69.
29 Ean Begg, *Myth and Today's Consciousness* (London: Sigo Press, 1991).
30 Ibid; see also *CW5:* §369.
31 Begg, 85.
32 Ibid., 87.
33 Ibid., 79-96.
34 Shirley Stave, "Tony Morrison's Beloved and the Vindication of Lilith," in *South Atlantic Review,* January 1993, 49-66.
35 Barbara Black Koltuv, *The Book of Lilith* (York Beach, ME: Nicholas Hays, Inc., 1986), 122.
36 S. Liddell McGregor Mathers, translator of portions of the Zohar, quoted in Israel Regardie, *A Garden of Pomegranates,* (St. Paul, MN: Lewellyn Publications, 1970), 48.
37 Regardie, 50.
38 Ibid., 51.
39 Jung's dream of the *hieros gamos* was of the marriage of Malkus and Tephiroth (Sixth Sephirah—Beauty and Harmony), in *MDR,* 294.
40 Paris, *Pagan Grace,* 84-85.
41 Bolen, *Gods in Everyman, Goddesses in Every Woman,* 295-305.
42 See McNeely, "Anger and Creativity," in *Animus Aeternus* (Toronto: Inner City, 1991); also see Koltuv, *The Book of Lilith.*

43 See *CW13*, frontispiece of Mercurius with three heads: Sol, Luna, and Coniunctio of the two in Taurus, under Venus.
44 *CW5*, §577.
45 Kerényi, *Hermes*, 65.
46 Nancy Qualls-Corbett, *The Sacred Prostitute* (Toronto: Inner City, 1988).
47 Pupul Jayakur, *The Earth Mother: Legends, Ritual Arts, and Goddesses of India* (New York: Harper & Row, 1990), 85.
48 See John Stratton Hawley, "The Thief in Krishna," in *Parabola*, Summer 1984, 6-13.
49 Pupul Jayaka, 54.
50 Ulanov, *The Witch and the Clown*, 29.
51 Steven McFadden, *Profiles in Wisdom: Native Elders Speak about the Earth* (Santa Fe, NM: Bear & Co., 1991). Interestingly, the same conclusion was arrived at by the Jungian scholar Phyllis Moore. In her book, *No Other Gods*, (Wilmette, IL: Chiron Publications, 1992), Moore holds that the patriarchy of Yahweh was a necessary stage of development in the collective consciousness, and must be accepted and worked through before collective consciousness can move forward.
52 Jack Kornfield, "New Dimensions," National Public Radio, Feb. 11, 1994.
53 Andrew Harvey, *Hidden Journey* (New York: Viking Penguin, 1992).
54 Khetsun Rinbochay, *Tantric Practice in Nying-Ma*, tr. Jeffrey Hopkins (London: Rider and Co., 1982), 190.
55 Tsultrim Allione, *Women of Wisdom* (London: Arkana Paperbacks, an imprint of Routledge and Kegan Paul, 1984), 237.
56 Ibid., 237.
57 Nikolai Tolstoy, *The Quest for Merlin* (Boston: Little, Brown and Co., 1985), xvii.
58 *CW13*, §§239-303.
59 Jung, *MDR*, 225.
60 Ibid.
61 Jung, *MDR*, 228. In conclusion of his carvings is the inscription: "In remembrance of his seventy-fifth birthday C. G. Jung made and placed this here as a thanks offering, in the year 1950."
62 Verena Kast, *The Nature of Loving*, tr. Boris Matthews (Wilmette, IL: Chiron Publications, 1986), 62.
63 Ibid., 63.
64 Barry Lopez, *Giving Birth to Thunder, Sleeping with His Daughter*, 6.
65 Ibid., 179.

CHAPTER V. ETUDES IN PARANOIA

1 Kundera, *Immortality*, 22.
2 Innocent victim of Othello's jealous rage in Shakespeare's *Othello*.
3 Maria Rainer Rilke, *Selected Poems of Maria Rainer Rilke*, tr. Robert Bly (New York: Harper & Row Perennial Library, 1981), 25.
4 Pelton, *The Trickster in West Africa*, 141.
5 Ibid., 142
6 Edinger, *Creation of Consciousness*, 86.
7 Ibid., 113

8 Regardie, 40.
9 See Stein, *Solar Conscience, Lunar Conscience*, 77-78, for more on Jung and reflective instinct.
10 For example, "Guide, giver of good things," is how Hermes is greeted by Homer, while the Winnebago claim that Hare did away with all things that were abusive or evil to man, according to Paul Radin.
11 Rosemarie Tong, *Feminine and Feminist Ethics*, 113.
12 See *Jung Letters, vol. 1*. For historical perspectives of this debate from Augustine to post-modernity, see Walter J. Lowe, "Innocence and Experience," in *Evil: Self and Culture*, ed. M. C. Nelson and M. Eigen (New York: Human Sciences, 1984).
13 Karl Kerényi, "The Problem of Evil in Mythology," in *Evil*, ed. The Curatorium of the C. G. Jung Institute, Zürich (Evanston, IL: Northwestern University Press, 1967), 17.
14 Ibid., 14.
15 Estes, *Women Who Run with the Wolves*, 63-65.
16 James Hillman, *Loose Ends* (Woodstock, CT: Spring Publications, 1975), 68.
17 Kerényi, *Evil*, 17.
18 Armstrong, *A History of God*, 275.
19 Goldberg, *Monitor*, October, 1995, 13.
20 Estes, *Women Who Run with the Wolves*.
21 *Jung Letters*, vol. 1, 539-541, 555.
22 Widengren, "The Principle of Evil in the Eastern Religions," in *Evil*, 21-24.
23 Armstrong, *A History of God*, 249. For a psychological description of the development of evil in the self image, see James S. Grotstein, *Forgery of the Soul*.
24 Armstrong, *A History of God*, 124-129.
25 Ibid., 249.
26 Ibid., 77.
27 Ibid., 77-78.
28 *CW13*.
29 May Sarton, *The Muse as Medusa, Collected Poems, 1930-1973* (New York: W. W. Norton, 1974), 332.
30 Alice Walker quoted in Paula Bennett, *My Life a Loaded Gun* (Boston: Beacon Press, 1986), 242.
31 Steven Spielberg interview with Dotson Rader, *Parade Magazine*, March 27, 1994.
32 Martin Schlappner, "Evil in the Cinema," in *Evil*, 144.
33 Ibid., 144.
34 Ibid., 145.
35 Ibid., 145.
36 Ibid., 148.
37 Ibid., 150.
38 Grotstein, *Forgery of the Soul*, 223.
39 Paul Radin, *The Trickster: A Study in American Indian Mythology* (New York: Schocken), 22.
40 Kerényi, *Evil*, 15.
41 Grotstein, *Forgery of the Soul*, 221.
42 Hillman, *Loose Ends*, 43.

43 Thomas Moore, *Dark Eros*, 96.
44 One example is Medea; a more recent example occurs in Amy Tan, *The Joy Luck Club*, (Putnam's, 1989).
45 Charles Derber, *The Pursuit of Attention* (Oxford: Oxford University Press, 1979), 96.
46 John Shea, *Starlight* (New York: Crossroad Publishing Company, 1992), 143-145.

CHAPTER VI. THE ANIMATED TRICKSTER

1 Native American (Coyote/Earth Woman), Celtic (Merlin/Viviane), African (Legba/Mawu).
2 Janet Dallett, *Saturday's Child: Encounters with the Dark Gods* (Totonto: Inner City Books, 1991), 19.
3 Eigen, 368.
4 Norman O. Brown, *Love's Body* (New York: Random House, 1966).
5 *CW, Answer to Job*, §745 (see ch. 5, n. 17).
6 Jung: "Man's relationship to God probably has to undergo a certain important change: Instead of the propitiating praise for an unpredictable king or the child's prayer to a loving father, the responsible living and fulfilling of the divine will in us will be our form of worship of and commerce with God." *Letters, vol. 2*, 316, quoted in Edinger, *Transformation*, 78.
7 In 1992, for example, some Mardi Gras clubs founded by white European immigrants opened to other races for the first time in almost 300 years. At the same time, military schools were challenged to admit females for the first time in their histories.
8 Tong, *Feminine and Feminist Ethics*, 77.
9 Nell Noddings, *Caring: A Feminine Approach to Ethics and Moral Education* (Berkeley: University of California Press, 1984), 83.
10 Ibid., 83.
11 Ibid., 178-179.
12 Armstrong, *A History of God*, 391.
13 Anne Benvenuti, "To Lead Them Out: Taking 'The Business' Out of Education," in *Creation Spirituality*, vol. x, no. 1, Summer 1994, 37.
14 Tong, *Feminine and Feminist Ethics*, 119.
15 Edgar S. Cahn, "The Time Dollar," in *Spices of Life*, Ruth Fort and Associates, (Center for Study of Responsive Law, 1990), 133.
16 Dinnerstein, *The Mermaid and the Minotaur*, 103.
17 *Homeric Hymns*, tr. Charles Boer, 140.